Word, Chant, and Song

SUNY series in Religious Studies

Harold Coward, editor

Word, Chant, and Song

Spiritual Transformation in
Hinduism, Buddhism, Islam, and Sikhism

Harold Coward

Cover image from iStock / Kostins

Published by State University of New York Press, Albany

© 2019 State University of New York

All rights reserved

No part of this book may be used or reproduced in any manner whatsoever without written permission. No part of this book may be stored in a retrieval system or transmitted in any form or by any means including electronic, electrostatic, magnetic tape, mechanical, photocopying, recording, or otherwise without the prior permission in writing of the publisher.

For information, contact State University of New York Press, Albany, NY
www.sunypress.edu

Library of Congress Cataloging-in-Publication Data

Names: Coward, Harold G., author.
Title: Word, chant, and song : spiritual transformation in Hinduism, Buddhism, Islam, and Sikhism / Harold Coward.
Description: Albany : State University of New York Press, [2019] | Series: SUNY series in religious studies | Includes bibliographical references and index.
Identifiers: LCCN 2018045642 | ISBN 9781438475752 (hardcover) | ISBN 9781438475769 (pbk.) | ISBN 9781438475776 (ebook)
Subjects: LCSH: Hindu music—History and criticism. | Buddhist music—History and criticism. | Islamic music—History and criticism. | Sikh music—History and criticism.
Classification: LCC ML3197 .C68 2019 | DDC 203/.7—dc23
LC record available at https://lccn.loc.gov/2018045642

10 9 8 7 6 5 4 3 2 1

*To our mothers,
Frances Maiklem and Hazel Coward,
who loved music*

Contents

Acknowledgments	ix
Introduction	1
1. Hinduism: Mantra Chanting and Singing in Spiritual Transformation	9
2. Buddhism: Word, Chant, and Song in Spiritual Practice	47
3. Word, Chant, and Song on the Islamic Spiritual Path	91
4. Sikh Spiritual Practice: Word, Chant, and Song	127
Conclusion	151
References	165
Index	173

Acknowledgments

During the past several years my research and writing of this book has been made possible by the Centre for Studies in Religion and Society at the University of Victoria, where I am an associate research fellow. As my introduction to this volume makes clear, my own personal experience of religion has involved music as a key component, yet music is given little attention in our academic study of religion. For the last five years, I have been singing in the Victoria Mendelssohn Choir, which has sharpened my interest in music and led me to write this book.

My method developed during forty years of comparative religion scholarship, and used in previous volumes, is to engage my worldwide network of scholars of religion from various traditions in the following way. Before beginning research on a particular topic in each religion (e.g., chant and music in Buddhism or Islam), I contact two or three of my colleagues who are scholars and cultural participants of that religion to advise me of the key primary and secondary sources of their tradition that I should consult on the issue. After doing my research and drafting my chapter, I then send it to them for critical reading, revision, or addition of suggestions. I then revise on the basis of their suggestions. I then ask these same scholars for a critical reading of the revised chapter, which I also present to at least one or two conferences of specialized scholars in that tradition for critical discussion and suggestions for further revision. Once again, I revise before placing the chapter in my book manuscript. For example, the Islam chapter in this book was presented to a Canadian Society for the Study of Religions AGM Conference session for Islamic scholars in Canadian academia held in Calgary in 2016. It was well received by the many Islamic scholars present (most from Islamic cultures) with some suggestions for revision. Such suggestions were addressed before submitting the manuscript to the publisher.

I wish to acknowledge and thank scholars who helped me research and write the chapters in this book. They include the following: T. R. V. Murti, Kunjunni Raja, Anatanand Rambachan, Vasudha Narayanan, Guy Beck, Mitra Barva, Martin Adam, Sean Williams, Leslie Kawamura, Victor Hori, Graeme MacQueen, Robert Florida, Hanna Kassis, Regula Qureshi, Frederick Denny, Roland Miller, Earle Waugh, Mahmoud Ayoub, Bindu Mennon Mannil, Harjot Oberoi, and Pashaura Singh. This book would not have been possible without their generous help. Remaining errors are my own responsibility.

As always, Vicki Simmons, my manuscript assistant, carefully attended to the initial typing and various revisions required. Without her careful and efficient assistance, my continued scholarly work would not be possible. Thanks are also due to Angela Andersen who so thoughtfully prepared the index.

—Harold Coward
Centre for Studies in Religion and Society
University of Victoria
August 28, 2018

Introduction

For lay devotees of the various religions, the experience of word, chant, and song is often basic to their spiritual practice. Yet in academic religious studies and musicology we have given little attention to chanted word and hymns (Beck 2006, 4–6; Laack 2015, 223–225). In this book, I begin to address this gap in knowledge through a thematic study of music as it functions in word, chant, and song for devotees in the Hindu, Buddhist, Islamic, and Sikh religious traditions (the Jewish and Christian traditions will need a separate volume to cover their long and complex interdevelopment of the topic). Since I do not presume previous knowledge, I begin each chapter with a brief introduction to the tradition's understanding of word and follow with a study of the range of chant and song in the devotee's practice within the religious tradition. Since one cannot be exhaustive in a single chapter, I employ case studies to indicate the diversity of understanding and practice within each religion, and I offer examples of current trends.

Growing up in a Protestant Christian family in Canada gave me a great appreciation for the scriptural word of Jesus, the chanted psalms of the Scottish Psalter, and spiritual power present in the singing of great Methodist hymns. Hearing the parables of Jesus at my mother's knee, when I was too young to even go to school, formed the foundation of my religious life. These parables along with the psalms and other teachings became the core of the biblical word, which when chanted and sung remains the fundamental grounding of my life to this day. My singing of the word was inspired when, as a small boy, I would stand beside my father as we sang hymns such as "Guide Me O Thou Great Jehovah" in Sunday worship. The power and beauty of his strong baritone voice blending with the organ, choir, and congregation seemed to shake the foundations of the church building and carry me into a sense of spiritual unity with God and the universe that moved me deeply. In university, my scholarly curiosity naturally turned to wanting to understand how scriptural words in their chanting and singing could have such a powerful and transforming effect on one's life. At first I studied within my own Christian tradition, but it was when my study led me beyond the Jewish and Christian sources to an examination of Hindu texts, their chanting as *mantra*, and singing as *kirtan* that I finally began to understand the life-transforming spiritual power of the word.

My teacher of Hinduism, Professor T. R. V. Murti of Banaras Hindu University in India, introduced me to a new way of studying and experiencing the word. In the traditional teacher-student relationship of India, study proceeds in a quite different fashion than the classroom approach of the modern university. Of course, I did attend Professor Murti's classes at the university, but the "real study" of the scriptural text occurred when I would go to his home three afternoons a week for traditional guru-student-style study. We would study a text by reading it together line by line, not going on the next one until he was satisfied that I understood the first line. But "reading" is not really the right description of what was happening—it was more speaking and hearing. Professor Murti would chant the verse of Hindu scripture or commentary aloud in its original Sanskrit (he knew all these texts by heart, so used no books), then he would give me an English translation and finally an explanation of the meaning. I would ask questions if I did not understand, and sometimes he would question me to ensure I had understood. Only when he was satisfied that I had a full understanding would we move on to the next line of the text. After studying together in this fashion for about three hours, we would stop and he would make me tea. Over tea he would explain other aspects of the culture and tradition that provided the context for our textual study. The first book we read together was the *Yoga Sutras* of Patanjali (*Patanjali's Yoga Sutras* 1978), the foundation text for the Hindu Yoga spiritual tradition dating from between 200 BCE and 200 CE. It took us about two years to get through the *Yoga Sutras*, for often a line would refer to another scriptural tradition (e.g., Buddhist) necessitating time out for Professor Murti to teach me the

Buddhist position, for example, so that I could understand what was being said. I also had to learn Sanskrit, so that I could experience the text in its original sound and meaning before an English translation was attempted. It was through this method of study that I came to a new understanding of how Christian scripture worked in my own life.

One of the *Yoga Sutras* that particularly intrigued me was 11:44, "By study of the scriptures comes communion with the Lord": *svadhyaya*. To a Protestant boy this seemed to be a wonderful confirmation of the daily Bible study tradition in which I had been reared. But Vyasa's commentary, as elucidated by Murti, led to a severe challenging of that tradition and an opening up of the question of the power of mantra chanting. My Protestant practice of Bible study involved rising early in the morning and reading through the books of the Bible in a systematic way. I would do this at my desk with the commentaries spread out around me. After reading a verse I would consult the leading commentaries to determine the historical context, linguistic points, and the intellectual meaning of the passage. While all of this was a thoroughly acceptable Enlightenment approach to the text, it was clearly far from Patanjali's concept of study or svadhyaya.

The idea of leaving behind a rational, analytical approach in favor of a chanted immersion in the text was completely new to me. It did not go against the *sola scriptura* of my Protestant tradition—in fact, that aspect seemed reinforced. But the rational liberal Enlightenment method of Bible study, championed in my seminary training, was thoroughly challenged. Rather than intellectual analysis of the passage leading to a clear conceptual understanding, Patanjali's svadhyaya aimed at a stilling of the rational thinking activity of the mind so that the Bible verse itself became the sole occupant of one's consciousness. The power of the chanted revealed word itself, freed of the obstacles of the thinking processes, was then able to transform one's whole being. My Protestant tradition believed strongly in the transforming power of the Scripture, and I had occasionally experienced that power when the word of the Bible was powerfully spoken by a preacher like Martin Luther King Jr. But in my private daily Bible study, I was blocking out much of that power by turning it into a rational, intellectual exercise. Exposure to the Hindu *Yoga Sutras* taught me that while reason has a useful role, it is a minor one, namely, the removal of obstacles to the direct immersion of the mind in the revealed word. That is the purpose of svadhyaya—to chant and meditate on the chosen passage until one loses the subject-object separation with the word and it becomes the whole of one's conscious and unconscious experience. The test for mastery, says Patanjali, is that one's study will be blessed by a vision of the Lord. One's consciousness is so completely one with the word that it is the object of the scripture itself that is revealed (i.e., the Lord) rather than the object of the rational activity of the mind (i.e., conceptual thought about the Lord).

This discovery led me to a complete change in my approach to daily Bible study. I put away the commentaries from my desk and immersed myself only in the revealed word itself. My morning Bible study became less and less intellectual and more and more an opening of myself to the transforming power of the biblical word. Surprisingly, I found myself recovering an experience I had not had since when, as a young child, my mother would tell me the parables of Jesus. The hearing of those words of Jesus by my clear and open young mind, as yet uncluttered by rational thought, made a deep and lasting impression. The foundation of my faith was established. My new approach to Bible study opened the way to a recovery of the kind of direct and transforming experience of the word that I had had at my mother's knee. It did not mean that I gave up my intellectual study of the word—only that the rational, analytical approach to the word to which I devoted myself during my working hours as a scholar was balanced by a nonrational devotional experience of the word in my early morning svadhyaya study. The overbalance on the rational side was corrected and I was reconnected with the deep transforming power present in the direct devotional experience of chanting and singing the word. I felt my faith to be more nourished, my life to be more vital, and my intellectual academic study, in turn, became more fruitful. The intellectual and personal experience of my Christian religion had been returned to its formative basis in my childhood hearing of the parables of Jesus and singing hymns by my encounter with Patanjali's *Yoga Sutras*.

Unlike my modern Western training in scientific biblical criticism, the Hindu tradition sees the written text as corrected by the carefully transmitted oral word. This stress on the oral word led me to reexamine the history of the Christian experience of the word to see if there had been a similar period of dependence upon the oral over the written. Jesus himself left no writings. Our knowledge of his words and works came from his immediate followers or apostles and their disciples. At first this information circulated orally. Later it was written down and some of it became canonized. However, for the early Christians, it was the oral experience of scripture that had the power to transform persons. The importance of oral rhetoric in Greek culture came together with the oral practices of the Jewish rabbis (e.g., chanting the Torah in synagogue) to provide a strong oral context. Jesus, and some Jewish rabbis of his day, did not write but depended on oral teaching to communicate their messages. Jesus's teaching and much of the early Christian mission was by word of mouth, in Aramaic and Greek, the common languages of the day; sermons were neither written in advance nor copied down by the hearers. They listened and remembered. As was the case with the great Jewish rabbis and their academies, the cultural traditions of the day were more oral than written—although there was certainly writing going on. Jesus and his disciples followed this pattern. The oral nature of their teaching was not due to illiteracy but was consciously chosen by the rabbis because of its greater power for reaching and transforming the people of the day (Neusner 1985).

Although both the gospels and letters were widely circulated in the early Christian churches, the power came when they were spoken aloud in congregational worship. In a sense, they functioned much like the score does in a musical performance. It is the heard music, not the written score, that is the real thing. Similarly, it is the spoken word in scripture reading, sermon, chanting, or hymn singing that has transforming power. Unlike the merely written text, the oral speaking, chanting, or singing enters the hearts of individuals and joins speakers and hearers together into a fellowship of the word—a *logos* of giving and receiving (Philippians 4:15; Galatians 6:6). The obstacle to faith is a defective sense of hearing. It is through hearing and oral confession that salvation is realized. All of this is very close to the Hindu view that the obstacle to release (*moksa*) is the mind's *karma*, which is removed by the devotional hearing of the chanted or sung scripture. Indeed, it was the Hindu understanding of this process that sensitized me to the power of the spoken word in early Christian experience. Looking over Christian history, one sees that this continues to be true through Augustine, Luther, and the Puritans right up to the present day. All emphasize that God's word as written scripture is dead; only when it is spoken and sung can it be heard. As Luther put it, when we read and write books, we have not fulfilled our responsibility as Christians. The church is a "mouth-house, no pen-house" (Luther 1961, 201), and today Luther would surely add, "or computer house." In modern times, scholars such as Walter Ong and Paul Ricoeur have emphasized the importance of the preaching of the Scripture. Ricoeur describes preaching as "the permanent reinterpretation of the text which is regarded as grounding the community" (Ricoeur 1979, 275). Ong observes that in Protestantism, God is powerful through the spoken word, which may be heard in sermons or in prayer or in the imagination of the devotee reading the Bible in print (Ong 1967, 282). We are reminded of Paul's understanding of revelation. Paul does not say that the gospel is about revelation; rather, when the gospel is preached, revelation happens. From my own experience, I would add that when scripture is combined with music and sung in chant, anthem, or hymn, a most powerful oral-aural experience of the word can occur.

My study of Hinduism and its understanding of the power of the oral word resensitized me to the importance of chanted and sung scripture within the Christian tradition. However, Hinduism also opened my eyes to the spiritual merit of a Roman Catholic practice that I as a Protestant had always judged to be nothing more than superstitious ritual. I refer to the chanting of the rosary. As a university student, I used to listen to a French radio station that played good classical music but once a day broadcast a chanting of the rosary. This used to annoy me and I would dismiss it as a Roman Catholic superstition. In India, I was surrounded by ritual chanting. At first I viewed it as I had the Roman Catholic rosary chanting—an empty superstition. But as I studied Bhartrhari's philosophy of language, I came to understand for the first time the spiritual power present in devotional chant. Bhartrhari's analysis of language as functioning on the three levels of uttered sound (*vaikhari*), inner thought (*madhyama*), and the supersensuous seeing (*pasyanti*) of the meaning-whole (*sphota*) provided a theoretical basis for understanding ritual chanting as having spiritual power (see Coward and Raja 1990). Instead of empty repetition, each sounding of the chant or mantra is inherently meaningful in that each sound attempts to reveal the whole sphota until the obscuring ignorance is purged and the meaning-whole of the mantra is seen. If the scriptural word has power, which I as a Protestant had always believed, then the chanting of a mantra or rosary, far from being a superstitious ritual, was actually a powerful technique for focusing the mind on the word so that its spiritual power could work within one's consciousness.

Patanjali makes the psychological process at work even more explicit. Through the practice of fixed concentration (*samadhi*) consciousness is purified of karmic obstructions and the supersensuous reality is "seen." The chanting of the mantra is a form of fixed concentration that keeps it front and center in one's mind to the exclusion of everything else one might perceive or think. Through the chanting the devotee becomes one with the mantra, be it OM, the rosary, or the Jesus Prayer. It is as though one's whole world becomes only the mantra and for the period of the chanting the devotee becomes only the mantra—for the period of the chanting nothing else exists. The power of such mantra concentration is to induce a perfectly clear identity with the signified deity (be it Isvara, Mary, or Jesus) as given detailed psychological explanation in Yoga Sutra 1:42. With continued mantra concentration all traces of uttered sounds and conceptual meaning are purged until only direct, pure perception of the deity or spiritual truth remains. The result is that not only does one intimately know the truth, but the truth becomes the motive of all of one's actions (*Isvarapranidhanam*, as Patanjali calls it in Yoga Sutra 11:45).

For me personally, the study of Hinduism has been both a confirming and deepening experience. It has confirmed my Protestant Christian experience of the power of the scriptural word but broadened my awareness of how that power functions in processes such as devotional chanting and singing. Study of the *Yoga Sutras* has led me to discover traditions of daily spiritual discipline within Christianity, of which I was previously unaware (e.g., the chanted Jesus Prayer in the Russian Orthodox Church). My daily Bible study has been changed from a rational to a devotional exercise and I have been resensitized to the roots of my spiritual foundation in the hearing of the parables of Jesus as a young child or singing the hymn "Guide Me O Thou Great Jehovah" at my father's side. A balance between an intellectual and a devotional experience of the word has been established in my life.

In our modern Western way of thinking, "scripture" as a written book is very familiar to us. Today most of us in the West simply take for granted that "scripture" means "holy writ," "holy writing," or "sacred book." Our focus both as laypeople and as scholars is on the written and printed character of the holy word. Little attention has been given to its function as chanted or sung sacred word. Reasons for this emphasis upon the written rather than the oral word are not hard to find. In our recent past, at least, the Jewish and Christian traditions have emphasized study of the written text for both scholarly and devotional purposes. Indeed, the very words "scripture" (from the Latin *scriptura*, "a writing") and "bible" (from the Latin *biblia*, "a collection of writings" or "book") have led us to think of divine revelation as a written or printed object. This conception of scripture as written word is bolstered in our culture by the great importance that we attach to the written or printed word. In so many areas of life today, we say that unless you have something in writing, it is not to be trusted. This valuation of the written over the oral-aural experience of language is, however, characteristic of only the most recent period of cultural history.

As we shall see, a recovery of the oral chanted and sung experience of the word would seem to be crucial if it is to function as a transforming power in people's lives. More than that, however, the scholarly study of scriptures of the various religions will remain seriously limited and one-sided if it does not become more sensitive to the fundamental oral character of scriptures such as the Veda, Buddhist Sutra, the Qur'an, and the Sikh Adi Granth. This book is directed toward that goal. Its analysis shows that "scripture" has been understood by more people in most times and places (other than in our own modern period) as including both the oral and the written word, and that of the two it is the oral word with its relational context in chant and song that has the greater power to transform lives.

CHAPTER 1

Hinduism

Mantra Chanting and Singing in Spiritual Transformation

> India is . . . the land of mantra. To know and love Indian religious life means coming to terms with mantric utterances.
>
> —Harvey Alper, *Understanding Mantras*

This chapter will examine how it is that Vedic words used in mantra chants and singing function as forces for spiritual transformation in the Hindu tradition. While mantra chanting was given careful analysis in Alper's *Understanding Mantras* (1989), the singing of kirtan and *bhajans* plays a powerful role in the practice of modern-day devotees. This chapter will examine the philosophy of word and practice underlying the formation of Hindu chant and singing and cite selected examples of important genres of chant and devotional music as powerful forms of spiritual transformation in Hinduism.

Spiritual Transformation via Mantra Practice

Just as Westerners are often put off by the strange shapes encountered in Hindu images, they also sometimes find the scripture, prayers, rituals, and chants that are constantly chanted to be a mystery. Indeed, for me as a Protestant boy deeply influenced by the Christian sense of sola scriptura, it was the Hindu sensitivity to the power of the spoken, chanted, or sung word to transform consciousness that first drew me to the study of Indian religious life. Technically referred to by the Sanskrit term *mantra*, this Indian ability to hear the divine sound, in the spoken words of the Veda (scripture) in ritual, in the chanting of Om, and the singing of hymns in the sounds of birds and nature—all of this is a continuing fascination for scholarly study.

In Indian cities one often feels engulfed in a sea of sound—trucks, cars, and motor scooters honk incessantly and one is surrounded by the crush of people. One soon longs for quiet and finds it by rising early and venturing out into the awakening day. Imagine yourself stepping into a small side street of Varanasi. The soft morning light is brightening to the East. All is quiet, and yet you begin to realize that around you the streets are full of activity. Forms of devout worshipers pass silently on their way to offer morning prayers and bathe in the Ganges. The merchants and traveling vendors with their distinctive cries of "Mangos," "Knives sharpened," or "Ice cream" have not yet appeared. But the morning quiet is broken by sounds of a different kind. From a second-floor window comes the sound of a morning prayer being chanted. As our ears become attuned to this chant, we hear it rising from houses all around us as we wind our way through the narrow streets. The golden globe of the sun is just cresting the horizon as we reach the ghats or steps leading down from the street level to the flowing water of the Ganges. The murmur of prayers being said around us steadily increases. A quietly chanted prayer is mixed with splashing of water from a man standing waist deep in the river. Sadhus, holy men, naked except for saffron loincloths, chant Sanskrit verses of the Veda, keeping count of their repetitions with prayer beads. Laypeople join in with their own chants—all seem to be different and yet somehow blend together. A harmonious hymn of sound is raised to welcome the auspicious moment of the rising of the sun—the dawning of a new day.

As the sun ascends from the horizon and its first rays are felt warm upon one's skin, the chanted prayers increase in their intensity. To the Indian the light and warmth of the sun is a manifestation of the divine, but so is the sound of the morning chant that rises heavenward as an invocation of the new day. Speaking the Vedic chants and seeing the sunrise are both important experiences of the divine in India. Indeed, we can say that Indians specialize in seeing the divine in nature, in images of gods and goddesses, and in hearing the divine in the sounds of daily life, from the morning prayer to the call of the crow, the screech of the ox cart axle or, in modern times, the incessant blaring of horns. In India, all sound is perceived as being divine in origin, since it all arises from the one sacred source. Some sounds, however, are more powerful in evoking the divine within and around oneself than are others. Sound intrinsically bears the power of the sacred in India. In the Hindu hierarchy of scripture, it is the *sruti*, the heard text, which is preserved in oral tradition, that is the highest manifestation of the creative word. Om is the supreme example, since it is the divine seed sound from which all other sounds are said to arise. Om is, therefore, taken as the root mantra or sacred sound for the whole universe of sound.

The rising sun also signals the start of activity in the major temples of Varanasi dedicated to the gods and goddesses of Hinduism. Within the imposing Vishvanath Temple, dedicated to Shiva, the priests begin to chant and dedicate offerings. Devotees crowd into the temple to have a view of the image of Shiva, a sight that is held to bring blessing, and to watch the colorful ceremony. Throughout the day, devotees stream to thousands of temples located all over Varanasi to worship their favorite gods and goddesses. The variety of images from which they can choose reflects the richness through which the divine has revealed itself in the Hindu tradition: Vishnu, the heavenly king who descends to the world from time to time in various incarnations (*avataras*) to maintain cosmic stability; Shiva, the ascetic god who dwells in yogic meditation in the Himalayas generating energy that can be released into the world to refresh its vigor; Krishna, the manifestation of the divine as lover; Hanuman, the monkey god, who embodies strength, courage, and loyalty; Ganesha, the elephant-headed god who removes all obstacles for his followers; Durga, the warrior goddess who periodically defeats the forces of evil in order to protect the world; and Kali, the black mother goddess who dwells in cremation grounds and takes you to herself at death.

Dawn is a busy time at the cremation grounds on the banks of the Ganges River. Family funeral processions carry their stretcher-borne corpses down the steps to the spot where several funeral pyres are always burning. Pious Hindus believe that death near the Ganges or Varanasi results in *moksa*, liberation, from the endless cycle of birth, death, and rebirth—the ultimate spiritual goal of most Hindus. Varanasi is also the home of many religious orders, including a large number of ascetics or world renouncers. These holy men or women may be seen spending their day in meditation on the steps leading to the Ganges or at the cremation grounds. Their only possessions are a staff and water pot. The males may be naked with long matted hair and bodies smeared with ash from the cremation grounds. The women may have shaved heads to show lack of concern for bodily appearance. All around them Hindu laypeople are busily going about their daily tasks as merchants, businesspeople, tradespeople, artists, students, and professors from Banaras Hindu University, all busy with everyday family life. In their midst, the ascetics look as if they are from another world, yet they are all part of the rich variety of lifestyles that Hindus may take on—one large extended family, as it were—full of diversity, including many languages, cultures, and religious traditions, yet with an underlying sense of unity.

Hindus living in North America cannot visit the Ganges at dawn, but many have a small pot of Ganges water on their home altar to help with morning prayers. Many of the same images (Vishnu, Shiva, Durga, Krishna, Ganesha, and Kali) will be present on the home altar, which is often located in an upstairs bedroom dedicated as the worship room. There the family may gather or pray individually, using the same chanted prayers or mantras and the same repetitions of Om that are said in India. Hindu temples have been built in many American cities, providing places for family and the whole community to gather on ceremonial occasions. Cremation takes place in funeral homes rather than on the banks of the Ganges. So, in many ways, the sacred practice of Hindus in Varanasi goes on in modified form in the West.

Just as the day begins with mantra chanting, so it also ends with an evening chant. At night, in India, the tropical birds join in with their "donc donc, donc donc." From the seashore comes the rhythmic roar of the waves. Not only is each day enclosed in sacred sound but so also is the whole of life. Indeed, it has been said, "From the mother's womb to the funeral pyre, a Hindu literally lives and dies in *mantra*" (Alper 1989a, 296). This saying appears to express a truth that has dominated India for the past thousand years. For generations of post-Vedic Indians mantra is not primarily a Vedic text but rather the symbolic source of sacred sound that overflows textual boundaries until it encloses all of life—not only the speaking of humans but also of animals, particularly of birds. Mantra is also heard in the voices of fire, thunder, and rain.

Diana Eck has shown that India is filled with visual experiences of the divine—images in homes, temples, or roadside shrines—that a central act of worship "is to stand in the presence of the deity and to behold the image with one's own eyes, to see and be seen by the deity" (Eck 1998, 3). That is now also happening in Hindu diaspora communities all over North America where temples have been built and images installed. But India is also permeated by sonic experiences of the divine. Drums, bells, gongs, cymbals, conches, flutes, and a wide variety of vocalizations are often heard, sometimes simultaneously, invoking and evoking the divine within temple, home, or sacred space. As suggested earlier, the first impression to the outsider may be one of chaos and cacophony, an ensemble of "noise" with no apparent rhyme or reason. But, if we empathize with the presuppositions of the Indian culture and religious traditions, we come to realize that there is an underlying religious foundation for the experience of sound in general and for the saying of specific mantras (words or sounds) in particular. Indeed, we could parallel Diana Eck's statement about the visual experience of the divine by saying that in Hinduism the central act of worship is hearing the mantra or sacred sound with one's own ears and chanting the mantra with one's voice (Coward and Goa 2004).

Hearing and saying the mantra is an act of worship and "tunes" one to the basic sound or vibration of the universe. By a continual hearing and chanting, one purifies and transforms one's life until it vibrates in harmony with the divine, which is itself pure sound. Indeed, we find Hindu religion filled with many different versions of "sonic theology." For Hindu India, then, *the act of worship* involves both seeing and being seen by the divine image (*darshan*) and also hearing and speaking the divine sound (mantra). Both are present and central to the worship of most lay people in India. For some more advanced worshipers, the sound may totally displace the image so that the concentration is on the sound alone. In this chapter, our focus will be on mantra, the hearing, chanting, and singing aspect of experiencing the divine by Hindu devotees.

It has been said that there is no parallel to the concept of darshan, of seeing and being seen by the divine in the Western religions (Bharati 1970, 102). As Diana Eck puts it, when the gaze of the huge eyes of the image of Lord Krishna meets those of the worshiper standing on tiptoe in the crowd, there is a special exchange of vision that is itself a form of "touching," of intimate knowing. Such an exchange of vision is darshan and is fundamental to Hindu worship. So also, the practice of hearing and speaking the mantra is an act in which the consciousness of the individual may experience a tuning into the divine sound of the cosmos. This is what Agehananda Bharati means when he says, "Mantra is not meaningful in any descriptive or even persuasive sense, but within the mystical universe of discourse" (Bharati 1970a, 102). Mantra chanting is verified not by what it describes or cognitively reveals but by the complex vibration or feeling tone it creates in the practicing person.

The Indian Worldview

From the Hindu perspective two presuppositions, *karma* and *samsara*, are basic to Indian thought and the spiritual function of mantra. *Karma* is a word that is fairly common in the West but often little understood. There are many definitions of karma in the Indian tradition, some making karma appear quite deterministic. One of the clearest descriptions, however, is found in the *Yoga-System of Patanjali* (Woods 1966). This concept is widely influential and makes room for free will. It runs as follows. Every time you do an action or think a thought a memory trace or karmic seed is laid down in the storehouse of your unconscious waiting for conditions to arise conducive to its sprouting fourth as an impulse, instinct, or predisposition to do the same action or think the same thought again (for a detailed analysis of the *Yoga Sutra* passages, see Coward 1983, 49–60). How does all of this apply to mantras? Speaking a mantra lays down a karmic memory trace in the unconscious. Chanting a mantra over and over reinforces that karmic trace (*samskara*) until a deep root or habit pattern (*vasana*) is established. Correctly chanting a mantra, such as Om or a Vedic verse, reinforces good karma and removes negative karmas or impulses by preventing their blossoming or maturing so that they wither away, leaving no trace behind. The more powerful the mantra the more good karma will be reinforced and negative karma will be removed from one's storehouse consciousness. In this way mantra chanting or singing can be seen to be a powerful tool for purifying and transforming consciousness.

Karma works together with the other basic presupposition of Hindu thought, namely, samsara or rebirth. Accordingly, your unconscious storehouse contains not only all the karmic traces from actions and thoughts done in this life but also in the life before this and so on, backward infinitely, since in Indian thought there is no absolute beginning. From this perspective, your unconscious is like a huge granary full of karmic seeds or memory traces that are constantly sprouting up, as conducive situations arise, impelling you toward good or evil actions or thoughts. No wonder we constantly feel ourselves being pulled and pushed by our karmic desires. But the possibility of free choice always allows us to take control over these impulses, and mantra chanting or singing gives us a powerful psychological tool to use in directing this process.

In Hinduism, the thing that causes one to be reborn is the karma within one's own consciousness. The chanting or singing of mantras is one of the most powerful practices for the purging of karmas, and when the last karma is removed, moksa is realized. Although conceptualized differently by different Hindu schools, moksa may generally be thought of as the removal of karmas that make us appear to be separate from Brahman (the divine). When the last veiling or obstructing karma is removed, the fact that one is, and has always been, nothing but Brahman is revealed. That is moksa—the direct realization of one's own oneness with the divine.

The concept of mantra as powerful sacred sound is associated with one of India's ancient scriptures, the Rgveda (Findly 1989, 15). India also shares with the rest of the world a fascination with what Rudolf Otto has called numinous sounds (Otto 1958, 4–7), sounds that go beyond the rational and the ethical to evoke direct, face-to-face contact with the holy. Otto conceived of the numinous with a typically Western emphasis on the experience of the distance, the separation, between human beings and God. For Hindus in the

Ṛgvedic context the cosmos is peopled by gods sometimes thought of in personal ways. For example, prayers or mantras are spoken to gods such as Varuna to maintain relationships with them so that they will act for the devotee. However, the Ṛgveda also saw mantras as the means by which the power of truth and order that is at the very center of the Vedic universe could be evoked. That truth, however, is not thought of as a personal God, like Yahweh or Allah, but as the impersonal *rta* or divine order of reality. In his classic article "The Indian *Mantra*," Gonda points out that mantras are not thought of as products of discursive thought, human wisdom, or poetic fantasy "but as flash-lights of the eternal truth, seen by those eminent men who have come into supersensuous contact with the Unseen" (Gonda 1963, 247). Sri Aurobindo puts it even more vividly: "The language of the *Veda* is itself a *sruti*, a rhythm not composed by the intellect but heard, a divine Word that came vibrating out of the Infinite to the inner audience of the man who had previously made himself fit for the impersonal knowledge" (Aurobindo 1971, 7). The Vedic seers supersensuously "heard" these divine mantras not as personal but as divinely rooted words and spoke them in the Hindu scripture or Veda as an aid to those less spiritually advanced. By concentrating one's mind upon such a mantra, the devotee invokes the power and truth inherent in the seers' divine intuition and so purifies his or her consciousness. It is this understanding that is behind the long-standing Indian practice of repeated chanting of mantras as a means for removing karmic ignorance or impurity from one's personality. The more difficulties to be overcome, the more repetitions are needed. The deeper one's separation from the Divine, the more one must invoke the mantra. Contrary to what our modern minds quickly tend to assume, the Hindu chanting a mantra in morning and evening worship is not simply engaging in an empty superstition. From the Hindu perspective, such chanted words have power to confirm and increase truth and order (rta) within one's character and in the wider universe. Chanting a Vedic mantra has a spiritually therapeutic effect upon the devotee and a cosmic significance as well. Hindus maintain that the holiness of the mantra or divine word is intrinsic, that one participates in it not by discursive understanding but by hearing, reciting, and singing it (Coburn 447).

The Hindu View of Language and Mantra in the Mimamsa, Grammarian, Patanjali's Yoga, Theistic, and Tantric Schools

The powerful function of words as mantras depends not only on Patanjali's psychological analysis of karma (as previously outlined) but also on the Hindu view of language as *Daivi Vak* or Divine Word. For the Hindu, the spoken scripture of the tradition is the Divine Word (Murti 1983, 361). The "sensitive soul" was the seer, or *rsi*, who had purged himself of ignorance, rendering his consciousness transparent to the Divine Word. The rsi was not the author of the Vedic hymn but, rather, the seer (*drasta*) of an eternal, authorless truth. The rsi's initial vision is of the Veda as one, which is then broken down and spoken as the words and sentences of scripture. In this Vedic idea of revelation there is no suggestion of the miraculous or supernatural. The rsi, by the progressive purifying of consciousness through the disciplines of yoga, had simply removed the mental obstructions to the revelation of the Divine Word. While the Divine Word is inherently present within the consciousness of all, it is the rsis who first reveal it and in so doing make it available to help all others achieve the same experience. The spoken Vedic words of the rsis act powerfully upon us to purify our consciousness and give to us that same full spiritual vision of the unitary Divine Word that the rsi first saw. This is the enlightenment experience, the purpose for which Hindu scripture exists.

As special words of revelation and power, mantras have received careful analysis by the scholars of India. Speculations begin in the oldest Hindu scripture, the Rgveda, where language has a prominent place. The words or mantras of language are described as the support of gods such as Indra, Agni, and the Asvins. *Vak* (language) bends Rudra's bows against the skeptic and gathers up all prayers. In the Satapatha Brahmana, Vak is identified with Sarasvati, who later becomes known as the goddess of learning, wisdom, and inspiration. The action of the rsis or sages in relation to the mantras of language is highlighted in Frits Staal's translation of Rgveda 10.71:

> Brhaspati! When they came forth to establish the first beginning of language, setting up names, what had

been hidden in them as their best and purest good became manifest through love.

Where the sages fashioned language with their thought, filtering it like parched grain through a sieve, friends recognized their friendship. Their beauty is marked on the language.

They traced the course of language through ritual; they found it embodied in the seers. They gained access to it and distributed it widely; the seven chanters cheered them.

Many who look do not see language, many who listen do not hear it. It reveals itself like a loving and well adorned wife to her husband . . .

Though all the friends have eyes and ears, their mental intuitions are uneven. Some are like shallow ponds, which reach up to the mouth or armpit, others are like ponds which are fit for bathing. (Staal 1977, 5–6)

Here the power of language is clearly contrasted in its two forms. To those who "see," as Staal explains, language (and meaning) is a manifestation, is widely distributed by the rsis, is seen and heard with understanding, is self-revealing and provides for deep intuitions; in contrast, to those who do not "see," who are obstructed by their own karmic ignorance, language is hidden, is mysteriously possessed by the rsis, is looked at and listened to without understanding, is wrongly used and is hidden in shallow intuitions. According to this hymn, the nature and function of language is to manifest or reveal the meaning of things.

The way in which mantras reveal the meaning and power of cosmic order (rta) is analyzed by various schools of Indian philosophy. Two principle schools, the Mimamsa and the Philosophy of Grammar, made the most significant contributions. Both of these schools follow the Brahmanic tradition stemming from the Veda, which takes language and mantras as of divine origin (daivi vak), as spirit descending and embodying itself in the vibrations of words. The well-known Rgveda verse (4.58.3) expresses this truth in poetic form. It symbolizes Speech as the Bellowing Bull of abundant fecundity, as the Great God descending into the world of mortals. Patanjali, the great Grammarian scholar, asks, "Who is this Great God?" and answers, "Speech itself" (*mahan devah sabda*) (Murti 1980, viii). To this view of mantra, the Hindu Mimamsa, Sankhya-Yoga, Grammarian, and Kashmir Saivism schools of philosophy are faithful.

In opposition to this high evaluation of mantra, there are the Indian schools that reject the Veda as an authoritative source of revelation—Jainism and Buddhism. Although the Jains and the Buddhists adopted a naturalistic view of language, namely, that it is but an arbitrary and conventional tool, the chanting of mantras, as we shall see in the next chapter, continued to play an important role in Buddhist spiritual practice.

Hindu thought sees a direct relationship between ritual action and mantras. Indeed, it has been suggested that in India, language is not something with which you *name* something; it is something with which you *do* something (Staal 1979, 9). Each spoken mantra corresponds to one ritual act. In post-Vedic India activities, such as bringing the goddess Kali into a stone image, bathing to wash away sins, sowing seeds in the fields, guarding the sown seeds, driving away evil spirits, and meditating to achieve release, all had to be accompanied by the chanting of mantras in order to achieve success (Gonda 1963, 261–268). In some situations, the ritual act itself was later modified or even abandoned, yet the action of mantra recitation was retained (Gonda 1963, 267). Within ritual action it is the uttered mantra that has central importance for release (moksa).

THE MIMAMSA THEORY OF MANTRA AS ETERNAL WORD (*SABDA*)

The task of providing a theoretical explanation for the power of spoken mantras was taken up by the Mimamsa school of philosophy as outlined by P. T. Raju (1985). The Mimamsa proposed a theory of sabda that suggests that the sound produced in pronouncing a word is not the result of human choice or construction; rather, every sabda or word has an eternal meaning. Each sabda is the sound-representative of some aspect of the eternal cosmic order. The mantras of the Vedas, therefore, are not words coined by humans. They are the sounds or vibrations of the eternal principles of the cosmic order itself. It is for this reason that the rsis or speakers of the Vedas are called "seers" or "hearers" of the mantras and not the authors of the mantras. Thus, the Hindu claim that the Vedas were not composed by human beings. They are not like other human literature. The Vedas, as the collection of the mantras, are not about everyday things. Rather, they give us negative and positive commands to ethical action in daily life that represent the eternal principles of rta (cosmic order) for ourselves and the universe around us. Even when the cosmic process ceases to be, between cycles of the universe, the mantras, as eternal truths, remain present in their seed state, ready to sound forth afresh as the eternal Veda in the next cycle of creation. Thus, the mantras are said by the Mimamsakas to be authorless and eternal. Another important aspect of this view is that these mantras are not written but passed on orally. The Vedic mantras are, thus, the eternal sounds of the ethical truth of the universe and ourselves. Words other than the Vedic mantras were regarded as human-made, with their meanings being established by human convention and, thus, incapable of giving us ethical guidance. Only the meaning content of the Vedic mantras can teach us the required continuous ethical action and enjoyment of its fruits that is the end goal in life.

For the Mimamsakas, ultimate reality is nothing other than the eternal words of the Vedas. They did not accept the existence of a single supreme creator god, who might have composed the Veda. According to the Mimamsa these gods named in the Vedas have no existence apart from the mantras that speak their names. The power of the gods, then, is nothing other than the power of the mantras that name them (Dasgupta 1977, 25). This concept of sabda, or word as divine, eternal, and authorless, is given further development in the Grammarian notion of *Sabdabrahman* and in the Tantric notion of mantra as mystical sounds that are "vehicles of salvation (*mantrayana*)"—an idea we see employed by the Buddhists in the next chapter (Eliade 1969, 212). Patanjali's *Yoga Sutras* seem to take over the Mimamsa view with little change and then identify it with the mind of Isvara, the master yogi. Let us examine each of these in turn.

The Grammarian Theory of Mantra as Sabdabrahman

We have seen that for the Mimamsa, mantra is sabda, the eternal authorless words of the Veda. The Grammarians adopt all of this but add to it the notion of Brahman, God as unitary pure consciousness. Consequently, the Grammarians offer a theory of mantra as a manifestation of Sabdabrahman or divine word-consciousness (Coward and Raja 1990). Although unitary in nature, this divine word-consciousness manifests itself in the diversity of words that make up speech. The mantra Om is identified by Bhartrhari in his *Vakyapadiya* (hereafter cited as *Vak*) as the root mantra out of which all other mantras arise (Iyer, 1965, 1:1 and 1:9). This sacred syllable is held to have flashed forth into the heart of Brahman, while absorbed in deep meditation, and to have given birth to the Vedas, which contain all knowledge. Om and the Vedic mantras are described as being at once a means of knowledge and a way of release (moksa) (*Vak*, 1:5). Fundamental to all of this is the notion that language and consciousness are inextricably intertwined. Indeed, the great Grammarian philosopher Bhartrhari puts it this way: "There is no cognition in the world in which the word does not figure. All knowledge is, as it were, intertwined with the word" (*Vak*, 1:123). Bhartrhari goes on to make clear that the word-meaning, as the essence of consciousness, urges all beings toward purposeful activity. If the word were absent, everything would be insentient, like a piece of wood. Thus, Bhartrhari describes the absolute or divine as Sabdabrahman (word-consciousness) (*Vak*, 1:1).

When everything is merged into Sabdabrahman, as in a high moment of mystical experience, no speaking takes place and no meaning is available through mantras. But, when the divine is awakened and meanings are manifested through words, then the knowledge and power that is intertwined with consciousness can be clearly perceived and known. Because consciousness is of the nature of word-meaning, the consciousness of any sentient being cannot go beyond or lack word-meaning (*Vak*, 1:126). When no meaning is understood, it is not due to a lack of word-meaning in consciousness but rather to ignorance or absent-mindedness obscuring the meaning inherently present (*Vak*, 1:332). For Bhartrhari and the Grammarians, words (mantras), meanings, and consciousness are eternally connected and, therefore, necessarily synonymous. If this eternal identity were to disappear, knowledge, communion, and the means to spiritual release would all cease to exist (*Vak*, 1:124). T. R. V. Murti concisely sums up the Grammarian position when he says it is not that we have a thought and then look for a word with which to express it, "or that we have a lonely word that we seek to connect with a thought. Word and thought develop together, or rather, they are expressions of one deep spiritual impulse to know and to communicate" (Murti 1974, 322).

The reason for the speaking of mantras is also traced to the nature of word-consciousness by Bhartrhari. He states that word-consciousness itself contains an inner energy (*kratu*) that seeks to burst forth into expression (*Vak*, 1:51). For example, the rsis see the Veda as a unitary truth, but, for the purpose of manifesting that truth to others, they allow the word's inner energy to assume the form of the various mantras. On an everyday level this inner energy or kratu is experienced when, at the moment of having an insight or idea, we feel ourselves impelled to express it, to share it with others by putting it into words. Indeed, the whole activity of scholarship and teaching is dependent upon this characteristic of consciousness.

Bhartrhari offers a detailed analysis of how the uttered sounds of the mantra reveal meaning. He describes three stages in the speaking and hearing of mantras on the analogy of a painter. Just as a painting is perceived as a whole over and above its different parts and colors, so our cognition of the mantra is of a meaning-whole over and above the sequence of uttered sounds. Sphota ("that from which meaning bursts or shines forth") is Bhartrhari's technical term designating mantra as a gestalt or meaning-whole that can be perceived by the mind as an immediate supersensuous intuition. Let us return to the example of the rsi. At the first moment of a Vedic mantra's revelation, the rsi is completely caught up in its unitary idea, gestalt, or sphota. But when under the expressive impulse (kratu) he starts to examine the idea (sphota) with an eye to its communication, he has withdrawn himself from the first intimate unity with the idea or inspiration itself and now experiences it in a twofold fashion. One the one hand, there is the objective meaning, which he is seeking to communicate, and on the other are the words and phrases he will utter. For Bhartrhari these two aspects of word-sound and word-meaning, differentiated in the mind and yet integrated like two sides of the same coin, constitute the sphota. Bhartrhari emphasizes the meaning-bearing or revelatory function of this two-sided gestalt, the sphota, that he maintains is eternal and inherent in consciousness (*Vak*, 1:23–26 and 122–123).

For the person hearing a mantra the process functions in reverse. Each repetition of the mantra removes karmic ignorance and brings further illumination. After sufficient repetitions (depending on the darkness of the person's karma) the sphota of the mantra stands clearly perceived—perhaps something like the "light bulb coming on" image we find in cartoons. As Bhartrhari puts it: "The sounds, while they manifest the word, leave impression-seeds progressively clearer and conducive to the clear perception of the word" (*Vak* 1:84, *Vrtti*).

The logic of Bhartrhari's philosophy is that the whole is prior to the parts. This results in an ascending hierarchy of mantra levels. Individual words are subsumed by the sentence or poetic phrase, the phrase by the Vedic poem, and so on until all speech is identified with Brahman. But Bhartrhari focuses upon the *vakya-sphota* or sentence-meaning as the true form of meaning. Although he sometimes speaks about letter sounds or individual words as meaning-bearing units (sphota), it is clear that for Bhartrhari the true form of the sphota is the meaning-whole. This has interesting implications for single-word mantras. Since the fundamental unit of meaning is a complete thought (vakya-sphota), single words must be single-word sentences with the missing words being understood. For example, when the young child says "Mama," it is clear that whole ideas are being expressed, for example, "I want mama." Even when a word is used merely in the form of a substantive noun (e.g., tree), the verb to be is always understood so that what is indicated is really a complete thought (e.g., "This is a tree") (*Vak*, 1:24–26, *Vrtti*). In this fashion Bhartrhari suggests a way to understand single-word mantras as meaningful. A devotee chanting "Shiva" may well be evoking the meaning "Come Shiva" or "Shiva possess me" with each repetition. Thus, such single-word mantras are far from being meaningless. They invoke a world of meaning.

In Vedic ritual mantra is experienced on various levels, from the loud chanting of the priest to silently rehearsed knowledge of the most esoteric formulas (Wheelock 1980, 358). Probably a good amount of the argument over the meaningfulness of mantras arises from a lack of awareness of the different levels of language. On one level, there is the intuitive flashlike understanding of the meaning of the mantra as a whole. At this level the fullness of intuited meaning is experienced in the "seen" unity of sound and thought in sphota. This is the direct supersensuous perception of the truth of the mantra that occurs at the mystical level of language—when "mystical" is understood in its classical sense as a special kind of perception marked by greater clarity than ordinary sense perception (Stace 1961, 15). Bhartrhari calls this level of mantra experience pasyanti (the seeing one) (*Vak*, 1:142)—the full meaning of the mantra, the reality it has evoked, stands revealed. This is the rsi's direct "seeing" of truth and the Tantric devotee's visionary experience of the deity. Yet, for the uninitiated, for the one who has not yet had the experience, it is precisely this level of mantra that will appear to be nonexistent and meaningless. If, due to one's ignorance, the pasyanti level is obscured from "sight," then the uttering of the mantra will indeed seem to be an empty exercise.

Bhartrhari calls the level of the uttered words of the sentence vaikhari. At the vaikhari level every sound is inherently meaningful in that each sound attempts to reveal the sphota. Repetition of the uttered sounds of the mantra, especially if spoken clearly and correctly, will each time evoke the sphota afresh until finally the obscuring ignorance is purged and the meaning-whole of the mantra is seen. Between these two levels of uttering (vaikhari) and supersensuous seeing (pasyanti) there is a middle level of madhyama corresponding to the meaning-whole in its mental separation into meaning and a sequence of manifesting sounds, none of which have yet been uttered. For Bhartrhari the silent practice of mantra is accounted for by madhyama and is, of course, both real and meaningful.

When all three levels of language are taken into account, as they are by Bhartrhari, it would seem that all Vedic and Tantric types of mantra practice can be analyzed and shown to be meaningful. In cases where the karmic ignorance of the speaker or the hearer obstructs the evocative power of the mantra, it may indeed be experienced as meaningless. But even then, the mantra is still inherently meaningful because it prepares the way for the sphota to be finally understood. Also, there is the fact that the cultured person, not afflicted by ignorance, hears and understands the meaning even though the person uttering the mantra does not (*Vak*, 152–154). The argument, of course, is circular, and if it were merely a theoretical argument, then Bhartrhari's explanation would have no power and would have been discarded long ago. However, Bhartrhari appeals not just to argument but also to empirical evidence—the direct perception of the meaning-whole (sphota) of the mantra. As long as such direct perception is reflected in the experience of people, Bhartrhari's explanation of the meaningfulness of mantras remains viable.

In the Indian experience the repeated chanting of mantras is an instrument of power (Gonda 1963, 271). The more difficulties there are to be overcome, the more repetitions are needed. Repeated use of correct mantras removes all impurities, purifies all knowledge, and leads to release. The psychological mechanism involved is described by Bhartrhari as a holding of the sphota in place by continued chanting. Just as from a distance or in semidarkness it takes repeated cognitions of an object before one sees it correctly, so also concentrated attention on the sphota by repeated chanting of the mantra results in the sphota finally being perceived in all its fullness (Vak, 1:89).

For Bhartrhari and the Grammarians, then, mantras are inherently meaningful, powerful in purging ignorance and revealing truth, and effective instruments for the realization of release (moksa). Indeed, Bhartrhari's theory helps our modern minds understand how the chanting or singing of mantras can be experienced as meaningful, powerful, and in fact a "yoga of the word" (Sabdapurvayoga) (Coward 1985, 1–13).

Mantra in *Patanjali's Yoga Sutras*

Patanjali, the great systematizer of the Yoga school, shares much in common with Bhartrhari, the Grammarian, when it comes to the understanding of mantra. In Patanjali's Yoga Sutras (1978, hereafter cited as YS), Isvara, like Sabdabrahman, is described as an eternal unity of meaning and consciousness from which all speech, including the Vedic mantras, evolves (YS, 1:24–29). Mantra, as the scriptural truth of the rsis, is taken to be the authoritative verbalization of Isvara's word-consciousness. All this is expressed in the sacred mantra, Om, which, when spoken, connotes Isvara and his omniscient consciousness. As was the case for Bhartrhari, it is the obscuring power of consciousness veiled by karmic ignorance that robs mantras of their inherent meaning and power (YS, 1:5). And as was the case for Bhartrhari, Patanjali states that this ignorance can be removed through a constant repetition of appropriate Vedic mantras. Says Patanjali, as a result of constant chanting or study (svadhyaya) upon mantras (including seed or *bija* syllables like Om) the desired deity becomes visible (YS, 2:44). Through the practice of fixed concentration (samadhi) upon an object, in this case an uttered mantra, consciousness is purified of karmic obstructions and the deity is "seen." Since for Patanjali Om is the mantra for Isvara, the devotee is advised that the *japa* or chanting of Om will result in the clear understanding of its meaning. Vyasa, a commentator on Patanjali, puts it in more psychological terms:

> The yogi who has come to know well the relation between word and meaning must constantly repeat it [the mantra] and habituate the mind to the manifestation therein of its meaning. The constant repetition is to be of the *pranava* (OM) and the habitual mental manifestation is to be that of what it signifies, Isvara. The mind of the Yogi who constantly repeats the *pranava* and habituates the mind to the constant manifestation of the idea it carries, becomes one-pointed. (YS, 1:28, *Bhasya*)

What does it mean for the mind to become "one-pointed"? The "point" is the mantra that is being chanted. "One-pointed" means that the continual chanting of the mantra is keeping it front and center in one's mind to the exclusion of everything else one might perceive or think. Through the chanting the devotee has become one with the mantra (Om in this case). It is as though one's whole world becomes only the mantra and for the period of the chanting nothing else exists. It is like the experience we sometimes have when we find ourselves "caught up" in a piece of music to which we are listening—for the moment your hearing of the music fills the whole universe. Or it is like the experience of being in a moment of love or sexual intercourse with another person—for the moment everything else ceases to exist. You are one-pointed. The yoga discipline described here involves becoming one-pointed or one with the mantra Om and what it signifies, Isvara.

The power of such mantra concentration (samadhi) to induce a perfectly clear identity with the signified deity is given detailed psychological analysis in the commentary on *Yoga Sutra* 1:42. With continued mantra concentration all traces of uttered sounds and conceptual meaning are purged until only the direct pure perception of Isvara remains. Patanjali's analysis supports Bhartrhari's claim that the repetition of mantra samadhi has the power to remove ignorance and reveal truth (YS, 1:17, *Tika*). This conclusion confirms the Vedic mantra experience (previously discussed) and the Tantric mantra experience to which we will turn shortly.

Since an additional aspect of the practice of mantra concentration is chanting, Patanjali prescribes the yogic discipline of making Isvara the motive of all one's actions (Isvarapranidhanam) (YS, 2:45). It is as though one is to become an "empty channel" through which Isvara (who is being held steady at the center of one's mind through the chanting or meditation upon Om) acts. In one's yoga practice one is attempting to emulate Isvara, the master yogi, so what better way than to attempt to act in every situation as though he were acting through you? It is rather like the young hockey player who tries to keep Gretzky uppermost in mind so that as he or she goes down the ice all moves will be those of the "great one." While chanting Om one "dedicates" all one's moves to Isvara. The result of such complete self-surrender, says the yoga text, is a vision of Isvara. In this way, says Oberhammer, the yoga of Patanjali is perhaps the oldest statement of theistic mantra meditation (Oberhammer 1989, 204). It is this actual face-to-face encounter with God that is given further development in theistic mantra meditation.

Theistic Mantra Meditation

The theistic traditions (e.g., worship of Shiva or Vishnu), which come to dominate Hinduism, use the meditation on mantras to effect an actual encounter with God. In the devotee who reverently disposes him or herself to an experience of transcendence, the mantra functions to take one out of or beyond one's spirit to an existential experience of the divine. The mantra has a sacramental function to make God present as an actual event. In Hindu theistic experience, mantras have both meaning and power—power to purify the mind and reveal the transcendent lord to the devotee in an existential encounter (Oberhammer 1989, 219).

Such mantras in the Hindu theistic traditions are held to have been created by the decree of the god involved—Shiva in the preceding examples. Shiva creates and empowers these mantras to be effective in communicating himself to his devotees for their salvation or release. When the practice of mantra chanting is put together with a concentrated seeing of the image of Shiva, the result is a powerful opening of the mind of the devotee in surrender to the god who is mediated through both sound and sight. Taken together, the mantra and the image have great power to remove distractions or mental impurities and open the way to direct hearing and seeing of the divine.

Mantra Theory in the Tantric Tradition

Unlike the philosophical and religious schools we have examined, Tantrism is a pan-India movement in that it is assimilated by all the great Indian religions (Hinduism, Buddhism, and Jainism) and by the various philosophical schools. There is a Buddhist Tantrism, a Hindu Tantrism, and to some extent even the Jains adopt Tantric methods. Strong Tantric influences are present in the Hindu sectarian movements of Saivism and Vaisnavism. According to Eliade, Tantrism begins to flower in fourth-century India and assumes a pan-Indian vogue from the sixth century onward (Eliade 1969, 200). What is the place of mantra in this new movement? Whereas the Vedic mantras serve to link the worshiper with the divine and to define the complex order (rta) of the universe, the Tantric mantra aims at the annihilation of all distinctions and affirmation of the worshiper's identity with the divine. "The mantras reflect this simplified worldview, recognizing fewer distinct beings, focusing on the one relation of man to God, and attempting to express sonically the collapse of the manifest universe into a single category" (Wheelock 1989, 117). As Eliade puts it, while the various Vedic mantras deal with different relationships between ourselves and the cosmic order (rta), the Tantric liturgy works to have us realize the one all-encompassing relationship, namely, worshiper = ritual = God. The divine, the worshiper, and the ritual all become one in the chanting of the mantra. While this bears much similarity with Grammarian and Yoga theory, which we have seen, there is one unique aspect that Tantrism highlights, namely, the power and function of the Great Goddess. No longer is the female merely an aspect that comes out of the male God; now the Goddess and her power (Sakti) are identified with the divine. And it is this female Sakti that the Tantric mantras seek to realize (Eliade 1969, 203). Particularly in

Hinduism, Sakti is elevated to the rank of the Divine Mother who sustains the universe and all its beings, including the gods. As the Great Goddess, woman incarnates the ultimate being of the universe: the great mystery of creation, living, dying, and being reborn. When danger threatens the cosmic order (rta), the gods appeal to Sakti the Great Goddess to put things right. And she usually does so, with a vengeance. Feminine divinities also made their way into Buddhism (Eliade 1969, 202–205) along with a focus upon the natural realities of life (eating, having sex, wearing clothes, and so on) as means of approaching and uniting oneself with the divine. Speech and sound, along with the rhythms of breathing, are natural processes upon which Tantric practice placed great emphasis. Another rule of Tantrism, however, is that the Tantric path begins with an initiation by a teacher or guru—one who knows all the secrets and can communicate them to you only from mouth to ear.

Eliade states, "It was tantrism, especially, Buddhistic as well as Sivaistic, that raised the mantras and *dharanis* to the dignity of a vehicle of salvation (*mantrayana*)" (Eliade 1969, 212). The term *dharani* literally means "she who upholds or encloses." Dharanis are sometimes partial or mutilated words (e.g., *vimale, hime, kale*) that express ideas of purity, but the majority of them are phonemes that seem to generate an inner echo when chanted during meditation (e.g., *hrim, hram, hrum*) (Eliade 1969, 213). Dharanis and mantras have to be specially received from the mouth of one's guru. They are thus different from the ordinary words that make up ordinary language or that we read in books. Once given by a guru, however, a mantra or dharani is claimed to have great power. Correctly pronounced and spoken according to the instructions (usually in synchronization with one's rhythm of respiration), union with Sakti, Shiva, or Buddhahood may be attained (Eliade 1969, 214). That the final goal could apparently be attained simply by repeated chanting seemed an easy path and this may at least partly account for the popularity of Tantrism right up to the present. Although it looks easy from the outside, this easiness is more apparent than real. Tantra, like the other yogas of India, is a long and difficult path. For example, uttering the mantra must be preceded by purification of thought. While speaking, one must concentrate on each of the letter sounds composing the mantra, avoid fatigue, and so on, observes Eliade (1969, 214).

In the Tantric view the power of mantras is that they can become the "objects" they represent. "Each god, for example, and each degree of sanctity have a *bija-mantra*, a 'mystic sound' which is their 'seed,' their 'support'—that is, their very being" (Bharati 1970a, 115–119). Each deity, suggests Bharati, has his or her bija-mantra often formed from the first three letters of the deity's name, for example, Gam for Ganesha, Dum for Durga, and so forth. By correctly chanting such a bija-mantra the devotee directly participates in its essence. He or she becomes the god or state of spiritual sanctity. In this sense the mantras are symbols that participate in that to which they point. The entire sonic universe, with all its gods, planes, and modes of being is manifested in a certain number of mantras. By chanting the mantra one awakens all the cosmic forces that correspond to it. The Tantric assumption is that there is a perfect correspondence between particular letter sounds (with accompanying image and color) and particular planes or degrees of sanctity. By chanting the sound that symbolizes it, the devotee evokes a particular plane of sanctity within his or her experience. The chanted sounds allow the devotee to assimilate the ontological state that he or she wishes to acquire. The Tantric worldview organizes these various ontological planes in a hierarchical continuity—each plane being correlated with a subtle center in the human body (the *Kundalini* cakras) and a bija-mantra. For example, the bija-mantra *Hang* evokes the god Shiva in his androgynous form and is physically centered in the *visuddha* cakra located in the throat (Eliade 1969, 242). In this way, a systematic mechanism is presented by which the devotee, under the guidance of a guru, can, through mantra chanting, awaken the various centers and experience identity with the spiritual planes or realities each center evokes. Eventually, identity with the whole cosmos may be realized.

The Tantric bija-mantras are also seen to function as a "shorthand" for metaphysical systems. This is especially the case for Buddhism, says Eliade, where the eight thousand stanzas of a voluminous Mahayana text, the *Astasahasrika-prajna-paramita*, were summarized in a few stanzas that were then further reduced to the few lines of the *prajna-paramita mantra* and finally reduced further to a single seed or bija-mantra: *pram* (Eliade 1969, 215). Thus, by chanting *pram*, one could be evoking in shorthand the whole of the Mahayana prajna-paramita metaphysics (see chapter 2 for more on this Buddhist example). This seems parallel to the Hindu practice encountered earlier where the chanting of the seed syllable Om was thought of as evoking the whole of the Veda. Some scholars have referred to such seed syllables as being meaningless or empty of meaning. Rather, it is their fullness of meaning—the whole meaning of the Vedas or the prajna-paramita—that is evoked by the chanting of the seed mantra. Indeed, it has been suggested that mantric utterances should be thought of as cognitive tools—as mental mechanisms for thinking a certain privileged class of thoughts (Alper 1989a, 268). In this sense a mantra functions something like a mathematical formula, meaningless to the uninitiated but evoking deep insight to those who understand. The powerful mantra Aram brings to the Shiva devotee the insight and direct realization "I am Shiva!" The various theoretical analyses of mantra offered in this chapter have made clear that the term mantra is not just a word or verse of scripture. It is that and something more—the divine truth in which the words and all of life partake.

Finding One's Mantra

In India, from a mother's womb to the funeral pyre, one literally lives and dies in chanted mantra. Having examined some of the theories of mantra we want now to sample some of the life experiences of mantra. These range from the traditional initiation of an individual by a guru to the singing of sacred mantras. Each of these experiences exemplifies different ways in which the divine is heard through mantras. Taken together they provide a menu of different ways in which one may find one's own mantra. They also indicate the social context in which people grow up and learn mantra practice by osmosis, as it were. As Harvey Alper has pointed out, the routine use of mantras presupposes specific convictions concerning the human condition, the ideal social order, and the purpose of existence (Alper 1989a, 258). Acceptance of these convictions provides the social and religious basis that has made and continues to make mantra practice possible. Although reasons may be offered to defend these convictions, they are also simply the social patterns and rituals within which life in

India is lived. The uttering of mantras would seem to be the most characteristic Hindu ritual gesture.

As we have seen, mantra chanting is essential to ritual action in Vedic, Yogic, and Tantric settings. Just as the gurus and the devotees following the final two stages of life complete everyday experience by transcending it, so too the chanting or singing of mantras may be understood to complete our everyday use of language by transcending it. Thus, mantras have both a social and individual function. In the earlier life stages, as, for example, in family and public rituals, they function as a kind of "sonic glue" to hold society together. In the later stages the mantras become highly refined instruments of personal inner transformation—transformation of exactly the kind that the earlier householder stage values and looks forward to as the ultimate completion of one's spiritual growth. In this sense mantras are not just mystical instruments of individual spiritual practice, they also form the basis of public worship or *puja*. Thus, mantras function at the intersection of "public" and "private" life in India. Indeed, the genius of Indian mantra practice is that even when it is used as a basis for withdrawal from ordinary worldly life, as in the last two stages of life, it is still affirming the order and values of everyday existence, for it is the expected and hoped for goal. Hence the joyful willingness of a family and village to provide food and shelter for the old uncle who has retired from his daily life as a lawyer to spend the last half of his life in increasingly private mantra chanting. His action is not seen as selfishness or as a drain on society, as it might well be judged in the modern West. Instead, his family and village take pride in the fact that one of their number is living out their social and religious ideal. Although transcending everyday life, the old uncle is also confirming it by being a living exemplification of its ideals.

Having a "living ideal" in one's midst also serves to keep one's lower and very worldly values of material possessions and sensual enjoyments in their proper perspective—namely, appropriate and necessary for the householder stage but not the values to which one should become permanently attached. Ultimately, material and sensual attachment must be transcended in the isolated spiritual life of a *sannyasin*. But to make such a transition one must find one's own mantra, and that can only be done under the guidance of a guru.

Finding One's Mantra through a Guru

One of the most ancient and important patterns present in Hindu society is the receiving of one's mantra from a guru. Although many manuals on mantras and their use may be found in India, mantra practice is never just a matter of the mechanical application of the rules found in such manuals. Rather, it depends on careful guidance by one's guru or spiritual master. Even in Tantric settings, which are sometimes more flexible, the use of a mantra is almost never "freelance" (Alper 1989a, 262). Hindu teaching has always maintained that mantras lose their power if not revealed by a guru and, indeed, that their unsupervised use may be dangerous. Mantras are the sound body of the deity, of cosmic energies, and it is necessary to balance these energies with the karmic predilections of the person. The central act of the guru is to bring about that balance, and so the "choice" of mantra is significant and particular indeed. The wrong mantra deepens instability or disharmony within. The right mantra guides one in another step toward union with the divine. And the question of which mantra is appropriate is really a question about what one's spiritual needs are. The guru is involved in the cure of persons; the guru is a spiritual physician.

It is not uncommon in India for people to have several gurus in their lifetime, although one guru will be of ultimate value for final release. Many Hindus have also spoken about chosen gurus who in the end turned out to be the wrong ones for them. The mantras employed under such a guru deepened disharmony. The guru apparently did not properly understand the source of disharmony within the person. In such cases the guru is clearly not the proper guru, the one who can reach within and discern what is needed for liberation. Infatuation governed the devotee's choice. Finally, when the right guru is found—or finds the devotee, as many say—the movement toward harmony and release is immediate.

It is for this reason that the Hindu tradition has maintained that mantras are esoteric knowledge that should be kept secret. Consequently, says Bharati, many traditional manuals were written in such a way that the mantra was spelled out in a disguised fashion that only an initiate would understand (Bharati 1970a, 119ff.). More recently, however, a mantra manual has been assembled that presents an encyclopedic compilation of Hindu mantras in straightforward fashion with no attempt at disguise (Bharati 1970a, 123–128). This new manual, widely used in cities like Mumbai, offers an indication of how modern influences are altering traditional mantra practice.

A traditional view, however, of the role of the guru is presented in the Kashmiri Saivite text *Sivasutravimarsini* by Ksemaraja (ca. eleventh century CE). The text states, "If one doesn't understand the hidden sense of a mantra, one will have to surrender to an authentic master (Alper 1989a, 249). It goes on to add that when it comes to making mantras work it is the guru who is the path. The guru is seen as the supreme mediator between the ordinary and the divine. As the text puts it, "It is the guru who is the supreme passageway (*tirtha*), in comparison to him any other passageway is of no use" (Alper 1989a, 263). As a passageway to the divine the combination of the guru's image and speech is especially powerful.

To find one's mantra, one must first find one's guru. From the guru one will receive the mantra specially selected to remove one's own impurities or karmic obstructions and advance one toward the realization of moksa or release.

As a perfected spiritual master, the guru's mind is completely pure and transparent (*sattvic*). Thus, when the devotee and the guru meet, the transparent mind of the guru is superimposed upon the devotee's mind with its ego-knots of karmic obstruction from actions in this and previous lives—and these are what the guru "sees." Having a clear understanding of the devotee's problem, the guru, like a doctor, prescribes the precise mantra that has the power to remove the particular karmic obstruction. When, after sufficient mantra chanting, that particular obstruction is removed, there is a direct realization of the divine and of spiritual freedom. The guru's prescription of a mantra has effectively transformed the devotee from the beginning state of a consciousness dominated by worldly concerns to a final state in which the mantra evokes a full and complete experience of the divine. However, this may well have required many years of chanting the mantra by the devotee. Then, in the context of the text we are discussing, one has become equivalent to Shiva and all one's speaking is the repetition of Shiva's name. Ksemaraja, author of the text, explains: "[The discourse of a master is japa] because he truly has constant inner realization of being the supreme 'I.' This is in accordance with the maxim: I myself am the supreme Hamsa, Siva, the primal cause" (Alper 1989a, 281). So, one sign of the highest spiritual attainment is the constant japa or chanting of sacred syllables. But of course, the context is important. Under the prescription of the guru, if I were directed to utter the mantra Hamsa eighteen thousand times, the first utterance ought to be qualitatively different from the last. The point of the endless repetition would be for me as a devotee not just to lose myself in trance but to remove the last karmic impurity and have the inner revelation of being Shiva.

The committing of oneself to such a rigorous spiritual discipline is a serious matter. It is marked by the ceremony of *diksa* or initiation of the devotee by a guru. The word diksa is defined by Bharati as dedication of oneself to the undertaking of religious practices, self-devotion to a person or god, or exclusive occupation with a spiritual goal (Bharati 1970a, 185). The most important aspect of diksa, however, is the receiving of a mantra from the guru. The mantra provides the content of the diksa or initiation (Bharati 1970a, 186). The practice of receiving a specially chosen mantra from a guru in an initiation ceremony is common to Hinduism, Buddhism, Jainism, and even to some tribal practice in India. Such a ceremony is always a one-to-one, interpersonal process between one guru and one disciple (Bharati 1970a, 187). The key part of this ceremony occurs when the guru whispers the mantra individually selected to suit the needs of a particular devotee into his or her ear.

Any practicing Hindu may receive mantra-diksa or initiation with a mantra. A person may go to a hereditary or family guru, or a person may "shop around." In the latter case the procedure is as follows. A person feels the desire for "spiritual practice" and goes to several teachers to listen to them. The guru whose teaching and personality has the most appeal is singled out. The devotee then tries to get that teacher interested in him or her by visiting frequently, bringing gifts of food and clothing, and discussing the possibility of diksa. When the guru feels the time is ripe, an auspicious day is selected when, according to the horoscopes of all involved, the particular deity desired will be easily accessible for worship. It is at this time that the mantra of the deity, as selected by the guru, is imparted to the disciple.

But before this time the disciple has had to prepare properly. This involves fasting for twelve hours, taking a bath, and bringing some fruits or other presents as a sacrificial fee to the guru's place. The guru sits facing East or South with the disciple facing him. The guru's deity is first invoked and then the disciple is instructed on the modes of meditation: keeping the mantra secret, breath control (*pranayama*), and concentrating the mind on the one point (*dharana*)—the one point in this case being the mantra. It is expected that the asana or sitting posture will have been mastered before the diksa or initiation takes place. The guru then "whispers the *mantra* into the disciple's right ear repeating it three times, and has it repeated three times by the disciple, first singly, then at one stretch" (Bharati 1970a, 189). The mantra must not be written down by the disciple or it will lose its power. Nor can it be passed on by the disciple to another person. Only after the disciple has achieved spiritual perfection and become a guru is he or she in a position to pass on mantras to others, and then it will be through the diksa or initiation ritual we have just described. After the mantra has been received, the disciple prostrates before the guru by lying face down on the ground with the forehead touching the guru's feet. The disciple then rises, circumambulates the guru three times, receives some sanctified food (*prasad*) from the guru, worships at the shrine, takes another bath, and withdraws.

The giving of the Gayatri Mantra with the sacred thread is a different kind of initiation from the Tantric diksa ceremony just described. The Vedic Gayatri is a standard mantra given to all boys of the upper three castes and was seen as an initiation that allowed him to master the Vedic knowledge needed for successfully entering the role of a householder. In Vedic times girls also were initiated (Coward, Lipner, and Young 1989, 13–14). By contrast to the Vedic Gayatri, the diksa initiation is most appropriate for those who have completed the householder stage and are dedicating themselves to the final goal of complete spiritual realization appropriate to the final two stages of life, the forest dweller and the sannyasin or holy wanderer. In the diksa initiation there is no common mantra, but, as described earlier, the guru carefully selects the appropriate mantra for the life situation or karma of each devotee.

Many Hindus have a guru whom they may know and consult in the flesh, while others may have a guru who died years ago or decades before the devotee was born. Their relationship to the guru, however, is no less intimate. The relationship is eternal in character and not bound by the normal understanding of time and space. We see a striking parallel with the relationship some pious Christians have with saints. The needs of one's soul are spoken to across time. The life of the soul does not know the bonds of death.

In the 1960s gurus began arriving in America from India bringing mantra practice, customized for Americans, with them. One of the first was Maharishi Mahesh Yogi, who taught a simple mantra meditation that he called Transcendental Meditation—often referred to as TM. He was widely recognized as the guru of the Beatles. The Maharishi, as he became known, started a university-based movement called the Student's International Meditation Society (SIMS) and soon had SIMS centers in over a thousand North American colleges and universities. Eck notes, "By the early 1980s, the society estimated that more than 1.5 million Americans had received a mantra and begun practicing TM under a teacher's instruction" (Eck 2001, 109). TM centers spread across North America, and a university, the Maharishi University of Management in Fairfield, Iowa, was established. Transcendental Meditation describes its approach as a simple, natural, easily learned mental technique of mantra meditation for fifteen to twenty minutes twice daily, sitting comfortably with the eyes closed. A mantra especially suited to the karma of the person is given by the TM teacher at the time of initiation. By following TM mantra practice, it is claimed, the meditator is able to realize a natural state of blissful, relaxed, yet fully alert consciousness. No difficult postures, special clothing, or cushions are required. One simply sits in a chair at home to do the TM mantra meditation. And it is open to everyone regardless of age, education, culture, or religion. In simplifying and adapting Hindu mantra practice for America, the Maharishi demonstrated a keen understanding of the American mind.

A quite different Indian mantra practice was brought to America in 1965 by A. C. Bhaktivedanta. Rather than adapting traditional practice to America, as the Maharishi did with TM, Bhaktivedanta retained the full Hindu approach to devotional or bhakti mantra chanting and also achieved success. From his humble beginning chanting "Hare Krishna, Hare Rama" in New York's Tompkins Square Park, Bhaktivedanta soon began to attract followers to his joyful, colorful, ecstatic chanting. Soon he opened his first Krishna temple in a Second Avenue storefront on the Lower East Side. In five years, he and his followers had temples in some thirty American cities. His movement was named the International Society for Krishna Consciousness (ISKCON). Unlike TM, this was not a comfortable use of mantra practice that meshed easily with North American life. Rather, ISKCON introduced a very traditional Hindu devotional approach with a completely different worldview and lifestyle involving Hindu dress, worship, chanting, singing, and dancing. Yet Bhaktivedanta, with his counterculture and fervent piety, succeeded in attracting a dedicated group of young followers that steadily increased in size during the 1970s and 1980s, spreading their message everywhere from "drug row" and working-class streets to university campuses.

Bhaktivedanta followed the approach of Caitanya, a sixteenth-century ecstatic saint who lived in Bengal, India, and popularized a form of mantra worship called kirtan—the chanting and singing of the Lord Krishna's holy name, for example, "Hare Krishna, Hare Krishna, Krishna, Krishna, Hare, Hare." This devotional practice could be done by anyone regardless of caste, gender, or financial status. "The singing of God's name required only love and broke down the barriers that divided people from one another. The followers of Caitanya were not only caste Hindus but untouchables, even Muslims (Eck 2001, 117). It was this approach that Bhaktivedanta introduced to America with its rigorous discipline and demand for complete commitment. Devotees rise at dawn and chant the name of Krishna in traditional temple rituals involving the offering of food, flowers, water, and sweets to the divine presence of Krishna so that the Lord's grace may be received in return. After offering food and fruit to Krishna, they eat together what has been consecrated by his presence. Incense is lit and used to circle the image of Krishna as mantra chanting of the Lord's name continues. This sensuous approach to mantra involving not only sound but also sight, smell, movement, singing, and dancing has saved many young Americans from lives they described as filled with drugs and meaninglessness.

Although it never attracted the large numbers of TM, ISKCON, with its demanding lifestyle, has become a permanent part of American religious culture. Senior devotees of the Hare Krishna movement have gone on to become serious scholars of Hinduism, undertaking graduate studies at universities such as Harvard. Dressed in their orange-colored robes, senior ISKCON leaders participate regularly in scholarly interfaith organizations such as the Society for

Hindu-Christian Studies, which meets annually with the American Academy of Religion. At the grassroots level the Hare Krishna temples have found themselves serving not only North American converts but also the needs of Hindu immigrants who settled in North America in significant numbers during the 1970s and 1980s. To begin with, the Hare Krishna temples were the only Hindu worship places to be found in local communities. When the Hindu immigrants showed up there on Sunday afternoons to engage in devotion to Lord Krishna, they would find a worship service in which they felt quite at home, complete with mantra chanting and a lecture on the Gita delivered by a well-trained Caucasian devotee dressed in the ochre robes of a Hindu monk (Eck 2001, 119). Thus, the newly arrived Hindu immigrants could enjoy a fairly traditional Hindu worship followed by a vegetarian meal served Indian cultural style. In addition, ISKCON temples observe the birthday of Krishna, the Diwali festival of lights, and other festivals that made the Hindu immigrants feel that they had found something of their religious and cultural identity in America. By the 1990s, when the North American–born children of the Hindu immigrants were coming of age, ISKCON played another role—namely, interpreting Hindu mantra theory and practice to second-generation Hindu South Asian young people in a way more in tune with their American and Canadian upbringing (Coward 2010, 882).

Finding One's Mantra through Kirtan Singing

The chanted mantra often seems to increase in its power to evoke the divine when it is sung. The major Indian religions have devised different techniques for doing this. The singing of mantras as hymns or kirtans is common to Hindus and Sikhs. A number of Hindu movements rely primarily on the sung mantra as a way to release or moksa. Throughout much of popular Hinduism a rich tradition of singing kirtan to the god or goddess of one's heart flourishes. It is done in homes and temples and in the streets on festive occasions (Smith 1976).

Guy Beck in his fine study of "Hinduism and Music" (Beck 2006) notes that the collective singing of the names of God or *nam-kirtan*, as in "Hare Krishna, Hare Rama," is very popular in Hinduism. The

"Hare Krishna" chant, known as the "Mahamantra" or "Great Mantra for Deliverance," was introduced by Caitanya in the 1500s and has continued to be chanted and sung by pious Hindus down through the years—and today has spread worldwide thanks to ISKCON. Other sung chants of God's names that are popular include the chant to "Rama and Sita" and the "chant to Siva." Beck translates these three chants as follows:

1. Hare Krishna, Hare Krishna, Krishna, Krishna, Hare Hare
   Hare Rama, Hare Rama, Rama Rama, Hare Hare.

2. Sita Ram, Sita Ram, Sita Ram Jaya Sita Ram
   All Glories to Lord Rama and his consort Sita.

3. Om namah Sivaya
   I bow to Lord Siva. (Beck 2006, 135)

Like most Hindu religious music, says Beck, the collective singing of the names of God is done to simple melodies accompanied by drums and cymbals. Such congregational nam-kirtan allows persons not schooled in classical music to experience fervent devotion and serves as an important means of spiritual transformation and release (moksa). It is performed with participants seated on the floor and led by a lead singer who often plays a harmonium for accompaniment— generally, a separate area of the temple facing a deity or picture is set aside for singing. Congregational members "usually repeat the lines in unison after the leader in call and response format" (Beck 2006, 135). Sometimes the leader may sing solo with occasional refrains sung by the group.

Musical sounds and instruments have been part of Hindu spiritual practice since the early Vedic period (ca. 1500–800 BCE), but musical engagement of the Hindu masses in devotional singing seems to have had a major development during the early Bhakti devotional movements in South India (from the seventh to the tenth centuries CE). During that period, ordinary devotees (including women) engaged in bhakti spiritual practice, and, says Beck, "musical texts such as Matanga's *Brhaddesi* began to incorporate the theories of sacred sound as *Nada-Brahman*" (Beck 2006, 124). Speculations of the Nada-Yoga and the Tantric traditions began interpreting all music as a direct manifestation of Brahman in the form of *Nada* (sound)-*Brahman*. Of course, this followed on very nicely from Bhartrhari's Grammarian theory (ca. 500 BCE) of Brahman as Sabdabrahman, as Beck demonstrates in his *Sonic Theology: Hinduism and Sacred Sound* (1993). Just as the chanting of Vedic mantras such as Om can remove karmic obscuration and lead to moksa or release from rebirth, so also can the singing of music. As a manifestation of Nada-Brahman, music is seen as a means of access to the highest reality and open to all caste levels. As such, music in Hinduism is viewed both as entertainment and a path for the realization of moksa—Nada-Yoga, a yoga of using music to remove karma and achieve release from rebirth. Thinkers influenced by Matanga see Nada-Brahman as manifesting spiritual song through all the gods as well as all living beings and all of nature. As Beck notes, the *Sangita-Ratnakara* of Sarngadeva (ca. 1200–1250 CE), perhaps the most important musical text of India, opens with the salutation "We worship *Nada-Brahman*, that incomparable bliss which is immanent in all the creatures as intelligence and is manifest in the phenomena of this universe" (Beck 2006, 124). Down through the centuries, and still today, the musical chanting of portions or all of the Hindu scripture, the Bhagavad Gita, is a favorite devotional yoga practice of educated Hindu laypeople in groups or in private. Says Beck, many pious Hindus have memorized the entire Bhagavad Gita and chant it regularly using a simple repetition of melodic motifs, with verses in strophic form. Hindus believe that regular chant/singing of sacred texts, like the chanting of God's names (*Nam-yoga*) will powerfully purge one's obscuring karma, bring one to the state of oneness with *Nam-Brahman*, and release one from rebirth (Beck 2006, 124–125). Such a bhakti or devotional spiritual practice rapidly came to be seen by the majority of Hindus in South India from the seventh century on as the favored means for moksa realization. While some song-texts were composed in Sanskrit, the majority were in vernacular dialects. Two main groups of poet singer-saints led this South India bhakti movement in Tamilnadu—the Saivite Nayanars (devotion to Siva) and the Vaishnava Alvars (devotion to Vishnu). Says Beck, "The collections of their devotional poetry in Tamil represents the oldest surviving verses in Indian vernaculars, and became the first hymnals of devotional music" (Beck 2006, 125).

In technical terms the musical scales and melody patterns of Hindu music are called *ragas* or emotional moods that are said to be timeless and transcendental (Beck, 2006, 126). Since they are preexistent in Nada-Brahman, they must be discovered and spoken/sung like the Vedas. Notes Beck, "Each *raga* possesses a particular mood or flavor (*rasa*) mysteriously embodied within it, and is capable of generating those same feelings within the minds of the listener and performer when properly invoked. When those feelings are directed toward God as Brahman or Isvara (Lord), the result is higher attachment. . . . And, if the music is both understood as *Nada-Brahman* and performed properly in the spirit of *Bhakti*, then the musician and the listener are said to gain momentum for eventual release and [communion] with God in both this life and the next" (Beck 2006, 126). In Hindu music, rhythm, or *tala*, also plays an important role in spiritual transformation. As Beck explains, just as Vedic chant was metrical (with the metrical units marked off by the playing of drums and hand cymbals—each unit conveying a portion of unseen merit to the performer and serious listener), so also in Bhakti music, the rhythm or tala gives benefits to the performer and listener of removing karma and ultimately enabling communion with the Lord and the realization of moksa (Beck 2006, 126). As Beck summarizes, "The developing notion of release (*moksa*) within most forms of *Bhakti* music retained this same idea, and also included the special emotional states and experiences of the practitioners as cultivated in their relationship with their chosen deity" (Beck 2006, 126). Bhakti or devotional singing for the Hindu masses rapidly spread throughout India. From the fourteenth century on there was an outpouring of devotional song from almost every linguistic region of India—each with its own composer of songs (high and low caste, male and female) to a favored manifestation of Nada-Brahman such as Vishnu and his incarnations of Krishna and Rama. For example, says Beck, "in the North, Sur Das wrote in Braj Bhasha about Krishna; Tulasi Das addressed Lord Rama in Avadhi; Tukaram and Namdev in Marathi expressed devotion to Krishna; Mira Bai in Rayasthani addressed Krishna; Govinda Das wrote about Krishna in Brajbuli; and Chandidas in Bengali expressed devotion to Radha and Krishna. In the South, Purandaradasa wrote in Kannada expressing devotion to Vishnu; Syama Sastri in Telugu devoted to the Goddess; Annamacharya in Telugu to Lord Vishnu; and Tyagaraja in Telugu to Lord Rama" (Beck 2006, 127). These composers, along with others, are held to have realized release (moksa) through their singing and opened the way for Hindu devotees of all ranks and gender to follow (right up to the present). They also helped provide the context for the arising of the Sikh tradition of chant and song (see chapter 4).

In Hindu temples, chant and music were always integral parts of worship. Pujas or daily worship (focused on a *murti* or divine image) included Sanskrit chants and vernacular hymns and songs with accompanying instruments often based upon ragas especially in the South.

Individual singer-saints have been very influential in Hindu music. Swami Harida (ca. 1500–1595 CE), called "the Father of Hindustani Music," composed many *dhrupad* songs for the pleasure of Lord Krishna. His student Tansen sang at the court of Emperor Asoka and had students who spread Hindustani music throughout the Mughal empire. Sur Das (sixteenth century CE) was a blind musician-poet of the Vallabha sect who composed and performed songs to Krishna. Says Beck, in his work *Sur-Sagar*, in the Braj Bhasha language, Sur Das maintains that singing to the Lord is as close as one can come to moksa understood as complete communion with the divine (Beck 2006, 130). The *Padavali-kirtan* of Bengal and Orissa is another distinctive style of devotional music. It combines religious narratives with songs composed by bhakti saints in Bengal and includes short improvised phrases called *akhar*, which interpret the meaning of the song in the local language for the benefit of the audience. Beck notes that "today there are many skilled singers of *kirtan*, both male and female, who have the ability to freely improvise *akhars* on the spot" (Beck 2006, 132). A sample akhar in a Bengali kirtan to Krishna is: "He has come, the one who previously was black is now golden." Sung in the local dialect it is a little like a spontaneous improvisation in a modern jazz performance (Beck, 2006, 132).

In Hindu religious gatherings today, *bhajan* or informal styles of devotional singing have largely replaced earlier more formal types of song (e.g., dhrupad or kriti). Bhajan elicits more audience participation and bhajan sessions stress egalitarianism—openness to men and women of all classes, castes, and social backgrounds. They may take place anytime and go on continuously for several days. Bhajan sessions have become popular and widespread across India and throughout the Hindu diaspora. Says Beck, "Distinct from other Hindu occasions such as specialized rites of passage, the atmosphere of the *bhajan* session, where all participants sit, sing and eat together regardless of caste, gender, or religious viewpoint, fosters intimate and informal social relationships" (Beck 2006, 133). All types of musical instruments, including drums, hand cymbals, and harmonium or *sarangi*, may accompany the singing. "Beginning with the chanting of Om, a typical *bhajan* session proceeds with invocations in Sanskrit in honor of a guru or deity, followed by sequences of *bhajan* songs that reflect the distinct or eclectic religious outlook; these are sometimes punctuated by short sermons. . . . Toward the closing, a special ceremony called *arati* is conducted as part of the *puja* which includes offerings of food, flowers, incense and lamps, and blowing of conches. The distribution of food, flowers, lampwicks, and holy water concludes the session" (Beck 2006, 133). In addition to the temple and informal group forms of bhajan, the term is also used for individual practices of spiritually advanced devotees. Such private practice involves the use of a rosary (to count repetitions) in the singing and chanting of scripture (e.g., verses from the Bhagavad Gita) before a home altar upon which the devotee's chosen form of God resides. Such sadhana or private spiritual practice is often customized to deal with the particular karmic obscurations of a devotee by a guru, "in an admixture of *japa mantra* chant, *nam-kirtan*, scriptural readings, prayers, puja (worship) of a personal or family deity [e.g., Vishnu, Kali, Siva, or Sita] with a series of offerings (incense, food, water, sandalwood paste, collyrium, camphor, and flowers), ritual bathing, and ablutions" (Beck 2006, 136). Since there is no required temple attendance in Hinduism, there is a strong tendency for devout persons to practice private spiritual devotions. Says Beck (who is himself a professional Hindu musician) serious Hindu musicians set aside a daily alone time for their six-hour practice in a private space, often in front of a deity like the goddess Sarasvati or a picture of a guru, so that musical practice has a sacred aura and may be referred to as a *svara-sadhana* (a spiritual exercise involving musical notes) (Beck 2006, 136).

During the twentieth century, Hindu renaissance movements have been permeated by religious and devotional music. Movements founded by figures such as Swami Vivekananda, Swami Sivananda, Sri Aurobindo, Swami Muktananda, Satya Sai Baba, Anandamayi Ma, Swami Rama, and A. C. Bhaktivedanta Swami Prabhupada spread to the West and brought with them their own styles of chants and bhajans. Hindu bhajans, says Beck, are also sung by yogic and New

Age Groups. Pop bhajans along with devotional songs sung by male and female singers have achieved great success in Indian films. Beck notes that "film *aratis* or worship songs such as 'Om Jaya Jagadisha Hari' (featured in the Hindu film *Purab aur Pacchim*) are now widely used by Hindus in home and temple worship practices all over the world" (Beck 2006, 137).

Conclusion

Mantric word, chant, and devotional song are key components of Hindu religious practice and spiritual transformation as it persists today throughout India and the worldwide diaspora. As Swami Satyananda taught his Western student John Main, through your practice you are seeking a state of consciousness in which the only sound in your heart and mind "will be the sound of your mantra, your word. The mantra is like a harmonic . . . which builds up a resonance . . . that leads us forward to our own wholeness . . . a resonance between you and all creation . . . and a unity between you and your Creator" (Main 1977, 4). Mantra chanting and singing leads to a "recollection" of the self, free from karmic obscurations, and union or communion with the Divine. As Bhartrhari puts it in the *Vakyapadiya*:

> After taking his stand on the word which lies beyond the activity of breath, after having taken rest in oneself by the union resulting in the suppression of sequence, after having purified speech and after having rested it on the mind, after having broken its bonds and made it bond-free, having reached the inner light, he with his knots cut, becomes united with the Supreme Light. (*Vak*, 1:131, *Vrtti*)

Or as Matanga put it in his analysis of sacred sound, all word, chant, and song is a direct manifestation of Nada-Brahman and a mode of communion with the Divine and realization of moksa or release from rebirth (Beck 2006, 124). Thus, music, especially in its bhakti or devotional forms of nam-japa, dhrupad, kirtan, and bhajan is today perhaps the most significant component of spiritual transformation for the vast majority of Hindus of all castes, classes, and genders throughout India and the diaspora (Beck 2006, 137–138). As Vasudha Narayanan observes, "The performers of music and dance, the transmitters of the religious traditions, speak for Hinduism. We should listen to them" (Narayanan 2000, 776). For the Hindu devotee, it is not traditional textual scholarship by itself that has spiritual power, but the scriptural word that is chanted and sung.

CHAPTER 2

Buddhism

Word, Chant, and Song in Spiritual Practice

> Through a regulated life in accordance with the *Vinaya* rules, to study doctrinal statements attributed to the Buddha as presented in the *sutras*, to practice the teaching and to reflect on some of the points in the light of commentaries are the consistent directives in Buddhist tradition. It is only through this threefold effort, the religious goal of Buddhahood, or *Nirvana*, might be attainable.
>
> —J. Yun-Hua, "Dimensions of Indian Buddhism"

Unlike Hinduism, Judaism, Christianity, or Islam, Buddhism has no "revealed" words or scripture, yet as the preceding quotation makes clear, the Buddhist life is lived from within Buddhist words and texts. Also, in their philosophy of language, Buddhists see words as useful for conventional everyday transactions and scientific knowledge, but not for transcendental knowledge. As Garfield puts it, the limit of articulate speech is well stated in the Madhyamika position of Nagarjuna (Garfield 2002, 171–172). Language, thought and spoken, is merely conventional—at best it can point to, but cannot explicitly say, the ultimate nature of reality.

How is it then that words come to function as mantras or powerful chants for realizing the ultimate in Buddhist traditions such as Tibetan Buddhism or Japanese Jodo Shinshu? That is the question this chapter attempts to answer through three case studies of Buddhist mantra practice: 1) the Triple Refuge in Theravada; 2) the Om Manipadme Hum of Tibetan Buddhism; and 3) the Nembutsu of Pure Land Chinese and Japanese practice. This will require us to follow Buddhism in India from its early development through the arising of Mahayana and especially the Mantrayana traditions from the seventh to the eleventh centuries CE in our attempt to understand how some words change from being seen as created by humans for the purpose of solving practical problems in everyday life to being powerful mantras that, when chanted repeatedly, can purify karma and bring spiritual transformation, even *Nirvana*. But before moving to the case studies and the development of Mantrayana, let us begin with a brief look at Gautama the Buddha as the founder of the tradition and the development of Buddhist scripture.

Buddha, Buddhist Scripture, Revelation, and Inspiration

The extant versions of Gautama the Buddha's life were all composed many years after his death. Even though legend was added to the historical elements, the intent of the early writers was to celebrate his deeds—they were poets rather than historians. Still, Ashvaghosa, in his first-century *Acts of the Buddha*, saw Gautama as a real human being—experiencing conflicts and temptations, and exercising his own choices motivated by compassion for suffering human beings (Robinson 1970, 13). This image of Gautama is likely as close to the historical person as Ashvaghosa could make it. As is the case for Jesus, we cannot get back behind the portraits developed of the founder by the early community. As Robinson puts it, "Though the Community (*Sangha*) created the image of the Buddha, the Buddha created the Community and in so doing impressed upon it his personality" (Robinson 1970, 3). Gautama was born (ca. 560 BCE) a *Ksatriya*, or warrior, to a princely family living on the edge of the foothills of the Himalayas. Growing up as an educated young man in Hindu culture, he would likely have had instruction in the Vedas. A study of the *sutras*, or sayings of Buddha, indicated he had definite views in regard to Vedic revelation (Jayatilleke 1980, 183ff.). In Buddha's view, none of the teachers of the Vedic tradition, not even the original rsis, have experienced a direct vision of Brahman. Thus, the Vedic claim to scriptural knowledge of Brahman is not trustworthy because it is not founded on direct experience of Brahman by one of the rsis. The Veda, therefore, cannot be accepted as a revelation. Buddha does not seem to be denying the possibility of scriptural revelation altogether, although the admission of the possibility of such a revelation in a theistic form would be incompatible with the nontheistic character of Buddhism. In the Buddha's view, even if a Vedic revelation was a true experience of the rsi, it might be misremembered or a false "revelation" might be correctly remembered. For these reasons, claimed the Buddha, the Vedas cannot be accepted as trustworthy revelation. Rejecting the Hindu faith's acceptance of the Veda, the Buddha went out in search of his own direct personal experience of reality. The words he spoke, which became the Buddhist scriptures, were a description of his experience of striving for and finally achieving the state of Nirvana—the final goal of knowing reality and experiencing release from suffering. Having had the direct personal experience face-to-face as it were, the Buddha had none of the doubts that worried him regarding the experience of the Hindu rsis. The words he spoke (e.g., "The Four Noble Truths") were intended to exhort and instruct others to enter this same path and also to realize release (Nirvana). These words were seen as new and different from the handed-down doctrines of the Vedas:

> That this was the noble truth concerning sorrow, was not, O Bhikkus, among the doctrines handed down [i.e., the Vedas], but there arose within me the eye (to perceive it), there arose the knowledge (of its nature), there arose the understanding (of its cause), there arose wisdom (to guide in the path of tranquility), there arose the (light to dispel darkness from it). (Davids 1969, 150)

This passage is repeated twelve times to emphasize the newness of Buddha's enlightenment experience, and its discontinuity with the Vedas.

Concern for the survival of his teaching is shown by Gautama just before his death. The *Maha-Parinibbana-Sutta* reports that Gautama's disciple Ananda feared that the death of his teacher would mean the end of the teaching (*Dharma*), and thus the end of the opportunity for release from samsara (rebirth). Gautama reassures Ananda and directs his followers that henceforth his Dharma would be their leader: "The truth and the rules of the order which I have set forth and laid down for you all, let them, after I am gone, be the Teacher to you" (Davids 1969, 112). In this way, Gautama took the lead in establishing the basis for the canon of Buddhist scripture and sowing the seeds for the view that the truth or Dharma embodied in his words had special power (the mantra idea). While Buddha's followers judged him to speak with an authority that arose from his own enlightenment experience, they seemed not to think that his words represented divine revelation or that they were dictated by God. Lewis Lancaster puts it well:

> While the followers of Buddha considered that his words possessed special power, the idea that the teaching arose from insights achieved in a special state of yogic development, a state open and available to all who have the ability and the desire to exert the tremendous effort needed to achieve it, meant that the words based on the experience need not be considered as unique or limited to one person in time. Indeed, the Buddhists held that Sakyamuni was but one of a line of Buddhas who have appeared in this world system to expound the Dharma, and that there would be others to follow. (Lancaster 1979, 216)

For Buddhism, as was the case for Hinduism, the truth taught by the scriptures is understood to be beginningless or eternal. Like the Hindu rsis (as they are understood within Hinduism), Gautama acts to clear away the obstructions that obscure the eternal truth. Other Buddhas have done this before him and will do it again after him. But always it is the same truth that is revealed. Revelation in this Buddhist sense is *parivartina*—turning something over, explaining it, making plain the hidden. This is the role of the Buddhas: to make visible the timeless truth to the unenlightened; to point out the path to Nirvana and guide the way. In the Buddhist view, each of us is a potential Buddha obscured in karmic ignorance, but with the possibility for enlightenment within us. Over time, Buddha's followers evolved two traditions (Theravada and Mahayana), each with somewhat different ideas regarding the Buddhist scripture and the transforming power of words, chants (mantra), and songs.

The Canon and the Monastic Communities

The Buddha was one of the first religious founders to establish monastic communities, and it was within these communities that the Buddhist canon was given shape. The different monastic groups tended to give the canon a different shape, and these diversities became more pronounced as the religion spread over a wide geographical area into many cultures. Controversy developed among the various groups regarding the substance and the character of the scriptures. Some limited the canon to those words of the Buddha remembered by his closest follower and relative, Ananda. Apparently, none of these had been written down during the Buddha's years of teaching, which covered four decades. Tradition records that within the year Buddha died (perhaps 480 BCE), five hundred monks gathered together at Rajagrha (the capital of the Magadha Kingdom) to agree on Buddha's teachings and to codify the Rule of the Monastic Order (Matics 1970, 16). Ananda is credited with recalling and reciting the discourses or "remembered words," which were then approved by the whole community (*Sangha*). These words were passed on orally for several centuries until they were finally compiled and codified into treatises called sutras (Buddha's teachings). Along with these sutras the rules of conduct for the monastic community (*Vinaya*) were also recorded (apparently by Upali, the Buddha's barber) and included as a part of the canon, since they were also considered to be the words of Buddha. Ananda is said to have recited in order each of the five *Nikayas* (also called *Agamas*) in the *Sutra Pitaka*, or the "Basket of Discourses." The sutras written on palm leaves were actually kept in a basket—thus the name. Each sutra begins with the words: "Thus I have heard at one time. The Lord dwelt at . . ." with the "I" here referring to Ananda, the reciter of Buddha's words. These texts are chiefly in prose. Robinson comments:

> In the prose texts the early disciples seem to have been more concerned with the substantive content rather than

the exact words. Everyone was allowed to recite the scriptures in his own dialect. . . . Sectarian bias undoubtedly has occasioned distortions, additions, and omissions. Nevertheless, a large fund is common to all versions, and the Sangha seems from the first to have striven to exclude spurious texts and to maintain purity of transmission. Strictness in preserving the essential kernel, and liberty to expand, vary, and embellish the expression, characterize Buddhist attitudes through the ages toward not only texts but art, ritual, discipline, and doctrine. The perennial difficulty lies in distinguishing the kernel from its embodiment. The Buddha is said to have told Ananda that if the Sangha wished it might revoke the minor rules; but Ananda forgot to ask which rules were minor, so the First Council, it is said, decided to retain everything in the Vinaya. (Robinson 1970, 36–37)

Many Buddhists felt that only these memorized and transmitted sayings of the Buddha could be part of scripture; others took a much more flexible approach to the canon. One school formed around the *arhat* monks and called themselves the School of Elders (*Theravada*). They took a conservative approach to the canon and argued that only the "remembered words" of the Buddha in the sutras should be included. In these "remembered words" would be found the "seeds" of the Dharma, or Buddhist teaching, which could then be amplified and developed. They considered their philosophic treatises expanding on the "seed words" of the Buddha to be also part of the Dharma. The origins of Mahayana Buddhism are not clear, and scholarly views have been significantly changing over the past fifty years. At the end of the 1960s, Richard Robinson, a leading scholar of his time, offered the following analysis.

The Theravada monks tended to form an elite community insisting that they alone knew the true Dharma and were thus in a position to pass judgment on the views of others. Some opposed this by arguing that a householder could become an arhat (Buddhist "saint") and keep his or her lay status. The Mahasanghikas admitted laypeople and non-arhat monks to their meetings and were more open to popular religious values (Robinson 1970, 37). They were the religious innovators and formed the main basis out of which Mahayana Buddhism arose. They maintained the open approach of the Buddha, but they carried the transfiguration of the Buddha much further than the Theravada in maintaining, "His body is infinite, his power is boundless, and his life is endless. He educates living beings tirelessly, awakening pure faith in them" (Robinson 1970, 38). Between 100 BCE and 100 CE, the Mahayana movement arose from within the Mahasanghika groups.

In contrast to Robinson's 1970 outline of the origins of Mahayana, Paul Williams's 2000 survey of more recent scholars offers a quite different picture. In this new view, says Williams, "Mahayana Buddhism has nothing to do with Vinaya differences, and is not the result of a schism. . . . Mahayana is very diverse. It is united perhaps solely by a vision of the ultimate goal of attaining full Buddhahood for the benefit of all sentient beings (the 'bodhisattva ideal') and also (or eventually) a belief that Buddhas are still around and can be contacted (hence the possibility of an ongoing revelation)" (P. Williams 2000, 103). Williams groups scholars such as Gregory Schopen and Paul Harrison into this new approach in which the origins of Mahayana may have been centered on "sutra cults" involving the promulgation and worship of particular sutras containing new revelation from the Buddha (or a Buddha) and does not involve the laity in any widespread way. Using both archeological and literary sources, Schopen and Harrison suggest that the origins of Mahayana in Northern India may be found within second-century CE monasticism itself, in a "hard-core" ascetic attempt to return to the original inspiration of Buddhism, namely, the search for full Buddhahood in an austere forest-retreat revivalist movement. Central to perfect Buddhahood is taking upon oneself the vow of the bodhisattva—one who lives for the benefit of all living beings—rather than the arhat's lesser vow of gaining liberation from merely one's own personal suffering (P. Williams, 96–111). Williams notes that this more recent scholarship sees in the Mahayana sutras a highly *conservative* monastic vision of Buddhism, centered on the inferiority of the laity and austere practice in the forest as the ideal. Also, in some of this literature is the idea "that the Buddha (or Buddhas) could still be contacted, and is really still teaching out of his immense compassion" (P. Williams, 108). In this Mahayana view, the Buddha is not dead but still around, able to be contacted through various meditation practices, and has the potential to offer continuing new revelation. It was in these ways, it is suggested by recent scholars such as Schopen, Harrison, and Williams, that the Mahayana monastic vision focused not on the remembrance of the historical Buddha, but on "an awareness of his continuing if rather invisible presence in the monastery" (P. Williams, 111).

With this survey of the formation of the canon and the evolution of the monastic communities in mind, let us now begin our examination of the function of words in the scriptures, chants, and songs of the Theravada and Mahayana traditions in turn.

Words in Theravada Buddhism: Chanting the Triple Refuge

As Asanga Tilakaratne puts it, "To be a follower of the Buddha is to 'take refuge' or 'go to refuge' in the Buddha, the Dhamma, and the Sangha—the Triple Gem" (Tilakaratne, 19). Tilakaratne suggests that the "taking refuge" practice originated when two passing merchants gave food to the newly enlightened Buddha. It is said that "they took refuge only in the Buddha and the Dhamma, for the third gem—the order of monks—had not yet come into existence" (Tilakaratne, 19). Tilakaratne describes the evolution of the practice as follows:

> It was customary for attendees at the Buddha's sermons to indicate their acceptance of what he taught by seeking refuge in the Triple Gem. That marked the beginning of one's life as a "Buddhist," as either a monastic or a household follower. Apart from this simple religious act there was no elaborate initiation ceremony to mark one's conversion to Buddhism. What was at this early stage a once-in-a-lifetime activity has now become a regular practice among Theravada Buddhists. (Tilakaratne, 20)

Accordingly, most Theravadins begin the day by repeating three times the taking refuge chant, followed by the *panca-sila* or five basic rules of Buddhist life, and end the day similarly. These recitations are also chanted by devotees at the start of any public Buddhist function usually led by a monk. This individual and community practice is basic to Theravada tradition: taking refuge in the Buddha, the Dhamma (his teaching), and the Sangha (the community of followers). The simple chant used to take refuge runs as follows in Pali:

Buddham saranam gacchami	I go for refuge to the Buddha
Dhamman saranam gacchami	I go for refuge to the Dhamma
Sangham saranam gacchami	I go for refuge to the Sangha
	(Tilakaratne, 25)

These chants for taking refuge along with associated virtues are among the first things learned by heart by a Theravadin, and they are used throughout life. These chants are done in Pali, the liturgical language of all Theravada Buddhists. Many devotees may never be able to reach a clear understanding of the Triple Gem chant and its associated virtues, yet they recognize the importance of this religious practice for their life. Tilakaratne concludes by noting that it has become customary for devotees to use a rosary in their chanting of the Triple Refuge and its associated virtues or rules for good conduct. This practice of taking refuge through chanting helps the Buddhist to overcome the fear of samsara—of living the repeated cycle of birth, suffering, aging, and dying, and rebirth over countless lifetimes. Fear of samsara is overcome through taking refuge or trust in the Buddha and his path in order to attain deathlessness or release from rebirth (Nirvana).

For many laypeople, chanting of the Triple Gem also helps to overcome fear by providing protection against everyday experiences such as nightmares, bad things happening, and evil in general. In this sense, for the ordinary devotee the chanting of the Triple Gem is felt to have almost magical power. Similarly, failure to follow the Triple Gem can result in a deviation from the Buddha's path and a loss of the merit-making (*punya-karma*) power offered by chanting. For Theravadains, daily chanting of the Triple Gem helps keep devotees on track in embodying the virtues of the Buddha in their daily lives.

In Theravada Buddhism, the taking of refuge is associated with the concept of trust (*saddha*) rather than faith in the Buddha. It is through trust in the Buddha that one is able to follow the path of the Triple Refuge. In traditional Theravada Buddhist societies, trust in the Buddha is generated by the culture and family upbringing in which devotion to learning and chanting the Triple Refuge plays a major role (Tilakaratne, 26–28). Yet even the most uneducated Buddhist would not expect the Buddha to play the role of a divine being or God who is able to grant wishes or answer prayers. The constant presence of Buddha statues in Theravada societies, says Tilakaratne, are not symbols of the living presence of the compassionate Buddha (as for, e.g., Kuan Yin in Mahayana). Rather, for the Theravada devotee Buddha statues "are simply visual aids to preserve the memory of the Buddha" (Tilakaratne, 29). For the Theravada Buddhist, the Buddha, in his lifetime, was a real person who could be seen and heard. However, what is significant is that through the path he pioneered the Buddha became an *awakened* person and thus offers an example and a path for others to follow. It is because of his awakened state that the Buddha is seen as worthy of being approached as a refuge—as is done in the chanting of the Triple Refuge, which keeps the memory of the Buddha, his teachings, and his community front and center in one's life as an example to be emulated. Constant repetition of the chant helps to keep one on track. This is done in daily morning and evening worship at home in a space or room with an altar and statue set aside for that purpose (Tilakaratne, 111). On occasions such as full-moon days each month, large numbers of people visit the temple or monastery to worship by chanting and reflecting on the Triple Refuge and its attached virtues for action in life (e.g., to abstain from destroying life, to abstain from sexual misconduct, and to abstain from false speech) (Tilakaratne, 155).

With regard to its musical aspect, Sean Williams notes that Theravada chanting, including chanting of the Three Refuges, is "limited to a few basic notes that resemble in principle the Vedic cantillation from which it was primarily derived. The principal chanter is followed line by line in response by the other monks. Chanting of the Three Refuges is normally preceded by a short drum sequence and an invocation" (S. Williams, 173). However, says Williams, music in Theravada Buddhism is appropriate only when it is subordinated to the message. "Music has little liturgical function, yet chanting continues to be central to the preservation of the Pali Canon. The Buddha's First Sermon . . . is regularly chanted . . . as a unison chant without call and response" (S. Williams, 175). Williams concludes that although music has no formal place within this tradition, it is accepted "as an authentic form of religious expression insofar as it points beyond itself as an art form" (S. Williams, 176).

Chanting the Triple Refuge is seen as an important part of the "Merit Making" practice for both householders and monks as they struggle through the beginningless and seemingly endless cycles of birth, death, and rebirth (samsara) until Nirvana is realized. While chanting of the "triple gem" formula occurs in most formal Theravada practices (e.g., *dana*, giving to monks or laypeople, and *sila*, morality), it is in *bhavana* or meditation that oral recitation of the Triple Gem is highlighted as the concluding part of the worship. Also, when there is a death the monks administer the last rites, which can take days or weeks of chanting depending on the financial resources of the family, and the cultural tradition of the Theravada devotee (e.g., Laotian or Sinhalese). Says Tilakaratne, "Monks are invited to chant appropriate passages in Pali, morning and evening, until the funeral takes place, and offerings are made to the monks who provide this service" (Tilakaratne, 117). Chanting is also involved in the monk's role as physician. *Paritta* (protection) chanting in Theravadin societies is a blessing of the people by chanting a collection of texts and formulae invoking the Triple Gem. In addition to receiving such blessings when they visit the monastery, "people specifically seek blessings on birthdays, weddings, when starting a new business venture, ground breaking for a new home, starting a new job, joining a new workplace, starting school, sitting for an examination, going for a job interview, embarking on foreign travel, for pregnancy, illness, and the like" (Tilakaratne, 119). Devotees often go to the monastery to receive such blessings of Paritta chanting, but monks may also visit homes or hospitals in cases of illness or when invited for a special purpose. Usually these sessions of chanting are short, lasting less than an hour, but on special occasions they may go on all night or, for example, as part of last rites, for seven days or more. Blessings and protection, or Paritta chanting, compose a significant dimension of Theravada practice. These chants are comprised of different parts from the Pali Canon. For example, a popular Paritta (verse) chant from the Maha Piritha or "Great Book of Protection" runs as follows:

> May all blessings be yours;
> May all gods protect you.
> By the power of all Dharmas;
> May all happiness be yours. (S. Williams, 176)

Such ceremonies of Paritta chanting provide opportunities for a monk's involvement with the day-to-day well-being of laypeople. Ideally, monks should follow the example of the Buddha and provide such services free of charge as acts of compassion.

Paritta chanting and ritual in Sri Lanka has been given detailed examination by Ariyapala Perera in his book *Buddhist Paritta Chanting Ritual*. Perera finds that Paritta chanting ceremonies may be dated from the fourth century CE, the Polonnaruwa period, and have been the most popular Buddhist ceremonies in Sri Lanka with both royalty and laypeople (Perera, 32). Perera describes "Paritta" as "a chanting of Buddha Vacana—Buddhist texts and Discourses to invoke blessings to ward off illness and danger to individuals and also for the health and welfare of the world. Paritta is regarded as a safeguard against fear and malady" (Perera, 1). Most of these chants have been taken from the sermons of the Buddha, who introduced their use as blessing or protection parittas himself. Says Perera, the chanting of Buddha's sayings as parittas was begun by Theravada monks as a simple ritual to add to the Triple Gem chants as a way of providing protection and refuge for laypeople. He also claims that the Buddha approved Paritta chanting as a healing therapy to overcome physical and mental ailments (Perera, 25). As Paritta practice developed through the centuries, it was influenced by the Hindu Arthaveda tradition and by Mahayana, Tantrayana, and Vajrayana ritual practices. However, Perera concludes that the Theravada elders "were clever enough to protect their own values and traditional characteristics of the Paritta Ritual" (Perera, 230).

A Canadian colleague and former Theravada monk, postdoctoral scholar D. Mitra Barua, describes paritta as the powerful words of the Theravada tradition. He says that the Theravada devotees trust that paritta contain the power to heal, protect, and to invoke well-being and prosperity—and that these powers derive mainly from the virtues of chanting the Triple Gem. Mitra Barua puts it as follows:

Paritta chanting is considered an act of truth or "truth assertion" (*Saccakiriya*). The truth uttered in Paritta chanting often relates to the virtues of the triple gem. The Pali three refuges (*tisarana*) chanting implies the virtues of the triple gem but does not necessarily verbalize the virtues (24 of them). Paritta chanting often includes a few discourses derived from the Pali canon, i.e., the Patana Sutta, Dhajagga Sutta, Khanda Paritta, etc. Particularly the Dhajagga Sutta lays out all the 24 virtues of the triple gem and those exact Pali phrases are chanted in everyday liturgical services in Theravada temples, homes, and public ceremonies. (Personal communication from Mitra Barua, August 3, 2014)

The preceding quotation is supported by the PhD thesis of Choy Fah Kong, "Saccakiriya: The Belief in the Power of True Speech in Theravada Buddhist Tradition." As Choy puts it, in the Theravada tradition the reason Paritta chanting is believed to be effective is because it is considered to be the recitation of the Buddha's true speech which has the power of *sacca* or "truth utterance"—a concept taken over from Hindu Vedic practice of power being present in the utterance of a name or mantra (Choy, 3–5, 10). From talking to Theravada colleagues in Canada, I understand that the Paritta chant rituals are alive and well in diaspora communities, especially in end-of-life rites.

Words and Chant in Mahayana Buddhism

Graeme MacQueen, in his article "Inspired Speech in Early Mahayana Buddhism," shows how the Theravada tradition's historically closed view of the Buddha's words or sutras (those recited by Ananda after the death of Buddha at the First Council) is opened up by the early Indian Mahayana monastic communities in various ways. At the First Council, Ananda's reciting of the entire collection of the Buddha's words or sutras from memory establishes them as the authoritative collection, and the door to further production of sutras is closed (MacQueen, 314). This is the Theravada narrow position as to the definition of the *buddhavacana* or words of the Buddha—those rendered to the First Council by Ananda as "a final and closed corpus, the *sutra-pitaka* which represents the revelation as possessed by the community" (MacQueen, 315). MacQueen offers a detailed analysis of how words spoken by those other than the Buddha (e.g., some of his followers) are to be judged in relation to the buddhavacana—remembering that the Buddha's words were considered authoritative because they were firsthand reports of his direct experience (*pratibha*) in his "awakened state." MacQueen, following Lamotte, shows that according to the First Council buddhavacana is the ideal, but it can be extended through a process of certification to include the utterances of others—thus assuming the Buddha's presence in the world after his death and opening the door to the Mahayana expansions of what can be included in the categories of inspired and revealed words. "Inspired" is the English term MacQueen uses to translate the Sanskrit *pratibha*, which, as Gonda has shown, was understood in Hindu thought to be the direct "seeing" of the Vedic rsis of Brahman or reality in a flash of insight as it were. It is this understanding of pratibha or direct perception (clear of obstructing karma) that MacQueen finds present as inspired speech in the Buddhist canon (MacQueen, 319–324). He concludes:

> To sum up, we have in the *sutra-pitaka* two major sorts of *prati-bha* construction, which refer to two sorts of creative speech by people other than the Buddha, this speech being acceptable under certain circumstances as the basis of sutra. These two kinds of creative speech share the important characteristic of coming freely from a state of mind different from, and higher than, the normal. They differ in these respects: the first kind tends to be connected with the mental states that are ideally open to all who strive correctly . . . the second kind tends to be connected with mental states that arise from an inborn faculty (a natural gift), that are sporadic, and that are indicative of faith. (MacQueen, 323)

However, words arising from these two kinds of pratibha mental states still had to be certified by the Buddha in order to be acceptable as sutra. As set forth in the *Uttaravipatti Sutra*, "certification by the Buddha" is a defined concept that states that personal pratibha is subordinate to buddhavacana and is authoritative only when transformed into extended buddhavacana. Criteria for certification include being "well spoken" and "speech of greatest spiritual worth" rather than needing to be the actual words of the Buddha. Such utterances are also to be checked against the existing Dharma (teaching of the Buddha) and Vinaya to see if it harmonizes in import, and accepted only if it does. Thus, says MacQueen, the approach in the sutra-pitaka moves from historical checks to a purely functional understanding of buddhavacana while yet maintaining itself as a stable body of literature established quite early. Changes in the existing sutras (from the First Council) tended to be minor and conservative. There was a strong conviction "that the time when the Buddha revealed the truth was past and that no such revelation would come again (at least for a very long time). . . . Thus the concept of buddhavacana, historically understood, put strong limits on the contribution people's pratibhana could make to the corpus of revealed truth" (MacQueen, 324).

Extension of Buddhavacana and Pratibhana in Early Mahayana

MacQueen's analysis shows that in the early Mahayana text, the *Astasahasrika Prajnaparamita*, the relation between buddhavacana and pratibhana is seen in a radically new way (MacQueen, 324–329). In this text, the issue is explained of how someone such as a bodhisattva (and not the historical Buddha) can have a direct experience of the perfection of wisdom such that it can have the status of sutra. Says MacQueen, "Being now familiar with *prati-bha* constructions as used in earlier Buddha literature [as outlined in the preceding section], we know that when the Buddha invites Subhuti to speak [in the *Astasahasrika Prajnaparamita* text], with the words 'may it be clear to you' (*pratibhatute*), he is asking that a (doctrinal) discourse flow freely from Subhuti's purified [karma-free] consciousness. The invitation constitutes a certification before the event and indicates that the discourse is a form of extended *buddhavacana*" (MacQueen, 325). This indicates that: 1) the sutra (and perhaps all Mahayana sutras) are extended buddhavacana or the words of people other than the Buddha but certified by him; and 2) this certified speech comes freely from or through the disciple's purified mind. According to the

Astasahasrika whatever the Buddha's disciples teach is an outpouring (*nisyanda*) of the Tathagata's demonstration of dharma. Consequently, says MacQueen, when the early Mahayana describe their sutras as buddhavacana, they do not mean that these texts are the words of the historical Buddha. How then do they account for the presence of the Buddha in their extended sutras—for the presence of the Buddha was viewed as the prerequisite for all buddhavacana, whether simple or extended? MacQueen suggests that the early Mahayana sutras adopt two main positions regarding the presence of the Buddha:

1. *The Theistic Viewpoint* which is strongly evident in the *Lotus Sutra*. The Buddha, it is held, is still present, has never gone away. Only the faithful are aware of this. . . . Sakyamuni Buddha and the countless Buddhas who support him are, therefore, fully present and capable of speaking and of certifying what others say. Not only can *sutra* legitimately be produced, but this revelation supersedes that given through the Buddha's corporeal form; that was the first turning of the wheel of *dharma*, this is the second.

2. *The Non-Theistic Viewpoint* is central to the Astasahasrika and answers two questions. [First] is there that which is even more worthy of attention and honour than the Buddha . . . and more rightly regarded as authoritative than the Buddha? The answer given is that liberating wisdom (or the perfection of wisdom, *prajnaparamita*) is the mother of all Buddhas. . . . The function of a Buddha is precisely to make known such wisdom to others, and this function implies its priority. [Second] Did the Buddha appoint a successor to whom one could turn after his passing away? The answer given is that the Buddha refused to appoint a human successor, saying instead that the *dharma* would succeed him. . . . The Buddha arose in the world because of his training in the perfection of wisdom; after his passing away one must take refuge in that very perfection of wisdom. (MacQueen, 328)

For the early Mahayana, says MacQueen, although the Buddha is no longer physically with us, the perfection of wisdom, the mother sutra of all Buddhas, is. Thus, the door to revelation did not close with the death of Sakyamuni Buddha but is still present and open to later bodhisattvas, as it was to the Tathagata. The perfection of wisdom is the Teacher, the source of all pratibha or direct revelation experience, and turns the wheel of dharma. Through it (the perfection of wisdom, the mother sutra) the Buddha lives on and is present in the world. Thus, when a text such as the *Astasahasrika* refers to "the Buddha's words," says MacQueen, "it does not primarily refer to what Gautama said in the sixth or fifth century B.C.E. but to the fresh revelation obtained via perfect wisdom" (MacQueen, 329). How does this perfection of wisdom, the mother source of all Buddhas, speak? For the Mahayanists it speaks through the medium of the dharma preacher who has the major task of raising up bodhisattvas by converting people through the experience of the rise of aspiration for Buddhahood (*bodhicittotapada*). One who has had it is a bodhisattva and belongs to the Mahayana, while one who has not had it is not. The role of the dharma preacher was to bring about bodhicittotapada in his hearers and help bring them to Buddhahood. "This meant that the sacred duty of all *bodhisattvas* was to set people on the path to Buddhahood—to give them the gift of *bodhicitta*" (MacQueen, 329).

The move by nontheistic Mahayana of identifying the *prajnaparamita* or the perfection of wisdom as the revelation source for all Buddhas, including the Tathagata, the Buddhas that existed before him, and the Teacher source of pratibha or direct experience of buddhavacana of the bodhisattvas, is important for our goal of understanding how words come to have life-transforming power when chanted as mantra in Mahayana Buddhism. Understanding the prajnaparamita or perfection of wisdom as the "mother source of all Buddhas" (as MacQueen puts it) allows one to ascribe liberating power to the words of all Buddhas when spoken as sutras. In this way of thinking, words revealed from the direct experience (pratibha) of the prajnaparamita or mother source manifest liberating wisdom and thus have power to purify and transform one's consciousness. Here the Mahayana view seems functionally parallel to the Hindu understanding of Brahman-consciousness as the source for the direct experience (pratibha) of the Vedic rsis. The rsis spoke their "Brahman truth" as the Vedas, which had purifying power, when chanted, to purge obstructing karma and enable one to realize moksa or release from rebirth (Gonda, 1963a, 14ff.). Indeed, as I have shown in chapter 1, this Hindu practice of Vedic words or syllables such as "Om" was formalized by the Grammarian philosophers and called Sabdapurvayoga or the yoga of the word (*Vak Yoga*), and Vak Yoga is shown to be a means to liberation (moksa) (Coward and Raja, 44–50).

The Mahayana move (in its nontheistic approach as outlined earlier) seems functionally parallel and perhaps had some Hindu influence. As with the Vedic rsi, the dharma preacher is described as getting directly in touch with and communicating the truth that the sutra itself manifests. This, says MacQueen, is especially clear in the *Astasahasrika* where the bodhisattva Sadaprarudita is told, when searching for the perfection of wisdom, that the person from whom you will hear the perfection of wisdom is one who has within him, so to speak, the perfection of wisdom itself—one who is not a mere reciter but an extempore speaker who rocks his hearers with inspired speech born of his intimacy with liberating wisdom. In nontheistic Mahayana, it is the clear mind of the speaker that is the instrument of the extended buddhavacana (the prajnaparamita). However, in theistic Mahayana, the dharma preacher is seen as the deputy and messenger of the Buddha—the preacher in visions and dreams who hears the Buddha expound the dharma and catches the true meaning, which he presents to others as both text (sutra) and interpretation (as for example in the *Lotus Sutra*, where the preacher is both the transmitter of a sutra and an inspired extempore exegete) (MacQueen, 331–332). Whether theistically or nontheistically conceived, it is the reachieved presence of the Buddha that is directly experienced through the dharma preacher or via the liberating wisdom of the prajnaparamita as the mother source of all Buddhas and bodhisattvas. As such, the Mahayana words and texts are experienced as inspired and filled with liberating power—opening the door to the idea of mantra chanting as a powerful spiritual yoga or practice (MacQueen, 337).

The Sociopolitical Fostering of Powerful Words in Medieval India

MacQueen's analysis demonstrated an understanding of words as having the inherent possibilities for inspired speech and revealed sutra when spoken by a Buddha or bodhisattva in early Indian Mahayana. Another scholar, Ronald Davidson, adds an external or contextual dimension to our understanding of how chanted words became powerful. In his sociopolitical study, Davidson shows how Mahayana Buddhism in post-Gupta India (seventh–twelfth centuries CE) came to reflect the political and social models of the surrounding feudal society in the esoteric practice of monks and *siddhas* (yogis or "perfected" independent laypersons) (Davidson, 2). Davidson demonstrates that the developing Mahayana use of language and scripture is found in its response to the feudalization of Indian society in the early medieval period—"a response that involves the sacralisation of much of that period's social world . . . [seen in] the tension between forms of esoterism that evolved within the hallowed halls of Buddhist monasteries and those forms synthesized by the peripatetic figures of the Buddhist 'Perfected' (*siddha*)" (Davidson, 2–3). For his analysis, Davidson used the hagiographies of both monks and siddhas together with the sociopolitical matrices of the Indian environment in determining how chanting of words and texts came to constitute a powerful new system of spiritual practice in the minority Buddhist culture of medieval India (concentrated in the northern and southern corners of the country) (Davidson, 76). Because of its focus on the use of mantras or chants as a method of gaining enlightenment, this new form of Mahayana practice was called Mantrayana Buddhism (Long, 177). According to Davidson, "the Mantrayana was at once the most socially and politically involved of the Buddhist systems and the variety of Buddhism most acculturated to the medieval landscape" (Davidson, 76).

During the Gupta period, Buddhist monks had been very successful in establishing themselves in positions of patronage through their provision of rituals by which kings or key persons would establish their positions of authority (e.g., ceremonies for the installation of a king). However, this pattern changed in the eighth century when the Buddha was displaced by Hindu gods and Buddhist rites were replaced by Puranic coronation ceremonies. Saiva ascetics, working in conjunction with Hindu Brahmins, replaced the patronage positions previously held by Buddhist monks. Buddhist patronage was also disrupted by the arrival of Islam during the eighth century (see chapter 3). Muslims replaced traditional Buddhists in social and economic roles with merchants and kings so that after the seventh–eighth centuries, Buddhism was no longer dominant through much of India, especially where Saiva patronage flourished. Buddhist monastic activity, however, did survive but mainly in the east, west, and north (Davidson, 81–90).

Davidson also argues that along with the loss of patronage there was a parallel erosion of the Buddhist intellectual and philosophical perception of reality—including the composition of scriptures as the word of the Buddha (buddhavacana). This erosion, says Davidson, was the result of the introduction of Buddhist skepticism by Nagarjuna's teaching that no technical or philosophical propositions may be adopted in the middle way. "Only the level of truth available in the world (samvyavahara) is the proper basis for speaking and communication" (Davidson, 99). According to Nagarjuna's Madhyamika philosophy, liberation from suffering can only be gained by insight into the ultimate nature of things. In terms of words and language, this insight can only be "grasped through language and thought which are thoroughly conventional and which can only be interpreted literally at the conventional level" (see his *Mulamadhyamakakarika* 24:10) (Garfield, 1995, 298). Thus, says Garfield in his commentary on the verse, the result is a shift of focus from the ultimate to the conventional use of words in this world as the locus for enlightenment. This shift in focus from the ultimate (paramartha) to the conventional truth (samvriti) in Buddhist philosophy had an unintended result, says Davidson, "in that it was perceived as validation of an ethical standard established by the lowest common denominator in Indian society and the restriction of vocabulary to a common-language assessment of reality" (Davidson, 100). This perception eroded the role Buddhist language and philosophy played in social, political, and economic infrastructure in Indian society. Nagarjuna's view of language ushered in a skepticism and relativism in ethics.

Even in Buddhist monasteries the teachings of Nagarjuna were employed by some monks to justify their unwillingness to adhere to the ethical teachings in the Vinaya regarding abstinence from drinking of alcohol and the pursuit of women. Davison notes that by the seventh century CE, the Hindu philosopher Sankara says that "the disparate elements in the Buddhadharma, and especially that of the Madhyamika made all attempts at a socially approved ethical system impossible" (Davidson, 101). As Davidson demonstrates, by the mid-seventh century, the twin movements within Indian Mahayana of Nagarjuna's skepticism and Dignaga's epistemology led to a public perception of the Buddhadharma as "given to quibbling about shades of gray . . . a form of presentation that political and military leaders found unhelpful and incomprehensible" (Davidson, 102–105). Yet the voices of these two lines of thought were dominant in the centers of monastic instruction from the mid-seventh century forward, resulting in a continued erosion of support to the Buddhist monasteries from their traditional sources of support, namely, the merchant guilds and minority kings. Saiva kings were displacing Buddhists in the Deccan, Buddhist dynasties were disappearing in the East, and in the West Islamic armies were taking control. Retrenching their populations to the Northeast, West, and South India, the major Buddhist monasteries modeled themselves on the *samata* feudal system—relying on kings for land grants and establishing branch operations where they had responsibility for villages, courts, and education (e.g., Nalanda). While they were not required to supply troops, Buddhist monasteries provided ritual, cultural, and educative services. Allegiance was maintained by the services the monks provided for the lord or king and villages of the area. Davidson concludes that through this process, early medieval Buddhist institutions, with their land grants and feudal responsibilities, assumed the characteristics of Indian life around them. These are the external contextual developments that, together with the intrinsic power of the word as analyzed by MacQueen, established the basis for the astonishing rise of esoteric Buddhism—"the form defined as a separate method or vehicle employing *mantras*" (Davidson, 114).

The Rise of Mantrayana

According to Davidson, the rise of Mantrayana is a process that represents the sacralization of the sociopolitical environment of the day in eighth-century India. Just as kings functioned in feudal India, in Mantrayana the practitioner becomes the controller of the mantras performed so as to ensure spiritual and secular success. Monks are doing this in their monasteries but also engaging with military generals and tribal leaders. Mantrayana practice also functioned as a socialization system for laypeople. Thus, a unified culture arose under monastic leadership and rule. But mantras were also employed by the anti-institutional siddha tradition functioning on the margins of Indian social institutions. These siddhas or "perfected saints"—often scruffy, long-haired anarchical practitioners—were fewer in number than the monks yet had high visibility and also cultivated political patronage. Both monks and siddhas were equally important to Mantrayana development. Says Davidson, this Mantrayana system "reflects the internalization of the medieval conceptual and social environment [after the fall of the Guptas], rather than being the revealed system that orthodoxy portrays" (Davidson, 115). Mantrayana demonstrated its high political and cultural sensitivity in its successful introduction into other cultures/countries such as Tibet, China, and Japan. Mantrayana also engaged people from a wide variety of strata in society and caste groups, both high and low. Davidson concludes that through the rise of Mantrayana practice, Mahayana Buddhism "moved toward multifaceted development after the fall of the Guptas, being pressed on by a sense of urgency and of crises within and without. Many of the directions taken were consistent with fundamental Buddhist principles, but in the rapidly changing environment of new political and military realities, they took on forms of signification unforeseen by their progenitors" (Davidson, 116).

We have seen that MacQueen's analysis of speech in early Mahayana demonstrated that powers of inspiration and revelation (intrinsic to the early Buddhist philosophy of language) were at work in the development of the bodhisattva path and the formation of new sutras. Although Davidson does not mention MacQueen, it does seem that both approaches can work together in helping one understand how chanted words and sutra come to have transforming power in Mahayana Buddhism. While MacQueen highlights internal inspiration and revelation qualities of speech itself in the Mahayana perspective, Davidson explores the influence of the changing sociopolitical context that fostered the rise of mantra practice. Both come together in the Mantrayana bodhisattva and the new canon of scripture. Mahayanists followed the traditional idea of scripture arising from the preaching of the Buddha, but in new circumstances such as to an audience composed of great bodhisattvas (such as Manjusri, Avalokitesvara, or Maitreya), who then recited his new teaching in the Mahayana sutras (Davidson, 147). Engagement with challenges from the Hindu Saiva context are seen in stories such as the bodhisattva Vajrapani's use of superior mantras and righteousness to defeat Siva (Mahesvara) and his deluded

Hindu doctrines and so establish the Buddhist dharma within a new territory (Davidson, 150–151). Davidson notes that such Mantrayana scriptures and their rituals were supported, performed, interpreted, and transmitted by Buddhist monks. Rather than the Theravada notion of the words of the Buddha functioning to help one remember and focus on his teachings, the Mahayana texts introduce to the monks the idea of Buddha mantras as having power to win cosmic battles in defense of the dharma and to transform individual earthly lives. While the ideas of bodhisattvas as subordinate Buddhas and possessors of powerful mantras had been around for some centuries in India, it was the Mantrayana that gave these ideas new development in the seventh century (Davidson, 117). The Mantrayana reshaped the older bodhisattva notion into a new path with new rituals based on their possession of secret powerful mantras (*mantrin/vajrin*) and ultimately institutionalized this material in Buddhist monasteries. These texts were copied and mantras performed on the feudal model of the person metaphorically becoming the overlord (*rajadhiraja*) or the universal ruler. Says Davidson, this is "the Buddhist version of the early medieval feudalization of divinity seen in the [Hindu] Puranas and elsewhere, applied to the Buddhist path by its ritual enactment in which either monks or laypeople may participate" (Davidson, 117). Let us see how this plays out in two case studies—the Tibetan Om Manipadme Hum, and the Japanese Nembutsu.

Om Manipadme Hum

In his book *The Origins of Om Manipadme Hum*, Alexander Studholme points out the importance of the constant chanting of Om Manipadme Hum in Tibetan life. Not only is the chant basic to virtually all the rites and rituals of Tibetan Buddhism, it is also the foundation for individual spiritual practice. It is the basic practice taught to children and beginners and a chant of advanced practitioners usually accompanied by the counting of prayer beads. The mantra is a central pillar of Tibetan Buddhism and is held to be "a powerful means of spiritual development in its own right" (Studholme 2002, 2). The repetition of Om Manipadme Hum is connected with the visualization of the bodhisattva Avalokitesvara. Each chanting of the mantra is thought to generate spiritual power and this is augmented by group forms of religious practice. On set occasions, people will gather to chant Om Manipadme Hum as many times as they are able, with the number of repetitions being counted. At the end of the week, each person's total is forwarded to the monastery in charge and the grand total calculated as an accumulation of blessings that might be dedicated, for example, to the well-being of the Dalai Lama. Studholme reports attending such an event and being woken early each morning by the landlord and his two young children busily chanting the mantra. He also experienced a group of elderly people at a temple in Lhasa also reciting Om Manipadme Hum in order that the accumulated number of repetitions might be sent to the Dalai Lama (Studholme 2002, 3). Of course, a devotee would also engage in the chant on a daily basis for his or her own spiritual development.

In his study, Studholme offers a historical analysis suggesting that the Om Manipadme Hum mantra is a Buddhist adaptation from the Hindu Saivite formula *Namah Sivaya* (Studholme 2002, 4). He also argues that just as Namah Sivaya is held to be a sui generis means of attaining liberation for Hindu devotees, so also is Om Manipadme Hum for Tibetan Buddhists. In both traditions, the chants are held to be powerful forms of spiritual practice "that are available to everyone, regardless of social or religious status" (Studholme 2002, 5). Evidence for this claim is found in the author's analysis of the Buddhist text *Karandavyuha Sutra* (dated at the fifth century CE in Kashmir). There, says Studholme, the treatment of Om Manipadme Hum "represents the reconfiguration in the Mahayana monastic establishment, of a practice first propagated by lay Buddhist tantric practitioners" (Studholme 2002, 6). This Buddhist adaptation from Hinduism is thought to have first occurred in early fifth-century Kashmir (Studholme 2002, 17). Says Studholme, just as in the Hindu tradition the Bhagavad Gita fosters *bhakti* (devotion) through the use of the Vedic Om as a means of evoking the vision of the Vaisnavite Isvara, so in the Buddhist tradition the *Karandavyuha* "promotes the namanusmrti of the Buddhist pranava *Om Manipadme Hum* as a means of entering the vision of the Buddhist *Isvara*. The vision of the cosmic Avalokitesvara is itself assimilated with the central Mahayana doctrine of Sukhavati, when this manifestation of the bodhisattva is said, in the sutra, to lead beings to Amitabha's pure land: the puranic doctrine of 'seeing' (*darsana*) the *Isvara* is syncretized with the Mahayana doctrine of rebirth in the

Buddha's pure land" (Studholme 2002, 7). According to Studholme, the meaning of the chant Om Manipadme Hum is understood as "in the lotus made of jewels," describing the manner in which a person is said to arrive in Sukhavati or the Pure Land of the Buddha. Says Studholme, "The image given in the *sutras* is that of a practitioner seated cross-legged in the calyx of a lotus flower made of jewels, which then unfolds its petals to reveal the splendour of one or other of the pure lands . . . [and] is also an expression of the aspiration to be reborn in Sukhavati" (Studholme 2002, 7). Repeated chanting of the mantra, Om Manipadme Hum, keeps one's mind focused on the goal to be realized and simultaneously removes obstructing karma. The more the chant is repeated, the greater its accumulation of merit and power—from the earliest learning of the chant in childhood through middle age and into one's senior years to the moment of death. In such practice, the mantra is seen as having the power to purify and transform one's own life, and also to be able to produce an accumulation of merit that can be dedicated to someone else (e.g., the Dalai Lama). The spiritual power of the Om Manipadme Hum chant is established at the beginning of the second part of the *Karandavyuha Sutra*. There the Buddha Sakyamuni reveals that in a former life he was liberated from the fear of death by the bodhisattva Avalokitesvara, who had accrued an infinite amount of merit. Sakyamuni offers a discourse on the merit found in the individual hair pores of Avalokitesvara. Studholme comments, "A description of the different lands contained within these pores ensues. Sakyamuni then says that those who bring to mind the six-syllable formula will be born in one of these very hair pores never again to wander in *samsara*, traveling from one pore to another until they achieve the state of *nirvana*. This is then the cue for a long section describing the qualities [powers] of Om *Manipadme Hum*" (Studholme 2002, 78). What this story does, says Studholme, is to reset the six-syllable formula into a thoroughly Mahayana Buddhist context, thus separating it from its originating Namah Sivaya Hindu influence. This is done by presenting the mantra in the same terms used to describe the Perfection of Wisdom in earlier Wisdom Sutras. Om Manipadme Hum, the sutra implies, has taken the place of the Perfection of Wisdom as the supreme principle of the Mahayana. Chanting of Om Manipadme Hum is held to lead to the accomplishment of the six perfections (of the Perfection of Wisdom), the vision quest experience of the bodhisattva Avalokitesvara, and rebirth in the pure land of Sukhavati leading directly to Buddhahood and nirvana. It is no wonder then that the *Karandavyuha Sutra* claims that Om Manipadme Hum, when recited, is second to none. Studholme concludes, "As a Buddhist *pranava*, the formula may be said to supersede the Perfection of Wisdom as the supreme principle of Mahayana" (Studholme 2002, 91). How is it that the Mahayana view of language and words as "empty" (as per Nagarjuna's philosophy of language) is now reversed into a set of syllables so pregnant with meaning and power as to take one to nirvana? Studholme convincingly demonstrates that in the *Karandavyuha Sutra*, this transformation occurs through a conscious adaptation of Hindu Saivite tantric thought and practice into Buddhist forms (Studholme 2002, 77–104). In terms of language, the six-syllable mantra Om Manipadme Hum is seen to have a "shorthand" function of manifesting the Buddhist pranava, or dharma, just as Om functions in Hinduism as a shorthand symbol containing the whole of the Vedic revelation of Brahman.

In his *Tibetan Buddhist Chant*, Walter Kaufmann supports influence from India. "For many centuries Tibetans looked at India as the paragon in religious, cultural, and artistic matters" (Kaufmann 1975, 3). India was seen by Tibetans as the home of the great teachers, of vedic chant, tantric mysticism, and of the raga concept in the making of music. Says Kaufmann, all of this was introduced into Tibet during the seventh century (Kaufmann 1975, 4). Although subject to change, it has stayed alive through the centuries right up to the present. Today, Buddhism in Tibet is characterized by adherence to Mantrayana and its focus upon the transformation of consciousness through mantra or sacred sound formulas often expressed in musical chant through which one can quickly accomplish enlightenment even in a single lifetime. As we have seen, the quickest and most powerful way to do this is to link one's mind to the mind of Avalokitesvara, the Bodhisattva of Compassion, through chanting Om Manipadme Hum. This mantra is translated by Sean Williams as: "Behold! The Jewel is in the Lotus: The practice of Compassion is united with Wisdom to achieve the Buddha nature" (S. Williams 2006, 180). According to Sean Williams, "all of the teachings of the Buddha are believed to be contained in this short, six syllable mantra which does not require initiation by a lama and is the most widely used of all Tibetan Buddhist prayers. . . . the act of chanting which may be repeated indefinitely, enlarges the circle of compassion beyond oneself to all sentient beings, and completely removes attention from the desires of the individual ego" (S. Williams 2006, 179–180).

Regarding the musical elements of Tibetan Buddhist chant, says Williams, it is necessary to rethink the concepts of melody and rhythm as a sequence of rising or falling pitches. In Tibetan chanting, it is in the shift of timbre or tone color that the melodic content and forward movement occur . . . including very deep sounds and resonance" (S. Williams 2006, 180). Regarding rhythm, it is necessary to go beyond the modern grouping of beats in twos and threes to "extremely complicated, logo-rhythmic formulas that extend into the hundreds of beats. . . . These rhythms not only form a link between song, ritual, dance, and drama, but also serve to enact or manifest aspects of Buddhist cosmology" (S. Williams 2006, 179–180). In addition to the chanting of individual persons, monks engage in choral chanting in daily services, in which the monks sit facing each other in rows with a leader who also plays percussion. Williams lists three categories of Tibetan chant: *don* (recitation chant), *rta* (melodic change), and *dkyangs* (tone contour chant). The last, dkyangs, the chant with which outsiders are most familiar, includes a very deep tone, a mid-level tone, and an upper harmonic tone. It sounds as if each singer is producing two or three pitches simultaneously, D, F#, and A (the D major chord), called "chordal chant," and is usually performed in association with instrumental music or *rol mo*, including cymbals (*sil snyan*), oboes (*rhga gling*), and long trumpets (*dung chen*). In Mantrayana practice, musical chants allow sacred sounds to work closely with ritual gestures (*mudras*) and instrumental expressions to symbolize religious truth, which cannot be explicitly stated. Whereas Theravada chant relies more on nonmusical chant, Mahayana Buddhism uses a wide variety of wind (horns, flutes, and conches) and percussion instruments. In this type of Mahayana ritual performance, chant is understood as an act of proclaiming the Buddha's teaching and is traditionally known as "sounding the drum of the Dharma" (S. Williams 2006, 178). All of the teachings of the Buddha are believed to be contained in the short six-syllable mantra Om Manipadme Hum that, when chanted, links one's mind to the mind of Avalokitesvara (the Bodhisattva of Compassion) and, according to the Mantrayana tradition of Tibet, is the quickest and most powerful way to transform one's consciousness and attain enlightenment (S. Williams 2006, 179–180).

NEMBUTSU

Having seen how the Tibetan chant Om Manipadme Hum is one example of Mantrayana Buddhism reshaping the older bodhisattva notion into a new path of powerful mantras open to both monks and laypeople, let us now examine a second example—the Japanese Pure Land practice of Shinran. Shinran's goal is to save the masses and not just the monastics, thus the practice of Nembutsu chanting is open to all. In this way, says Shojun Bando, the Nembutsu may be considered to be the culmination of the Buddhist mantra tradition, "a means solely intended to further the universal salvation of all men, as distinct from the more circumscribed monastic and scholastic ideal prevailing in the earlier centuries of Buddhism" (Bando 2014, 2). Victor Hori notes that Nembutsu originally meant "meditation on the Buddha and is the Japanese-Chinese translation of *buddhanusmriti*." But in China, Nembutsu acquired two meanings: "meditation" and "recitation." Some people taught that Nembutsu as meditation was for superior people and that recitation was for inferior people. This ambiguity in meaning continued until the time of Shinran (Hori 2014). Today, says Bando, the Nembutsu is seen to have the dual significance of "thinking of/remembering the Buddha" and "pronouncing the name of the Buddha," especially the name of Amida Buddha, or the Buddha of Infinite Light and Eternal Life. In the Japanese Jodo Shinshu or True Pure Land School, the label "Nembutsu" is given to the chanting of the mantra "*Namu Amida Butsu*" (Bando 2014, 2). The transforming power of this chant is attributed by Tzu-min, the Chinese Pure Land master of the eighth century, to the boundless compassion of Amida, the bodhisattva of Immeasurable Light and Life, as follows:

> Not choosing the learned and those upholding pure precepts,
> Not rejecting those who break precepts and whose evil karma is profound,

> Solely making beings turn about and abundantly say the nembutsu,
> I can make bits of rubble change into gold. (As quoted by Unno 2002, 12)

Victor Hori describes the Nembutsu as having the power to change rubble into gold as a new and different account of mantric power:

> Instead of thinking of mantric power as the power of a blessing to make changes in the physical world, this image suggests that mantra has the power to effect change in how one experiences the world. Where the ordinary person sees rubble, the person who chants nembutsu sees gold.
>
> In nembutsu, the practitioner finally realizes that his calling out to Amida is not his own act, it is Amida who originates the call. Using his voice, Amida is calling out to Amida. In nembutsu, his self is there but it has become empty, functioning only as a conduit for Amida. When the self with its constant calculation of everything it experiences is finally emptied, then even rubble appears as gold. That is the final power of *nembutsu*. (Hori 2014)

This transforming power of Amida, evoked by chanting the Nembutsu, is experienced as being: boundless compassion, nonjudgmental, and all-inclusive.

The all-inclusive nature of the *Jodo-shin-shu* (True Pure Land School) is highlighted by looking at the progressively more inclusive history of the sangha in the development of Buddhism. Leslie Kawamura summarizes as follows: "In India, the term *sangha* referred to a gathering of monks and nuns and only by extension did it include the laity. In China and in Japan, especially with the development of the Jodo-shu (Pure Land School), the congregation comprised both monks and laymen. It was Shinran (1173–1262) who emphasized the fact that enlightenment was not limited to monks, nuns, and ascetics, but that the Buddha's teaching was meant for all walks of life" (Kawamura 1977, 37). Indeed, after trying the path of rigorous monastic practice on Mt. Hiei outside Kyoto for many years, Shinran gave up the priestly life and got married. Kawamura comments, "Contrary to the lifestyle of a monk for whom celibacy was the custom, Shinran's marriage to Eshinni was revolutionary" (Kawamura 1977, 38). Shinran made this revolutionary move after a careful study of the Buddhist doctrine of karma and through his own existential life experience. While Buddhists rejected the Hindu conception of *varna* or caste divisions in society, they did adopt the Hindu ideas of karma and rebirth, including the notion that one's karma determined what one was (Sutta-Nipata 3.9.57). Rejecting the Hindu idea of a permanent underlying self (*atman*) as the apparent possessor of one's karma, Buddhists reinterpreted karma in terms of mental "intention"—as the thoughts and acts that constitute, lead, and control one (Dhammapada 1.1–2). Such karma is the cause of one's present frustration or happiness. Vasubandhu describes these karmic patterns as our *cetana* or mental drives that can be experienced as painful or pleasant and become obstacles to the attainment of nirvana (enlightenment) because they constantly reinforce one's egoism, which Buddhism sees as the source of suffering. As Kawamura puts it, such was the spiritual dilemma in which Shinran found himself after twenty years of meditative practices as a monk. Try as he might to rid himself of karmic emotional afflictions and reach enlightenment, Shinran found that the more diligently he applied himself to meditative practices the more ego-bound he became. Thus, the attainment of enlightenment through such self-motivated practices seemed to take him in the opposite direction. This led him to leave Mt. Hiei, the center of Buddhist learning at that time, and go into the city of Kyoto where he was inspired to visit Honen, who was also struggling with the spiritual dilemma of karma (Kawamura 1986, 192–194).

In his own way, Honen had already resolved the deep problem that confronted Shinran. Kawamura describes Honen's experience as follows. Like Shinran, Honen understood himself to be emotionally afflicted, being bound to past karma just like all other sentient beings, and he determined that no one was better off than another. For Honen, his interest was not in efforts to improve his lot but in renouncing the world. Part of this feeling of hopelessness likely came from the circumstances around him—the declining power of the imperial government and the increasing decadence of the nobility. Due to these feelings, Honen turned to the practice of Nembutsu, believing that the only way to release was through the good merits accumulated from the chanting of the Buddha's name that would bring him happiness by rebirth in the Pure Land of Amida Buddha. This was so because of Amida's compassionate vow to save everyone:

> If, after my obtaining Buddhahood, all beings in the ten quarters should not desire in sincerity and trustfulness to be born in my country, and if they should not be born by only thinking of me for ten times, except those who have committed five grave offences and those who are abusive of the true Dharma, may I not attain the Highest Enlightenment. (18th Vow as quoted by Bloom 1965, 2)

Kawamura comments, "It was through Honen's guidance that Shinran came to know of the power of Buddha's Fundamental Vow as the only means for salvation. . . . Simply by believing in the power of Amida's vow to save, salvation was assured" (Kawamura 1986, 197).

But Shinran developed differences from his teacher Honen. For Honen, chanting the Nembutsu was the only means to rebirth in the Pure Land, but this alone left open the interpretation that recitation of the Nembutsu generated merit that got one to the Pure Land. Indeed, among Honen's disciples, competitions developed over how many times the Nembutsu was chanted daily until it was quantity rather than quality that counted (Bando 2014, 4). This Shinran rejected. For him, one was enlightened not by the merit that one's own saying of the chant could generate, for that self-effort would leave one stuck in the seemingly endless round of ego-generated karma that would obstruct enlightenment. Rather, Shinran focused on seeing the Nembutsu as the embodiment of Vow-Power or Other Power. As Kawamura puts it, "To say that salvation derives from the Vow-Power is to say that one has reached one's utter incapacity to attain enlightenment after having tried diligently to attain it through every possible channel . . . thus no religious practice—not even the recitation of the *nembutsu*—could give assurance for Birth in the Land of Bliss, because salvation was not determined by self-motivated, self-righteous, good or evil actions done for the sake of gaining it" (Kawamura 1986, 197). Says Kawamura, Shinran's greatest contribution was his focus on karma as the key to understanding the human existential dilemma. Shinran also saw Honen's failure to fully understand the true vow-power or

Other Power of the Nembutsu (Kawamura 1986, 198). Victor Hori summarizes the result as follows: "For many people in Chinese and Japanese Pure Land, nembutsu was a self-power (jiriki) practice. 'I' initiated it and 'I' accumulated merit for it. Many monks were famous for chanting the name of Amida tens of thousands of times a day. But for Shinran, nembutsu was an other power (tariki) practice. Amida Buddha originates it. . . . In nembutsu, it is not I who calls Amida, it is Amida who calls Amida" (Hori 2014). In Shinran's practice, Nembutsu is done completely without calculation or self-consciousness, no jiriki. As it is nothing but Other Power detached from self-power, says Hori, "it is neither a religious practice nor a good act on the part of the practitioner" (Hori 2014).

Shinran's radical rejection of the traditional monastic approach symbolized by Mt. Hiei (and its emphasis on elaborate disciplinary and philosophic approaches to enlightenment) resulted in his banishment from Kyoto along with his teacher Honen. The charge against them by the community and the monastic orders was "irreligious behavior." Honen was sent to Tosa on Shikoku and Shinran to Kokubu in Echigo. Shinran remained in exile from 1207 to 1245. During this period, he married and had several children. He was a villager and lived the life of common people. Bloom says, "It was in this context that Shinran probably came to realize that the common man could attain Buddhist ideals in his ordinary life. . . . On this basis he rejected the duality of religious and lay life and took seriously the Buddhist principle 'Samsara is Nirvana' as something to be applied concretely in the common life. Existentially and philosophically Shinran merged the secular and religious spheres" (Bloom 1965, xi). In 1211, Shinran and Honen were pardoned and Shinran moved his family to the newly developing Kanto region, where he attracted a considerable following. There he developed the *Kyogyoshinsho*, a systematic compilation of various passages from Pure Land texts, as the basis of his teaching. In 1235, Shinran returned to Kyoto, spending his final years in writing and correspondence before dying in 1262. While dying, he constantly chanted the name of Amida (Bloom 1965, xiv).

In his major work, the *Kyogyoshinsho*, Shinran traces the teaching on the original vow of Amida Buddha for the salvation of all sentient beings as having been brought to earth by Sakyamuni Buddha and passed down by the seven patriarchs: Nagarjuna and Vasubandhu in

India; T'an-luan, Tao-ch'o, and Shan-tao of China; and Genshin and Honen in Japan. "Thus, according to Shinran, Pure Land teaching proceeded from the eternal, compassionate mind of Buddha, that appeared in history and spanned three countries, India, China and Japan" (Bloom 1965, 23). Today, one would have to add North America to the list. In his study of the patriarchs, Shinran's conclusion was that in their teachings regarding Amida's bodhisattva vow, all focused on making release from the entrapping round of karma possible for common persons, with whom Shinran realized he was at-one. Bloom notes that while recitation of Amida's name in the Nembutsu came to be the central practice of the Pure Land school, from T'an-luan to Honen "the practice was regarded as a *means for acquiring the necessary merit to gain birth* in the Pure Land. The devotee could view his practice as his own effort to attain it, albeit the practice was given by Amida Buddha and rooted in Other Power. The practice as established by Amida Buddha is Other Power, because its ultimate effect is dependent on the virtue of Amida Buddha's name resident in the formula" (Bloom 1965, 25). Before Shinran there had been an implicit reliance on self in the attainment of release from the karmic round and rebirth in the Pure Land. Shinran's radical step was to see that the only way out of the degenerate age in which he lived was to give up all attempts at self-power and surrender to the Other Power mind, "entrusting or surrendering" to the arising of "the true mind" (as Shinran calls it) from within. Rather than trying to define "the true mind," it may be easier to begin with its opposite. As sentient beings, says Shinran, from the beginning we are filled with blind passions, we lack a mind true and real, and have no heart of purity. Due to our self-motivated karmic drives and impulses, it is impossible for us to accord with Amida's vow. All our attempts to make ourselves worthy of being saved by chanting Amida's name are nothing but more clinging to our own powers and hopes for the generation of merit. *Shinjin* (the moment when the practitioner loses his self and is confirmed by Amida), however, signifies a religious awakening from entrapment in our own karma into the experience of Amida's sincere and true mind—a true mind state from which one cannot retrogress (4.61). As Bando paraphrases, "True mind is the *bodhicitta* which fulfils man's innermost wish to be what he is originally and in principle (metaphorically expressed as 'Birth in the Pure Land'), by attaining his original nature (Buddhahood), free from the egoistic drive or influence of karmic *klesha*" (Bando 2014, 3).

In his *Kyogyoshinsho* Shinran outlines the implications of this new understanding for faith and practice. Nembutsu practice or "Saying the Name" is described by Shinran as follows:

> Saying the Name breaks through all the ignorance of sentient beings and fulfills their aspirations. Saying the Name is the right act, supreme, true, and excellent. The right act is the nembutsu. The nembutsu is Namu-amida-butsu. Namu-amida-butsu is right-mindedness. (Shinran 2001, 2.12)

But what is right-mindedness? This question is answered in the next section of Shinran's *Kyogyoshinsho* entitled "The True Shinjin of the Pure Land Way." Usually *shinjin* has been translated into English as "faith." But I am wary of this because the term "faith" is loaded with modern Christian connotations that may well be misleading. Therefore, I will not use it. Instead, let us follow Shinran, who says, "Our attainment of *shinjin* arises from the heart and mind with which Amida Tathagata selected the Vow, and that the clarification of true mind has been taught for us through the skillful works of compassion of the Great Sage, Sakyamuni" (Shinran 2001, preface). Unlike a collection of religious beliefs (the modern Christian conceptions of "faith"), shinjin, or right-mindedness, is the giving up of our ego-directed and unwholesome mental tendencies. *Bodhicitta* directs the ordinary person toward what he or she essentially is (the Buddha). "Shinran showed explicitly that the *nembutsu* practice, as an expression of [Right Shinjin], is no other than this *bodhicitta*" (Bando 2014, 3). That is why, as Shinran taught, if practice is done with complete sincerity, only one chanting of the Nembutsu is needed, for then one's obstructing karma will be overcome in the realization of the Buddha Nature. But complete sincerity of mind and body is very difficult to realize, so this great practice of Shinran (requiring only one sincere recitation) is the very opposite of easy and can only be achieved through a shinjin of complete surrender. That is why such shinjin is not something *we do* but *Amida does* through us. As Bando puts it, *Namu Amida Butsu* fully translated means, I take refuge in the Buddha of Infinite Light (*prajna*, wisdom) and Eternal Life (*karuna*, all-embracing compassion). But in reality, there is no "I" apart from "Amida" and no "Amida" apart from "I." Both are neither self-existent or something real in a substantial sense—in the experience of Nembutsu the arising of both I and Amida is simultaneous (Bando 2014, 5). Yet here, as Nagarjuna taught, we bump against the limits of language. Even words such as Amida become "empty" when it comes to expressing the transcendent. Because Shinran knew this from Nagarjuna he understood the name of Amida in the Nembutsu as a limited relative secondary truth that can only point beyond itself to that which cannot be said—Suchness itself. Says Bando, "What mattered to Shinran was no longer 'Amida Buddha' as the object of worship, but *Namu Amida Butsu*. 'Amida Buddha' as *upaya* can be objectified, but not *Namu Amida Butsu* for it is the actual inter-relationship between subject and object: it is not a static 'thing' but a dynamic 'event.' Therefore, as Rennyo (1415–99), the eighth Patriarch of the Jodo Shin School . . . remarked . . . the myogo (the six characters of *Na mu a mi da butsu*) should be preferred to the picture of Amida" (Bando 2014, 6). The key for Shinran was that the Nembutsu, when chanted with complete sincerity, "reverberated in the mind" so powerfully that a common person would have the transformative experience of realizing his or her birth in the Pure Land. Through this kind of hearing and saying the Name—not just grasping it intellectually but being penetrated by the dynamic reality of the compassion that it embodies—shinjin is awakened in them. For Shinran, "genuine utterance of the *Nembutsu* and *shinjin* are not generated out of human will, but emerge together as manifestations of the Buddha's working. They are always interfused. Because the Name is given—is spread throughout the universe by all the Buddhas—sentient beings are able to hear it and come to know Amida's Primal Vow" (Shinran 2014, 4).

That the power of the Nembutsu is tied to being chanted in its original syllables was evident in research I conducted on the Jodo Shinshu community of Southern Alberta (Coward and Goa 1983). In 1981, along with my colleague David Goa, I attended services and obtained interviews with Jodo Shinshu followers in several Southern Alberta communities. While some changes from Jodo Shinshu practice in Japan were noticeable in the Canadian experience of the devotees, the Nembutsu chant remained the major practice. As a result of the protestantizing influence of seventy-five years in the Canadian context, the sermon had come to occupy a more central role than in Japan, but Nembutsu chanting remained the key self-definition practice for the Canadian Jodo Shinshu devotee. Of particular interest for this discussion was their experience of experimenting with changing the language of the Nembutsu chant to English. In the Raymond congregation, for example, when English chanting was introduced into the Sunday School, the children repeatedly objected and requested a return to the familiar Chinese Nembutsu, even though they did not understand it. English allowed some understanding of the meaning, but it did not make the chanting personally powerful. As one teacher noted, the children have been chanting in Chinese since they were babies, so for them the Nembutsu in English was strange. In the adult worship, the attempt at chanting the Nembutsu in English did not last long—it simply did not seem to have the right vibrations and the transforming power of the traditional syllables, which had been chanted in Pure Land Buddhism for centuries. In traditional Jodo Shinshu chanting it is the noncognitive rather than the rational discursive functions of the psyche that are dominant. This was especially evident in our study of the function of Nembutsu chanting at funeral services in the Southern Alberta community. Simply telling a wife that she will join her departed husband when she is reborn in the Pure Land and that they are one when she chants the Nembutsu is of little help. In the crisis of bereavement, it is the nonrational—the emotional and intuitive—aspects of the psyche that dominate. These are precisely the psychological processes actualized and satisfied in the Nembutsu ritual chant. Although the discursive meaning of Namu Amida Butsu may be "I surrender myself to Amida Buddha," it is through the emotional and intuitive processes of chanting that the existential experience of oneness is realized. Thus, says Reverend Y. Kawamura of Raymond, if there is too much sermon and too little chant in the funeral service, the result is a removal of the psychological mechanism by which the wife can identify with Amida and her deceased husband (Coward and Goa 1983, 374–375). Layperson Reyko Nishiyama of Raymond says of her experience of the chant: "You are one with Amida Buddha in the *nembutsu*" (Nishiyama 1981). During the chant, she also feels the presence of her deceased parents, and with regard to her husband she reports, "I feel closest to Mac when we chant the *nembutsu* together"

(Nishiyama 1981). In her view, Jodo Shinshu is not a religion of education but of the heart. Scholars may work out the meaning of the chant, she says, but it is the deep feeling the chant evokes that makes Jodo Shinshu special. This conforms with Shinran's enlightenment experience, which turned him from the highly intellectualized Tendai Buddhism of his day to a simple but sincere shinjin practice of complete surrender to or trusting in Amida Buddha. Ritual Nembutsu chanting, not intellectual analysis, thus characterizes the traditional Jodo Shinshu experience of the common person from the time of Shinran in the 1200s CE to today's Japanese Canadian Jodo Shinshu persons in Alberta.

The Reverend S. K. Ikuta of Calgary presents the following introspection into the psychology of the chant:

> When you identify with the chant it has the function of structuring spiritual space: the sound of the chant, the smell of the incense, and the action of putting hands together—all this through repeated experience becomes predictable and induces the spiritual.
>
> When I chant it brings memories of my father, of gatherings with other ministers . . . it sets your mind psychologically to hear the Buddha's teaching. It [the mind] opens . . . like flower buds being opened to receive the sun.
>
> Chanting out loud is also quite important. Shinran says rather than recite the nembutsu quietly within yourself, say it out loud: bring it out and then listen. Although I am chanting:
>
> > Amida speaks it,
> > Amida hears it,
> > And I am the union. (Ikuta 1981)

Another psychological function of the chant is as a mnemonic device. When scripture is poetic rather than discursive, it is much easier to memorize. The Buddhist tradition has always used chanting as a device for embedding scripture in the budding consciousness of the young child. Raised within this tradition, the Reverend Y. Kawamura reports: "My father taught me scripture. I would repeat after him.

After ten years, he taught me how to read and what it meant. Later on in the University I studied these texts." (Y. Kawamura 1981) Sean Williams (2006, 182) observes that in Japanese Buddhist chanting, music plays a limited role, but bells and chimes are used to establish the opening and closing of each section of chant.

The order indicated has psychological importance. The ritual chanting not only provides the mechanism for memorization, but it also etches the sound of the sacred words ever more deeply within consciousness. As Reyko Nishiyama aptly puts it: "To me [the chant] is meditative. It induces peace from the hustle and bustle of life. It is very comfortable. It has seeped in . . . it is part of my consciousness" (Nishiyama 1981). Indeed, I would go further and say chants such as the Nembutsu structure one's consciousness. As such, they become the foundation from which perception and discursive analysis can proceed. More importantly, they are constantly available for immediate guidance, inspiration, and solace in the crises of life.

Jodo Shinshu adaptation in the direction of protestantization may also be seen in the Canadian approach to congregational worship. A regular meeting on Sunday was instituted. This affected the way ministers carried out their functions, placing emphasis on the Sunday service and drawing attention from the memorial services traditionally held in the home. Participation in worship moved from a Japanese model, focusing on the individual family privately worshiping at the temple or around the *butsu dan* (shrine) in the home, principally in memorial for a recently departed relative or for the collective dead. Instead, it shifted to the whole community gathering for the regular service of thanksgiving at the church on Sunday morning. Though the context of worship shifted, the service itself continued to accent in structure and content the ideas Shinran introduced as reforms to Japanese Buddhism in the thirteenth century. The service of thanksgiving practiced in Alberta commonly takes place in the Buddhist church on Sunday morning. The ritual pattern is similar whether the service is conducted in Japanese or English and, like the eucharist for some branches of Christianity, forms the core of all special and festival services. Entry into the time of devotion is marked when a gong hanging in the entrance of the church is struck. Candles have been lit and offerings of rice, sweets, and cut flowers are in place on the main shrine. As devotees enter they *gassho* (put hands together in gratitude), repeat the Nembutsu, and walk up the centre aisle to the lesser altar. They offer incense in adoration of the Amida Buddha and in thanksgiving for the Original Vow (18th Vow of the Buddha) through which enlightenment is attained.

Once seated, the congregation chants the Nembutsu, accompanied by the piano, as a collective entrance to the service. One of the denomination's three principal sutras (the larger *Sukhavati-vyuha Sutra*, the *Amitayur-Dhyana Sutra*, and the smaller *Sykhavati-vyuha Sutra*) is chanted, then read in English. A *gatha* (hymn) is sung to piano accompaniment. The minister's sermon that follows occupies about one-half the time of the service and focuses on some aspect of Jodo Shinshu teaching. Another gatha, announcements of church activities, and a final meditation using the Nembutsu, with piano accompaniment, round out the service. In addition to the Sunday services, daily chanting of the Nembutsu around the butsu dan or home shrine (morning and evening) continues in Canada much as it did in Japan.

In traditional Jodo Shinshu life, the joining together of the whole community in ritual chant provides a unifying center for family and social life. Group chanting gives a sense of harmony and belonging; it induces a feeling of oneness to the whole congregation. Ministers may conflict with one another in their sermons and teachings, observes one respondent, but the chants, memorized in childhood and communally repeated, do not change (Nishiyama 1981). In all Jodo Shinshu festivals, group chanting has occupied an important place.

Let us conclude our discussion of the Nembutsu chant's power to transform the life of the common person by returning to Shinran's experience of his own obstructing egocentric karma, that was being made worse by his self-efforts to achieve enlightenment. In his twenty years of experience as a monk, and afterward as a layman, the more he tried through jiriki or self-power practice, the more karmically trapped and evil he became. Only by a total surrender of self to the compassion of Amida through the Other Power (tariki) of Amida was he rescued into the infinite life and light of Amida's Pure Land. As one of Shinran's gathas or hymns puts it,

> When we say "Namu-amida-butsu,"
> Which surpasses all virtues,
> Our heavy obstructions of evil—past, present, and future—
> Are all unfailingly transformed, becoming light. (Veda
>   1991, 83)

As Hori notes, "Shinran's notion of *nembutsu* is imbedded within his larger theory of *akunin shoki*, the evil person is the focus of Amida's grace. The person who says 'I admit I am evil' is the person who receives Amida's grace. The evil person who fully admits his evil has given up self; his actions are no longer *jiriki*. *Shinjin* is the moment, the experience, when the practitioner loses his self and is confirmed by Amida" (Hori 2014). Or as D. T. Suzuki suggests, Shinran's Nembutsu practice is neither practice nor even karmically good behaviour but simply "living" (*gyo*) in Amida. Suzuki says Shinran's sincere Nembutsu is "nonpractice because it is *tariki*" and is therefore *daigyo* or "great living" in Amida Buddha during our daily lives (Shinran 2012, 7).

Perhaps Shinran's existential experience of the evil self being rescued by Amida's grace through the Nembutsu is best captured in Fumio Niwa's novel, *The Buddha Tree*. At one point in the story there is a dialogue between the priest Soshu and an enquirer, Tachi, a professed communist who describes his spiritual experience in prison. Soshu, the priest, remembering his own struggles says,

> "When a man feels in his heart a desire to call upon the name of Buddha, this is the first motion in him of the divine mercy. All men have within them both a Buddha-nature, and that which is its enemy—the arrogant human intellect. When in times of danger we call on the name of Buddha, what makes us utter that involuntary cry, Shinran believed, is none other than the grace of Amida working within us. At such a time we have only to repeat that call [the Nembutsu], in simple faith; all questioning, all reasoning is vain . . ."
>
> Remembering his time in prison, Tachi says, "At first I thought I'd go mad when they locked me up, from the loneliness. The *nembutsu* was almost part of me, of course, I'd been so used to hearing and repeating it since I was a baby; but I never had any real faith. Then it happened in prison. Suddenly, without thinking, I found myself repeating 'Namu Amida Butsu' . . . In that moment I knew I had a Buddhanature. It was Mind becoming conscious of itself . . . I know all we have to do is to forget self and trust Him for everything . . ." (Quoted in Earhart 1997, 68 and 72)

Conclusion

We began this chapter asking the question "How is it that words come to function as *mantras* or powerful chants in Buddhism—a tradition that has no revealed scripture and a philosophy of language that sees words as useful for conventional but not transcendental knowledge?" To answer this question, we first looked at the formation of Buddhist scripture and then examined three case studies of Buddhist use of word and chant in spiritual transformation.

As writers of the *tripitaka*, the early followers of Gautama the Buddha set out to celebrate his deeds and record his teachings. They saw him as a real human being experiencing conflicts and making his own choices motivated by compassion for suffering human beings. In these writings, the community or Sangha created the image of the Buddha through his life and teachings. In the Buddha's view, revelation such as the Hindu Vedas, even if a true experience of the rsi, might be misremembered or might be false "revelation" correctly remembered. Thus, the only truth to be trusted came from one's own direct personal experience of reality. Thus, the words he spoke, which became Buddhist scripture, were a description of his own understanding of reality following his experience of striving for and finally achieving the state of nirvana—the final goal of knowing reality and experiencing release from suffering.

In our three case studies, the Theravada practice of chanting the Triple Refuge plays the role of a Buddhist identity marker. Nonmusical recitation of the Triple Refuge reinforces the fact that one is a Buddhist, and that is how it helps to keep the devotee on the right track of following the teaching and example of Gautama the Buddha. Graeme MacQueen shows how the Theravada historically closed view of the Buddha's words (i.e., those recited by Ananda) is opened up by the early Indian Mahayana monastic communities. He shows how the revelation between *buddhavacana* and *pratibhana* (direct perception clear of obstructing karma) is seen in a radically new way—to explain how someone such as a bodhisattva (and not the historical Buddha) can have a direct experience of the perfection of wisdom (prajnaparamita) such that it has the status of sutra with inspired words filled with liberating power. We also saw how Ronald Davidson's sociopolitical analysis of events in post-Gupta India from the seventh to the twelfth century added a contextual dimension to our understanding of how chanted words became powerful. During this period, Mahayana loses its dominant social position in India to the resurgent Hindus and responds by moving to reflect the political and social models of the surrounding feudal society in the esoteric practice of monks and siddhas, especially in the North and South where Buddhist monasteries provided ritual, cultural, and educational services. These contextual developments, together with the intrinsic power of the word (as described by MacQueen) established the basis for the rise of esoteric tantric Buddhism and its method of employing mantras as powerful practices to transform earthly lives. According to Davidson, it was the Mantrayana movement that reshaped older ideas of bodhisattvas as subordinate Buddhas and possessors of powerful mantras into a new path with new musically accompanied rituals institutionalized in Buddhist monasteries.

In our second case study, we examined Alexander Studholme's careful historical analysis of the Om Manipadme Hum chant that is basic to the rituals of Tibetan Buddhism and the foundation for individual as well as group spiritual practice. Repetitions are counted on a rosary and may be dedicated to the well-being of someone else (e.g., the Dalai Lama). Chanting of the Om Manipadme Hum is said to lead to accomplishment of the perfections (of the Perfection of Wisdom), the visualization experience of the bodhisattva Avalokitesvara, and rebirth in the pure land of Sukhavati leading to Buddhahood and nirvana. How did Nagarjuna's understanding of words as "empty" get reversed so that the Om Manipadme Hum musical chant is so filled with meaning and power as to take one to nirvana? Studholme shows that in the *Karandavyuha Sutra* this transformation occurs via a conscious adaptation of Hindu Saivite tantric thought and practice into Buddhist forms.

The third case study showed that in China and Japan the development of the Nembutsu mantra reaches deeper levels of karmic analysis and gives greater room for the equal engagement of laypeople. Until the time of Shinran, monastic practice seemed to focus on the number of repetitions as the way to generate greater merit for oneself so as to eventually realize nirvana. Both as a monk and later as a layman, Shinran found that the more he tried to reach nirvana through jiriki (self-power practice) the more karmically trapped and evil he became. Only after leaving the monastery, marrying, being exiled from Kyoto, and living in a rural area did Shinran become so aware of the decadence of his own karmic nature as to throw himself in total surrender on the compassion of Amida and be rescued into Amida's Pure Land—not due to his own act of surrender, but as a free gift of grace from Amida (tariki or Other Power). This understanding of tariki or Other Power is Shinran's most radical challenge to the traditional approach to Nembutsu chanting. For Shinran's own experience, it was not the *quantity* but the *quality* of the chant that was all important. Only when he opened himself in complete surrender was Amida able to speak through Shinran one completely sincere Nembutsu recitation, enabling him to realize liberation. As D. T. Suzuki suggests, Shinran's Nembutsu is neither practice nor karmically good behavior, it is simply living in Amida. As a Southern Alberta Jodo Shinshu minister we interviewed put it, "Although I am chanting: Amida speaks it, Amida hears it, and I am the union."

Overall then, this chapter charts the change from the Theravada's Triple Refuge of nonmusically chanted words as serving merely to keep one focused and on track, to the Mahayana musically accompanied chants (like Om Manipadme Hum and the Nembutsu) as having power to transform lives. This dramatic change is seen to have resulted from Hindu influence, contextual influences in medieval India, and through the Pure Land perception that the radical evil of human nature could only be overcome by chanting the Nembutsu and evoking the compassion of Amida.

CHAPTER 3

Word, Chant, and Song on the Islamic Spiritual Path

Sonic theology, the coming together of revealed word and oral/aural sound, forms the heart of the spiritual path in Islam. According to tradition, this begins with the Prophet Muhammad (610 CE) who receives the Qur'an, passage by passage, as a fully formed revelation directly from Allah through the angel Gabriel, who spoke the message to make it audible to the human ear. One traditional recounting of the revelation of the Qur'an is given by the Muslim historian al-Tabari (839–923 CE). Muhammad, following his usual practice, had gone to a cave on Mt. Hira, a few miles northeast of Mecca for contemplation. Tabari recounts the events as follows. Muhammad heard a voice from heaven saying: "'O Muhammad! You are God's messenger and I am Gabriel.' I lifted my head towards heaven and behold, there was Gabriel in human form. I stood there looking at him until he disappeared. Then I departed and returned to my family" (Tabari 2000, 1:1150). Muhammad later returned to Mt. Hira and listened as Gabriel recited to him verses that when collected together compose the Qur'an. Notice that Muhammad had no choice in deciding the time, content, or vocabulary of the revelations that he received. Among the first of these verses is:

> The revelation and the Messenger: "Say . . . 'This Koran has been revealed to me that I may warn you thereby.'" (6:19)

> Recite (*iqra*): In the Name of thy Lord who created,
> created Man of a blood-clot.
> Recite: And thy Lord is the Most Generous,
> who taught by the Pen,
> taught Man that he knew not. (96:1–5 in Arberry 1955)

Muhammad is commanded by God to hear the message recited by Gabriel in Arabic, memorize it, and then chant it to the people. Thus, the chain of revelation is from God to Gabriel, who recites the Qur'an to Muhammad, who memorizes what he hears and then, as commanded, recites it to the people. The people are to memorize the Qur'an verses they hear from Muhammad and in turn chant it as their devotional practice and their message to others. The beginning of the Muslim community and its continued existence come in response to the call to memorize and chant the Qur'an (Welch 1979, 620). More recently, Miriam Cooke and Bruce Lawrence have redescribed this process in terms of Muslim networks (Cooke and Lawrence, 2005).

Although recognizing that others such as Jews and Christians have received books from God, the Qur'an sees itself as superseding all previous books and creating a new "people of the Book" from a community that, until then, had had no book. Instead of sending to the Arabs a missionary from those who had already been given the book, God sent Muhammad, the prophet chosen from among those who had previously not been given the Book of God (Welch 1981, 403). The heart of Muslim spiritual practice involves committing the words of the Qur'an to heart in memory and recitation or chanting (Cragg 1969, 61). Despite his status as a prophet, Muhammad remained an ordinary man in the minds of his followers (3:144). As Kassis puts it, "He was but a prophet and a messenger of God, surpassed by the message he bore. That message was the Qur'an, the corpus of the revelations that continued to descend on him until 632 CE, the year of his death" (Kassis 2000, 69). For Muslims, the Qur'an is God's word revealed to the entire human race in clear Arabic, Muhammad's native language. Muslims, regardless of their different language backgrounds, ecstatically hear the Qur'an recited and chant it without necessarily understanding what is said, satisfied that for them it is the word of God (Kassis 2000, 70). Let us now turn our attention to the uniquely Muslim experience of the chanted Qur'an.

The Oral or Chanted Qur'an

Muhammad received the words of the Qur'an in retainable portions, kept them in his memory, and passed them on to his followers through oral recitation. By the time of his death many others had committed the entire message to memory. Tradition says that during the Prophet's lifetime the text of the Qur'an was written down by Muhammad's secretary, Zayd ibn Thabit, who is quoted as saying, "We were at the home of the Prophet . . . collating the Qur'an from written patches" (Kassis 2000, 74). However, the written copies of Muhammad's revelations were not compiled into a book during his lifetime. Qureshi notes that the written words of the Qur'an remained inseparably linked to their utterance in recitation. Muhammad "spread the message by sending out reciters, not texts, and Caliph Uthman (the third successor to Muhammad, 644–56 CE) compiled the first authoritative text, and sent with each copy a reciter who could teach its recitation" (Qureshi 2006, 90). Even today, says Qureshi, "the pages of the Qur'an are as much an aid for memory as a direct access to the message of Islam" (Qureshi 2006, 90). As in music where it is the voiced sound, not the written score, that is the music, so also in Islam is it the chanted word, not the written text, that is the experienced Qur'an or word of God. Thus, learning how to "read" the Qur'an means learning how to chant and remember the Arabic words as well as their meaning. So, Muslim children are taught to memorize and chant the Qur'an in its original Arabic form no matter where in the world they live. The goal of every pious Muslim is to be able to chant the entire Qur'an from memory before dying. Such reciters are honored with the title Hafiz al-Qur'an (Qureshi 2006, 90). Instructions regarding the importance of recitation are found in the Qur'an itself. Qureshi notes that the Qur'an was transmitted from Gabriel to Muhammad in the mode of recitation/chant (*tartilan*) (25:31), and "Muhammad was directed to recite it in the same manner (*wa rattili l-qurana tartilan*)" (Qureshi 2006, 91). To aid in its memorization and chanting, says Qureshi, "the Qur'an abounds in a wealth of rhyme, assonance, rhythmic patterns, and recurring phrases, all of which enhance the meaning, and provide structure to the text as well as its sonic impact" (Qureshi 2006, 91). Kristina Nelson in her classic study, *The Art of Reciting the Qur'an*, adds that important recognition of the orality of the revelation is given in its name as *al-qur'an* meaning "reciting"/"recitation" (Nelson 1985, 4). She notes.

> For purposes of memorizing and reciting, the text is divided into 30 approximately equal parts corresponding to the 30 days of Ramadan, the month of fasting. . . . Superimposed on this structure are the notations which guide correct recitation according to the rules of *tajwid*. These include signs indicating such details of performed recitation as places of stopping and beginning, points of extended duration, and elision of consonants. (Nelson 1985, 5)

Nelson further suggests that the experience of chanting itself when well done "evokes the moment of revelation, the sound of the revelation, . . . as Muhammad learned it, that the various manifestations of the Qur'an are at the same time the whole" (Nelson 1985, 7).

The traditional chanting of the Qur'an in public liturgy and witness as well as in personal prayer is grounded upon a well-developed theology of the oral word. The Qur'an is uttered to call others to it, to expiate sins, to protect against punishment, and to ensure blessings in paradise. "He who recites it [the Qur'an] shall have the reward of a thousand martyrs, and for every *sura* the reward of a prophet" (Ayoub 1984, 10). Like a prophet, the pious person will be called on the day of resurrection to rise up and recite. With every verse that is recited the person rises up one station until the rewards of everlasting life and the bliss of paradise are received (Ayoub, 9). In this way the pious reciter, to the extent that he or she knows the Qur'an by heart, is said to share in the status of the prophets. The difference between the pious person and the prophet is that, unlike the prophet, the reciter does not receive the Qur'an as revelation. But to the extent that the reciter memorizes it, he or she is said to "live in the Qur'an" (Ayoub 1984, 11). Mahmoud Ayoub observes that this is a very close parallel to the New Testament idea that the pious Christian is one who lives "in Christ" (Ayoub 1984, 11).

As the direct word of God, the uttered words of the Qur'an are judged to possess powerful numinous qualities. For example, sura 59:21 states, "Were we to cause this Qur'an to descend upon a mountain, you would see it humbled, torn asunder in awe of God" (Ayoub 1984, 8). In addition to its creative and destructive power, the words of the Qur'an are also a positive source for healing and tranquility. According to tradition, when the Qur'an is recited divine tranquility (*sakinah*) descends, mercy covers the reciters, angels draw near to them, and God remembers them (Ayoub 1984, 9). Tradition also tells how one of the companions of Muhammad came to him and reported seeing something like lamps between heaven and earth as he recited while riding horseback during the night. Muhammad is reported to have said that the lights were angels descended to hear the recitation of the Qur'an (Ayoub 1984, 8). For the pious Muslim, then, the chanted words of the Qur'an have the numinous power to create and destroy, to bring mercy, to provide protection, to give knowledge, and to evoke miraculous signs. Because they contain such power, the words of the Qur'an are described as a heavy burden for those who take them to heart.

To bear this holy burden requires that the chanters be pure in heart, mind, and action. The reciter must be prepared to sacrifice for the holy word by fasting, by chanting through the night, and by giving thanks. The possibility of spiritual pride infecting the chanting of the Qur'an has been recognized by the tradition. Is the virtuosity of the chanter designed to draw attention to the person or to the holy words? Qur'an scholars have been of two minds on this question: "Some have adduced *hadiths* extolling musical chanting (*taghanni*) of the Qur'an, and others have cited equally accepted traditions enjoining a simple chant (*tartil*). Two modes of Quranic recitations came to be accepted: *tajwid* (making good, that is musically beautiful) and *tartil* (a slow and deliberate, simple chant)" (Ayoub 1984, 13). Musical styles used in secular singing are ruled out. The Qur'an is to be recited with dignity of demeanor, softness of voice, and a sorrowful tone. Within Islam the argument is between those who would adorn the Qur'an with their voices, and those preferring the simple mode who reverse the injunction to read "adorn your voices with the Qur'an" (Ayoub 1984, 13). The latter see themselves as putting the emphasis upon the beauty of the sacred word rather than upon the reciter's voice, thus guarding against the sin of pride. The emotion to be evoked in chanting is one of subdued sadness rather than joyful ecstasy. Because

God sent down the Qur'an in sorrow due to the sinfulness of people, Muhammad charged his followers, "Weep, therefore, when you recite it" (Ayoub 1984, 14).

The pious and correct chanting of the Qur'an has been understood as meritorious within the tradition. Completing a recitation (*khatm*) of the full Qur'an is a time of celebration. For the Muslim, the Qur'an is not seen as a book in the usual sense, but as a living word and faithful companion in the journey through this life to the hereafter. As Ayoub puts it, "a Muslim journeys through this life in the Qur'an" (Ayoub 1984, 14). This recitation of the holy word not only purifies the life of the devotee but also is seen to be necessary for the well-being of the rest of humanity and the maintenance of order in nature. Such an exalted view of the power of the holy word parallels the Hindu experience of revelation as mantra, which maintains both personal and cosmic order (rta) (see chapter 1).

A contemporary Egyptian Muslim, Labib as-Said, in his book *The Recited Koran*, has underlined the importance of the oral Qur'an for Islamic life. Worried about the decreasing memorization of the oral text by young children, and the falling off of good teachers and reciters, Said proposed recording the chanted Qur'an and its reproduction on audio records as a way of preserving the oral text (as-Said 1975, 65–76). With support from the government of Egypt and the rector of the al-Azhar University, the recording project was begun in May 1960, using the *tartil* (less musically dramatic) style of chanting. The *al-Mushaf al-Murattal* reading of the Qur'an was made available in some twenty-eight records. Said feels that by safeguarding the oral text in this fashion the legacy of the Arabic Qur'an, which binds together Muslims from all over the world, will be maintained (as-Said 1975, 121–125). Said's thinking in this regard is grounded in the viewpoint that while the canonical written text has been a significant factor in the preservation of the Qur'an, equally if not more important has been its transmission from generation to generation by word of mouth. This high regard for the oral tradition also involves meticulous methods for preserving it. Transmission from the mouth of a teacher to a student through the oral mode is judged to avoid errors such as the misreading of words (*tashif*), which easily occurred in the early script when diacritical points and vocalization signs had not yet been developed (the so-called *scriptio defective*) (as-Said 1975, 55). As a safeguard against the oral text becoming corrupted in its transmission, each trustworthy teacher had to be identifiable as being in an unbroken chain (*isnad*) of teachers reaching back to Muhammad. Said identifies ten such schools, commonly called "Readings" (*qira'at*) (as-Said 1975, 53). Traditional scholars attribute the variations among the Ten Readings to the dialectical variation in the way they were originally spoken by Muhammad (as-Said 1975, 53). Safeguard against corruption of the original revelation or new materials creeping into the oral text is achieved by application of the principle of *tawatur*, namely, that a large number of readers scattered over a wide area could not possibly concur on an erroneous or fabricated reading (as-Said 1975, 54). Said's aim in his modern project was to record all Ten Readings of the Qur'an.

It might be supposed that once the ambiguities of the early script were overcome through the use of diacritical points and vocalization signs, the oral readings would no longer be judged essential. This has not happened and the reasons offered for the continuing need for the oral text are instructive. First, since the added points and signs are not judged to be part of the orthodox written canon as such, there is a continuing need for the oral as the criterion against which the written text is to be verified. In the view of Muslims like Said, experience of the oral word is more basic and trustworthy than the written: "Oral tradition, provided it satisfies those requirements which are subsumed under the concept of *tawatur*, is considered to be a virtual foolproof vehicle of transmission. Written marks and signs are simply a convenience to scholars who wish to study and compare the various authentic Readings. They should never be taken as a source from which to learn these Readings" (as-Said 1975, 56).

"Secondly," maintains Said, "only through the oral tradition can the Koran's essential character as something recited, something orally delivered be preserved" (as-Said 1975, 56). Just as the Qur'an was orally delivered to Muhammad by the angel Gabriel, so its ongoing reception and transmission must retain the oral form. In disseminating the Qur'an, Muhammad sent out reciters not books. Even later, when 'Uthman distributed copies of the canonical written text, reciters went along as well to teach the correct recitation.

"Thirdly," argues Said, "the art of chanting the Koran, known in Arabic as *tajwid*, cannot be conveyed except by means of oral tradition" (as-Said 1975, 56). Muhammad proclaimed the revelation by chanting the scripture and directed the people to follow his example of melodiously reciting the Qur'an. Such speaking is not ordinary speaking but a special style of chant suitable for the sacred words.

From our modern context, it is important to note the key role that memorization plays in the oral tradition. To avoid errors creeping in from the misreading of words (*tashif*), the Qur'an is not to be memorized from a written text but, rather, by the repetition of the recitation of an authoritative teacher. In traditional Islam, to learn the Qur'an is to learn it by heart. In this learning there is a personal linkage through one's teacher's chain of teachers back to Muhammad, Gabriel, and God. Thus, there is an experience of spiritual psychological immediacy that memorization from a printed page cannot duplicate. Like other religions with oral text traditions (e.g., Hinduism), Islam stresses the importance of memorizing the Qur'an early in life. Psychologically, this is sensible for two reasons. First, children possess the ability to memorize large amounts of text easily. Second, having learned the text by heart at a young age, it is intimately with one for the rest of one's life. Being present within the unconscious, assuming that we sleep and occupy our conscious minds with other activities, the text in the unconscious is—as Freud has shown us—all the while influencing our thought and action. Learned by rote in childhood, the meanings of the words are then gradually appropriated by a pious or reflective person throughout the adult life. Memorization of the Qur'an by children has been taught privately by parents and publicly in the *kuttab*, or schools devoted to memorization of the text. First established by 'Umar in 634, these schools (sometimes called madrasas) have flourished wherever Muslim civilization was dominant (as-Said 1975, 58). This practice, however, is being challenged in some modern Islamic cultures (e.g., present-day Egypt), thus leading to the worries that Said, through his recording project, is attempting to address.

The special eloquence and power of the oral recitation of the Arabic Qur'an has fostered the doctrine of its incomparability (*i'jaz*). Together with the tradition that Muhammad was an unlettered man, the idea that the verses he recited were so uniquely beautiful and powerful has led to the Qur'an being seen as a miracle that only God could have authored (von Denffer 1983, 149). Indeed, the Qur'an itself challenges others to bring forward revelations that could equal the Qur'an (e.g., sura 2:23–24). According to the Islamic tradition, this challenge has never been met and in fact cannot be met (von Denffer 1983, 151). The Muslim scholar al-Qurtubi in his commentary lists characteristics of the Qur'an's i'jaz, or incomparability, such as: its language excels all other Arabic language; its style excels all other Arabic style; its comprehensiveness cannot be matched; it has no contradiction with natural science; it has a profound effect upon the hearts of people (von Denffer 1983, 151).

Nelson observes that the concept of i'jaz adds an aesthetic dimension to the experience of the Qur'an. Not only is the Qur'an "an expression of the nature of the divine, and of the human in relation to the divine, it is a model of beauty to which human expression can only aspire" (Nelson 1985, 7). Nelson captures the power of the public recitation of the Qur'an—a familiar event in Egyptian daily life. The setting is a large tent on a Cairo street. It is evening:

> . . . a clear ribbon of sound separates itself from the street noise. . . . The sound is that of the recited Qur'an . . . the reciter is seated alone in a raised chair against a far wall. He recites with his eyes closed, one hand tensely shaping the sound . . . as he begins a high passage he catches their attention. Suddenly the power of the phrase seizes the scattered sensibility of the crowd, focusing it, and carrying it forward like a great wave, setting the listeners down gently after one phrase and lifting them up in the rising of the next. The recitation proceeds, the intensity grows. A man hides his face in his hands, another weeps quietly. Some listeners tense themselves as if in pain, while, in the pauses between phrases, others shout appreciative responses to the reciter. Time passes unnoticed. (Nelson 1985, xiii)

Nelson comments that chanting, such as this, by professional reciters in Egypt, is considered to set the standard for the Muslim world. Says Nelson, "The familiar sound of recitation is the Muslim's predominant and most immediate contact with the word of God . . . even in private, they usually read aloud. For many Muslims, recitation remains their only access to the Qur'an" (Nelson 1985, xiv).

Given that it is the eloquence of the chanted Arabic Qur'an that is unique and incomparable, it stands to reason that it should be judged also to be untranslatable. This is certainly the view of traditional scholars, and it is a position shared by many Western scholars. One of the most successful Western scholars in this regard, Arthur Arberry, carefully distinguishes his English rendition from a translation by titling it *The Koran Interpreted*. Commenting on the special qualities of the Arabic Qur'an, Arberry uses a music analogy: "There is a repertory of familiar themes running through the whole Koran. . . . Using the language of music, each Sura is a rhapsody composed of whole or fragmentary *leitmotivs*; the analogy is reinforced by the subtly varied rhythmical flow of the discourse" (Arberry 1955, 28). When to this literary insight the intangible qualities imparted by a well-trained chanter are added, the claim that the total Arabic experience of the Qur'an is untranslatable appears quite reasonable. This should caution those who, upon reading an attempted translation and finding it dull or repetitious, are then tempted to dismiss the Qur'an as incongruous or lacking in aesthetic qualities to think again. The strength of Arberry's rendering is that he has tried to transpose the rhapsodic patterns of the Arabic Qur'an into English parallels, thereby conveying much more of the lyrical style of the original. The message of the Qur'an, it seems, is contained both in its lyrical style and in its word-meanings. Cragg captures this understanding effectively: "The scripture is a miracle of eloquence and diction, as well as the repository of final truth. Meaning cannot be assured in such sacred and crucial fields of truth unless language is also verbally inspired and given. Once given, in the revelatory particular, which is Arabic, it cannot be undone or transposed" (Cragg 1969, 32).

The Qur'an in Daily Piety and Practice

It is the use of the Qur'an in daily life by pious Muslims that demonstrates its continuing presence in their lives. As Wilfred Cantwell Smith has emphasized, the Qur'an is not just a seventh-century Arabian document, as modern historians of religion often seem to maintain. For the Muslim, the Qur'an is equally a ninth-, a fourteenth-, an eighteenth-, and a twentieth-century document, which has been and still is intimately involved in the life not only of Arabia but also of Africa, India, China, and elsewhere (Smith 1980, 498). The continuing vitality of the Qur'an is well portrayed by Smith:

> The Qur'an has played a role—formative, dominating, liberating, spectacular—in the lives of millions of people, philosophers and peasants, politicians and merchants and housewives, saints and sinners, in Baghdad and Cordoba and Agra, in the Soviet Union since the Communist Revolution, and so on. That role is worth discerning and pondering. The attempt to understand the Qur'an is to understand how it has fired the imagination, and inspired the poetry, and formulated the inhibitions, and guided the ecstasies, and teased the intellects, and ordered the family relations and the legal chicaneries, and nurtured piety, of hundreds of millions of people in widely diverse climes and over a series of radically divergent centuries. (Smith 1971, 133)

"The meaning of the Qur'an as scripture," says Smith, "lies not in the text, but in the minds and hearts of Muslims" (Smith 1980, 505). By way of comparison, as Smith has suggested, "for the Muslim the Qur'an is what Jesus Christ, not the Bible, is to the believing Christian" (Kassis 2000, 79). Thus, the Qur'an is not understood as "divinely inspired" and then composed by human authors such as Matthew, Mark, or Luke, but rather a revelation dictated by Allah directly to Muhammad through the angel Gabriel. Thus, from the Muslim believer's perspective there is no human authorship involved and the resulting book, the Qur'an, cannot be subjected to higher critical study as is the Bible (Kassis 2000, 79).

This central role of the Qur'an is anchored and sustained in Muslim life by the practice of recitation (*qira'a*). Recitation of the Qur'an has been the one essential element of Muslim daily worship (*salat*). In addition to the opening sentences, it is expected that one or more shorter suras, or chapters, of the Qur'an will be recited. Recitation of the Qur'an is the preferred form of devotion in Islam at any time. The fact that the Qur'an is the sacred word of God has led Muslims to maintain that it should be recited in the original Arabic, even if that language is not understood. Thus, Muslim children of whatever linguistic or cultural background are taught to memorize by saying aloud the words of the Qur'an. Memorized knowledge of the key passages will allow them to participate in salat, or daily worship, throughout their lives. As one old teacher, who was teaching children the Qur'an in Singapore, put it: "The sons of the Prophet ought to have this Word in their memory so that they can repeat it often. These words are endowed with special virtue. . . . In translating them we might alter the meaning and that would be sacrilege" (Graham 1985, 37). Like the Vedic mantra, the recited Qur'an itself has power. But even more important is its memorization, which has been basic to education throughout the Muslim world. One of the greatest accomplishments open to a Muslim is to be designated hafiz, or one who has learned by heart the entire Qur'an. This is also a goal for any accomplished religious scholar (*'alim*). In a Muslim society, the lilting refrain of Qur'anic recitation occupies a prominent place, so that from birth to death people are continually reimmersed in the Qur'an (Graham 1985, 38). This has a powerful unifying and transforming effect on both the individual and communal psyche. This is especially evident in salat, the five-times-daily prayer.

SALAT OR DAILY PRAYER

Miller observes that together with Qur'an recitation, Muslim salat or five-times daily prayer also includes acted out statements of the believer's surrender to God in *sujud* or physical prostration—thus involving a combination of body and soul in a symbolic act of surrender. This principle underlies the physical aspect of prayer, while the second aspect is that one should be frequent in chanting the Qur'an in remembrance of God (Miller 1995, 213). That is why at least five daily occasions for prayer are called for by the Qur'an (7:206)—morning, evening, and midday prayers are mentioned so as to keep the remembrance of God front and center throughout the day. As sura 33:42 puts it, "O ye who have believed, mention your Lord much and praise him early and late." The aim is to live in the awareness of God the Qur'an teaches and evokes. As sura 2:153 says, "Remember Me and I will remember you" (Cragg 1969, 61).

The salat prayers are at set times or time periods established by tradition:

> First prayer (*Fajr*)—between dawn and sunrise, two cycles
> Second prayer (*Zuhr*)—just after noon, four cycles
> Third prayer (*'Asr*)—in the afternoon, four cycles
> Fourth prayer (*Maghrib*)—after sunset, three cycles
> Fifth prayer (*'Isha'*)—before retiring, four cycles.
> (For details on the chants and postures in the cycles, see
>   Miller 1995, 214 and 220–221)

Preparation for each prayer involves a statement of intention and ritual purification or washing prior to beginning prayer. If one is in a Muslim community, the call to prayer is given five times daily from the minaret of the mosque by a trained chanter or muezzin—a powerful Arabic chant: "Allah is most great!" (once in each direction); "I bear witness that there is no God but Allah!" (repeated once); "I bear witness that Muhammad is the messenger of Allah" (repeated once); "Come to prayer! Come to prayer! Come to salvation!" (repeat); "There is no God but Allah!" (Miller 1995, 217). The call is penetrating, stirring, and reminds Muslims that they should remember God. Wherever one prays, in the mosque, in a public place (e.g., the office, airport) or at home, one is to pray facing in the direction of Mecca. On Friday, the noon prayer becomes congregational and is extended to include a sermon. In addition to the preceding prayers Muslims are encouraged to engage in voluntary individual chanted prayers (*du'a*)—free, spontaneous petitions (e.g., of repentance or calling down blessings such as "May God bless Muhammad") (Miller 1995, 221).

STYLES OF PUBLIC CHANTING

William Graham (1985) reports two examples of different styles of public recitation. One is the *dhikr* (the "remembrance" of God through litanies of group recitation) practiced by Sufi brotherhoods and certain mosques, especially tomb mosques. Dhikr involves the chanting of texts steeped in the language of the Qur'an and usually begins with the recitation of verses of the Qur'an itself. In contrast to such group chanting are sessions in which listeners gather to hear the Qur'an recited by a series of individual practitioners of tajwid (musical recitation of the Qur'an). Cairo is especially known for its varied forms of this kind of session, which can take place in mosques or in private homes of devotees of the art.

In addition to sessions of public recitation, the individual activities of a pious Muslim's daily life are potentially accompanied by spoken words of the Qur'an, for example, the *basmala*, "In the name of God, the Merciful, the Compassionate," that precedes routine daily acts such as eating or drinking, just as it precedes all but one sura of the Qur'an. There are also longer passages heard in daily life, for example, the *Fatiha*, sura 1, which every Muslim knows by heart and recites not only in every salat, or daily worship, but also at virtually every formal occasion. Other suras, such as "The Cow" (*al-Baqara*), contain prayers for forgiveness and are often recited before going to sleep (Graham 1985, 39).

The result of all this activity—the memorization of the Qur'an in early youth and the constant participation in public and private recitation of such memorized passages throughout adulthood—is that Muslim life is lived in resonance to the Qur'an. What the Muslim scholar al-Ghazali said of the Qur'an long ago still holds today: "Much repetition cannot make it seem old and worn to those who recite it" (Graham 1985, 40). In much of modern society "the book lives on among its people, stuff of their daily lives, taking for them the place of a sacrament. For them these are not mere letters or mere words. They are the twigs of the burning bush, aflame with God" (Graham 1985, 40). In addition to this oral experience of God's sacred word, its written form also forms a valued part of daily experience. The written Qur'an provides the content of Islamic art and is visible in magnificent fashion. As Graham puts it:

> The tradition of manuscript illumination and calligraphic artistry is one of the wonders of the Islamic cultural heritage. The written qur'anic word embellishes virtually every Muslim religious building as the prime form of decorative art. Nor is the reverence and honor shown the written

Qur'an text in Muslim piety any less striking and impressive. All such facts simply underscore what has been argued here: that the scriptural word, even where its written form is most prominent, is always demonstrably a spoken word, a recited word, a word that makes itself felt in personal and communal life in large part through its living quality as sacred sound. (Graham 1985, 40)

Music in Islam

Instrumental music was rejected by the orthodox in the early stages of Islam. Muhammad was said to have been hostile to music, yet he may have tolerated functional music such as pilgrimage chants and festival songs ("Islamic Arts" 1989, 67). As for vocal music, which was popular in Arab society, in Islam its place was largely taken by a sophisticated and artistic form of the recitation of the Qur'an known as tajwid. However, in Muslim courts where music was supported, Arab music was influenced by Persian and Greek music. And, among the religious groups, "the Sufis introduced both vocal and instrumental music as part of their spiritual practices. The *sama*, as this music is called, was opposed by the orthodox Muslims at the beginning, but the Sufis persisted in this practice, which slowly won general recognition" ("Islamic Arts" 1989, 38). Indeed, the great Sufi poet Jalal al-Din Rumi (d. 1273) is revered equally by the orthodox and the Sufis.

Originally the term "music" was reserved for secular music separate from folk music and religious chanting ("Islamic Arts" 1989, 65). But over time as Islam spread and absorbed various ethnic groups (e.g., the Berbers in North Africa, the Mappilas in South India, and others in Indonesia), the core Arabian music and chant absorbed influences from these cultures and new forms of Islamic music arose.

The use of melody and rhythm in the performed chanting of the Qur'an has been briefly mentioned. We will begin by examining these developments with close attention to the musical elements involved in the chanting of Qur'an especially in performance recitation by professional chanters. Then we will look at the use of instrumental and song music in the historical evolution and spread of Islam to various cultures. While the space limitations of a book chapter prevent us from being exhaustive, case studies will give some indication of the range of musical song in Islam: Mappila Muslim Song in the Sunnis of South India, Shi'a hymn commemorating the martyrdom of Imam Hussain, munshid Sufi song, and chant in Morocco.

Tajwid

The opening discussion of Qur'an recitation offered in this chapter provides an introduction to the practice of chanting that is the general devotional requirement for all Muslims. When the question of how this changes with the addition of aesthetic practice in chant and song is asked, we find different responses from Sunni, Shi'a, and Sufi Muslims. Tajwid involves development of an elaborate system of rules regulating the correct recitation of the Qur'an—"believed to be the codification of the sound of the revelation as it was revealed to the Prophet Muhammad and which he subsequently rehearsed with the Angel Jibrail (Gabriel)" (Qureshi 2006, 93). In her classic study of the art of reciting the Qur'an, Kristina Nelson finds that within Islam there are different areas regarding chanting the Qur'an (Nelson 1985, 14). The first is that the Qur'an (the Revelation from God) is meant to be heard and recited according to the rules of tajwid—the practice of articulating each letter with full value so as to sound out the revelation exactly as God is said to have sent it down to Muhammad. Thus, says Nelson, learning to recite according to the rules of tajwid (as commanded in the Qur'an) is the acknowledged duty of every Muslim, and, logically, the foundation of Qur'anic studies (Nelson 1985, 15). A Muslim student of tajwid learns the correct sound of the recited Qur'an from a teacher orally—the student learns by repeating the teacher's chanted passages of Qur'an. The written rules of tajwid are considered to be memory aids to help the student remember and correctly chant what he or she has heard—which, if done well, is nothing other than God's living revelation of the Qur'an (Nelson 1985, 15). Thus, tajwid is the system that shapes the sound of the Qur'an being recited as close as possible to the sound of God's revelation, and it consequently is far more significant to the believer than the written text (Nelson 1985, 16). Tradition holds that Muhammad himself in 622 or 623 CE instituted the call to prayer chanted by a professional singer or muezzin, and that he chose the Abyssinian singer Bilal as the first muezzin ("Islamic Arts" 1989, 67).

While there are many different manuals of the rules of tajwid, Nelson identifies three major areas of focus: 1) vocal production of phonemes or letter sounds; 2) extended duration of syllables (from one to six beats); and 3) rules for sectioning of the phrasing through the use of pause and beginning. These are the main areas of rules for reciting included in tajwid manuals, which the student learns not from these texts but by imitating the chanted sound heard from one's teacher. Opening and closing formulae (e.g., "In the name of God the Merciful and Compassionate," and "God has spoken truly") and the general styles of reciting (e.g., *Tahqiq*, very slowly, or *Hadi*, very quick) are considered secondary since they are not included in all tajwid manuals. Also, there is some disagreement between the various Islamic schools of law as to whether the pronunciation of opening and closing formulae needs to be audible. Nelson concludes that the effect of rules of tajwid on the sound of recitation results in its characteristic nasal quality and allows the individual reciter/performer to manipulate the sound variables for maximum artistic advantage (Nelson 1985, 16–21).

The rules of tajwid are meant to highlight the key aspects of Qur'anic chanting for the devotee, namely: 1) the Qur'an is meant to be spoken/heard rather than read, thus oral transmission is primary; 2) the recited Qur'an is of divine and inimitable beauty, therefore listeners approach it with expectations of heightened experience; and 3) the Qur'an "is held to be the last of God's revelations—therefore, it must be preserved and high value is placed on its accurate transmission (Qureshi 2006, 93). Nelson adds that for Muslims the correct recitation, as regulated by tajwid rules, ensures the correct transmission of both the aural and semantic messages. Also, the unique sound of tajwid signals a text and event set apart from other religious texts and experiences as well as from aesthetic experience in general. "It is the *tajwid* itself which encodes and makes perceptible both the unique nature of the text and the unique significance of the sound" (Nelson 1985, 31). But beyond the semantic and aesthetic results, perhaps the most important role of tajwid in recitation is its emotional effect upon the listener—the ability of a reciter to make people weep, for weeping is seen as a response to truth. As the Qur'an puts it, "When they hear what has been sent down to the Messenger, thou seest their eyes overflow with tears, because of the truth they recognize" (sura 5:86). Qureshi notes that "reports testify to the Prophet and his companions weeping on hearing the Qur'an recited" (Qureshi 2006, 93).

Mappila Muslim Music

For a Sunni example of recitation we turn to the Mappila Muslims of South India using Roland Miller's *Mappila Muslim Culture* (2015) as a key source. Although not well known outside India, the Mappila Muslims are a major social group of over 8,900,000 people in the Kerala State of South India. Says Miller, this population "is larger in size than 22 out of the 44 Muslim majority countries in the world. . . . They represent a significant example of successful Muslim cultural adaptation. . . . They draw on their Malayalam [South Indian] heritage for their everyday life and at the same time on their Islamic heritage for their faith, religious ethos, and many customs" (Miller 2015, 5). Islam came early to South India when, in the seventh century, Arab Muslim traders from the South Arabian peninsula boarded Arab dhows and sailed them across the Indian ocean to Kerala's shores to trade for spices (especially pepper)—trade that had been going on for more than 2,500 years as a peaceful commercial enterprise. After the Prophet Muhammad's successful preaching in Arabia, the Arab traders came to Kerala's shores as followers of Islam to trade with their commercial partners, the region's Hindus. Some Arab traders stayed and married local women. Such marriage unions plus conversions resulted in the development and spread of the Mappila Muslims (Miller 2015, 26). The Arab traders from the Southern Arabian Peninsula learned the local Malayalam language to carry on their business, but for them Arabic had a sacred quality. The result was a hybrid Arabic-Malayalam form of Muslim culture that became strong in eighth-century Kerala (Miller 2015, 26–28). Miller notes that in the northern Malabar region, "the growth of Islam was marked by intermarriage with and the conversion of Nayars and other higher caste Hindu classes" (Miller 2015, 44).

    For the Mappilas, a major influence was the conservative heritage of the South Arabian area. This heritage of the Arabic language and the Qur'an is central to the Mappila experience of education, culture, and religion—without diminishing their love for Malayalam, their mother tongue. Although today few Mappilas are fluent in Arabic, there is a willingness to let Arabic be the focus of early education and for its sound to be revered especially when expressed in the repetition of sacred phrases such as the daily call to prayer, which begins:

> Allah is most great [four times]
> I bear witness that there is no God but Allah
> I bear witness that Muhammad is the messenger of Allah
> Come to prayer! Come to prayer! (Miller 2015, 76)

The five-times-daily prayer and the Friday mosque service resound with Arabic formulae, petitions, and Qur'an verses that are learned from youth. Says Miller, the Mappila "emphasis on Arabic stems from the belief that it is the vehicle of God's final revelation" (Miller 2015, 77). Due to their lack of literacy in Arabic, the Mappila approach to devotion was sound-centered rather than meaning-focused. From a young age the Qur'an was memorized and recited rather than read and understood. This Sunni approach, including its sharia (law) emphasis, led to a traditionalist clergy with close ties to Arabia and Egypt. This "by heart" and ritual chanting of the Qur'an shapes daily prayers, the mosque service, the elementary religious school curriculum, and is evident in everyday Mappila family life. Miller observes that among the Mappila Sunnis there is a live-and-let-live outlook in which some tend toward their traditional heritage while others look toward moderate changes (Miller 2015, 224–225). Miller also notes that within Islam today there is a critique of mere rote recitation by some Muslim reformers. Their basic contention is that the word of the Qur'an is meant to be understood as the Islamic principle of guidance (*hidayat*) requires. Rote parroting of sounds unaccompanied by exposition is not enough. Muhammad was a prophet with a message that called people to learning and obedience. Rote recitation alone becomes the power of traditionalism and must be overcome by education (Miller 2016).

In addition to their traditional chanting of prayers and Qur'an, the Mappila community is proud of its music, which includes songs, instruments, and dance. On the Arabian side of its heritage, an early and great Islamic musician was Ibn Misjah of Mecca. Often honored as the father of Islamic music, he was a skilled singer and lute player

("Islamic Arts" 1989, 67). The Mappilas love to listen to music and watch trained dancers. Traditional Mappila songs share influence from both the Arabic and Malayalam cultural streams, but it is the Arabian songs that dominate. Most often these are noninstrumental songs by Mappila women. Says Miller, "with powerful memories Mappila women learn the songs at home and pass them on to their daughters. . . . They usually sing the songs in groups in a rhythmic chant, at public performances such as marriage festivals, *mawluds*, and other occasions" (Miller 2015, 304). Songs are often of three types: 1) songs of praise and prayer—garlands for the saints; 2) song stories—for example, a religious narrative; and 3) miscellaneous songs—wedding airs, teaching refrains, and modern lyrics. Many heroic Mappila songs extol the lives of prophets such as Abraham (Ibrahim) or Joseph (Yusuf). "They also sing of the virtues of early companions of the Prophet Muhammad" (Miller 2015, 306). Early heroic songs developed into war songs reminding Mappilas of God's vindication of His people in early Islamic history (e.g., the battles of Hunayn and Khaybar). This tradition is carried forward in Mappila song celebration against their oppressors. Martyr-saint songs or *malas* bring together the qualities of a valiant faith and military sacrifice in Mappila life between 1498 and 1921 in songs of praise for gallant struggles against impossible odds. In addition to military martyr songs, the Mappilas also revere romantic and wedding songs, instructional songs (e.g., Kunyain Musaliar's 1738 song of admiration for the Prophet), and modern songs (e.g., expressing the social problems of contemporary life such as family separation due to Gulf employment of Mappila men—songs such as "The Dubai Pattic" and "Tears of Kuwait"). Miller concludes his review of Mappila Muslim songs by noting that Mappila women have now begun to sing their old religious songs on the Internet (Miller 2015, 312).

The power of singing for spirituality is illustrated in the saint-song "Moideen Mala," which memorializes Abd al-Qadir al-Jilani (1077–1166), noted for his sober piety and mystical nearness to God. Singing this song is clearly a meditational means of Muslim spiritual transformation. His song begins: "Be with God, the Mighty, the Glorious, as if no creation exists. And be with creation as if there is no self in you . . . and when you are with creation without yourself, you will do justice and help the path of virtue and remain safe from hardships of life" (Miller 2015, 305). After singing praises for God and the life of the saint, the song story adds an appeal for forgiveness based on intercession for the devotee by the saint and concludes with a prayer. Says Miller, the song describes the saint as having the sharia or legal knowledge on his right and *haqiqa*, esoteric truth, on his left (Miller 2015, 305). The saint in his song clearly declares his spiritual function of "mediating with God on behalf of the believer" (Miller 2015, 306).

Devotional Hymns in Pakistan and India

In addition to the Mappila songs of Kerala, Qureshi points out that vernacular devotional hymns are common Sunni, Shi'a, and Sufi practices in Pakistan and India, as well as among South Asian diasporic communities (Qureshi 2006, 96). Sung in Urdu using Indian raga scales and tala rhythms along with harmonium and barrel drum (*dholak*), these devotional song gatherings are held mostly in homes rather than mosques. Says Qureshi: "A lead reciter, often with a supporting group, presents a series of hymns to an audience of devotees, who respond in specific ways to the religious listening experience. While the three hymn genres [Sunni, Shi'a, Sufi] differ from each other and from the language and recitation of the Qur'an, they are invariably permeated with scriptural references and phrases in Arabic, so that the connection with the primary message of Islam remains audible" (Qureshi 2006, 96–97).

In the Sunni tradition, a *na't* is a poem chanted in the *milad* devotional assembly to celebrate the birth of the Prophet Muhammad. Many Muslims, especially Sunnis, also celebrate special family events, or a person's life, with a milad or sequence of hymns with a lead reciter and accompanists—sometimes preceded by a recited passage from the Qur'an, followed by a series of na't poems and prose passages relating to the birth of the Prophet. "Hymn recitation concludes with the *Salam*, in which verses of praise alternate with a verse of salutation in Arabic. Out of respect for the Prophet, everyone rises to a standing position and joins in reciting the refrain while the reciters present the verses" (Qureshi 2006, 97). Qureshi points out that "for most Muslim girls and women, such recitation is the only approved way of expressing musicality and regaling an audience with an attractive sonic rendering of pious words" (Qureshi 2006, 97). Na't are much loved by devotees and performed in private and public contexts. Poets compose and recite na't as acts of faith, says Qureshi. She also observes that musically, "*milad* hymns evoke feelings of both devotion and exultation; they convey an experience of veneration and submission before the Prophet" (Qureshi 2006, 97). Milad devotional assemblies may well achieve meditational states of spiritual transformation perhaps comparable to Hindu and Sikh practices of group singing.

SHI'A HYMNS

Majlis means a "session" or "assembly." In South Asian Shi'a use majlis to refers to a recitational and hymn assembly to commemorate the martyrdom of Imam Hussain and the tragedy of his massacre at Karbala (Qureshi 2006, 98). Performed in homes and *imambaras* (Shi'a meeting halls), majlis gatherings are the primary Shi'a religious observances held on significant days throughout the year and to mark Hussain's death on the tenth of Muharram (*ashura*). Throughout the year various hymns are sung to take the singer/listener from personal grief (*soz*) through elegiac lamentation (*marsiya*) and a sermon about the struggle, suffering, and death of devotees. "Then simple dirges of intense grief (*nauha*) build to a climax of participation, with everyone rising and beating their chest in mourning (*matam*) . . . followed by an Arabic salutation to the Prophet and his descendants to conclude the *majlis* event" (Qureshi 2006, 98). Says Qureshi, majlis recitation and hymn singing creates for the listeners "a deep involvement in suffering that is both deeply personal and spiritually transformative. Through the coordinated movement of chest beating (*matam*), it creates a participatory bond among Shi'as. . . . In the broadest sense, *majlis* hymns constitute a repository of Shi'a heritage, interpretation and sentiment which their recitation brings to life for the community" (Qureshi 2006, 98). In his detailed study of Shi'i devotional rituals in South Asia, Vernon Schubel (1993) notes that rhythmic and musical variations of lamentations (*gham*) sung in the last portion of the majlis have an especially powerful emotional effect upon the devotees. These lamentations are sung by young men who stand near the minbar (pulpit facing Mecca) with the congregation "joining in with a calling pattern of repetition. The rhythm of the *matam* [the physical act of mourning] is carried by the metrical striking of the hands against the chest . . . and is profoundly emotional" (Schubel 1993, 98). Says Schubel, the central motif of the Shi'a majlis is personal allegiance to Imam Husayn. "This is accomplished by gradually turning the attention of worshippers away from their own life experiences and on to the experiences of the *ahl al-bayt* [Husayn and other imams] so that those experiences become tools of reflection upon their own lives" (Schubel 1993, 100). Such manifestations of grief are deeply meditative and are understood to be spiritually transformative (Schubel 1993, 94).

Sufi *Sama* Assembly for Spiritual Advancement: *Qawwali*

Nelson observes that "the impulse to render Qur'anic text melodically has been irresistible from the beginning of its practice, although, apart from phonetics and rhythm, we do not know how Qur'anic recitation sounded before the advent of recording technology" (Nelson 1985, 32). The Arabic term *sama*, meaning "audition" or "listening," refers to listening to music and listening to a musical recitation of the Qur'an. However, there is a long-standing debate between Muslim legalists, literature scholars, and Sufi thinkers regarding any kind of musical addition to the recitation of the Qur'an (Nelson 1985, 32). Nelson provides a clear description of how this debate has developed. On the one hand, there are those who reject sama, or music, as a powerful aesthetic force that distracts from or interferes in the struggle of the listener to achieve God's will. On the other hand, "for *sama's* proponents, most notably the Sufis, music is a neutral force which, channeled and regulated, can just as well lead to God as away from Him" (Nelson 1985, 50). This debate, which attempts to bring music under the mantle of Islam, appeals to four sources of authority: 1) Qur'an; 2) Hadith; 3) pronouncements and behavior (*sunnah*) of companions of the Prophet, scholars of the legal schools, and people of pious reputation; and 4) scholarly and scientific studies of the effects of music on all living creatures. With regard to recitation, the goal is to place guidelines or limits on the use of music (Nelson 1985, 33–34).

Nelson notes that some Sufis see music as a means to spiritual union with the divine and even a physical response. In this connection, she quotes al-Ghazali (legalist, philosopher, and Sufi seeker, 1058–1111) saying, "Know that the listening comes first, and that it bears as fruit a state in the heart that is called ecstasy, and ecstasy bears as fruit a moving of the extremities of the body" (Nelson 1985, 32). It seems that the sama argument cannot be resolved by appealing to the Qur'an since it is not specific on the subject of music, and its verses have been interpreted as supporting both sides. In the Hadith support has been found for both points of view. Nelson concludes her comprehensive study of sama by saying that in current Egyptian practice music is seen as essentially morally neutral; however, most Egyptian Muslims never question the compatibility of music with Islamic principles. "Just as music flourished in the face of official disapproval, so has the melodic recitation of the Qur'an continued as a widespread practice and even, in Egypt, a source of pride" (Nelson 1985, 51). Especially in Sufi contexts, the beauty of the human voice (*al-swat al-hasan*) together with poetry is seen as a powerful force for spiritual transformation.

Since the thirteenth century, says Qureshi (2006, 98), Sufi mystics across North Africa, the Middle East, Iran, and South Asia have developed the practice of reciting and meditational listening to mystical poetry and words as a spiritual training to achieve nearness to God. In this tradition, sama or *qawwali* is "an assembly for listening" that uses mystical poetry set to music as a means of realizing ecstatic union with God. In this practice, melodic instruments, drum beats, and handclapping articulate the incessant repetition of divine names that can last all night. Within the Sufi tradition all of this occurs within the context of pursuing discipleship under a spiritual master.

In South Asia, says Qureshi, "*sama* is a very intimately spiritual experience among a brotherly circle of Sufi disciples" (Qureshi 2006, 99). The South Asian musical singing of Sufi poems is improvisational in style and responds to the listener's spiritual needs of the moment. The lead singer (a highly skilled professional) accompanies himself on the harmonium while a supporting reciter plays the dholak or barrel drum. The professional reciter is a highly trained specialist but can also be an amateur—the range is wide. Highly trained Qur'an reciters, says Qureshi, can literally move listeners to tears (Qureshi 2006, 99). South Asian samas or recitational assemblies (qawwali) are public and are held "throughout the year, both among exclusive spiritual groups in any location and at shrines before large public audiences. The principal occasion, however, is the anniversary of the numerous

Sufi saints, especially the great Chishti and Qadiri founders of Indic Sufism" (Qureshi 2006, 99). Such Sufi meditational assemblies begin in the name of God, uttered musically; recitation of a passage from the Qur'an; and the singing of a succession of moving hymns drawn from poetry in Persian, Hindi, and Urdu sources. These texts extol and evoke mystical love between the devotee and the divine. They also name the hierarchy of Sufi masters from living spiritual guides (shaikhs) to saints, to Hazrat Ali, and finally to Muhammad—the human person most closely connected to God (Qureshi 2006, 99).

To offer an indication of the range of Sufi musical practice, let us conclude with a brief description of the music of the munshidun Berbers of Morocco, using Earle Waugh's fine book *Memory, Music, and Religion: Morocco's Mystical Chanters* (2005) as our major source.

Moroccan Sufi Chanting

As in the aforementioned case of the Mappila Muslims of South India, in Morocco's ethnic makeup (Arab, Berber, African) it is Islam, in this case Sufi Islam, that provides the glue to hold the ethnic groups together and provide a national identity, religion, and culture as munshidun (Waugh 2005, xvi). The Berbers of North Africa were early converts (750 on) to Islam and Sufism, which reached them via Spain. Waugh's book focuses particularly on the munshidun chanter tradition and its loyalty to a remembered religious reality. Indeed, Waugh identifies memory as foundational for the Sufi chanter practices and their music. Says Waugh, Sufis often speak about memories as the basis for remembering the beneficence of God and achieving their own self-understanding, which, when shared with others, serves a social solidarity function—as in Sufi chanter ritual (Waugh 2005, 6–10). The ability of music to carry religious memory into articulation and yet not to limit its meaning is crucial for the munshidun. Waugh offers the following analysis: "They [the munshidun] see the music of the brethren as a ritual form rooted in the collective past and carried on in the dhikr and sama (meditational song) today. So far as the individual chanter is concerned, his work can be summarized this way: The munshid operates in the milieu of a Sufi encoding system, trying to utilize material from the tariqa's musical and textual tradition, but always retaining a memory of a previous powerful moment when an encounter was made with 'reality' and that reality became 'present' or tangible. Retaining that remembered moment is his goal" (Waugh 2005, 13–14). In providing a *tariqa* or pathway for devotees, says Waugh, the role of the *munshid* (master chanter) in dhikr and sama meditation sessions "is a remembering of past inspired occasions, reintroduced by means of his memory so that his memory of that peak moment provides a breakthrough from past time to the present time to all who participate" (Waugh 2005, 14). In Moroccan Sufism, master- or munshid-led disciple/devotee musical meditation may reach the ecstasy of such peak moments.

Dhikr refers to Sufi rites or meditational liturgy focused on the remembrance of God and leading ultimately into a personal encounter with God (Waugh 2005, 18). But the term dhikr implies not just to remember but also to praise by remembering, to rehearse, to commemorate, to cherish the memory as a precious possession. Our natural condition as humans is to be in a state of forgetfulness from which we must be rescued by constant remembrance of Allah (God)—the act of dhikr, as taught to us by the Qur'an and Hadith. Dhikr is a meditation ritual for those who are "on the way," the brotherhood of believers as approved to be present by the shaikh and held in a private location. Although women attended some Sufi functions, in Morocco traditionally only men who were members of the tariqa (the brotherhood of believers following a guide or shaikh) attended (Waugh 2005, 20). In contrast to large public celebrations (as on birth celebrations of the saint days in Morocco), dhikr is exclusive to the committed and functions within a secret society where the goal is to move from the self-centeredness of one's own forgetfulness into a larger context in which one's relationship to God is front and center.

The Sufi dhikr tradition seems to have begun in Baghdad where the famous scholar and Sufi saint al-Ghazali had a school at which Abd al-Qadir studied. Qadir's personal dhikr involved a meditational chanting of the names of God in his own cell (in the *zawiya* or Sufi retreat building) after the evening prayer and bears a functional similarity to Hindu and Buddhist mantra practice. His definition of dhikr follows: "Dhikr is the impact when God comes fully, by eternal grace, into the intimacy of the initiate's heart, which is in perpetual evolution towards 'God.' And this dhikr illuminates and enchants the heart of the devotee. Consequently, he desires never to forget God. . . . [Thus] the initiate must repeat the Qur'an . . . saying: 'O you who believe! Recall often the name of God; recall him, and celebrate his praises morning and night' (33:41). The best dhikr is therefore that which springs up from the depths of the heart, inspired by the Glorious Lord" (Waugh 2005, 23). Abd al-Qadir's definition and subsequent developments of dhikr practice were brought to Morocco by the descendants of al Qadir's sons who had settled in Spain but were forced to flee to Morocco before the Battle of Grenada (1492). "The khalwa [meditation room] is first noted in Fez in 1692 where the order is known by the name of Jilala" (Waugh 2005, 23). Other great dhikr masters include Ibn al-Arabi and the Moroccan mystic Mulay al-Arabi al-Darqawi, who said, "All men need only one thing, which is truly to practice the remembrance of God" (Waugh 2005, 24).

Movement and dhikr are enshrined together in Sufism. All dhikr sessions involve head or body movement. Waugh suggests that Sufism has a structure of movement that unites body, mind, and self in fundamental ways: "The first is the way in which the culture of the group has learned and carries out the whole program of gesture, a remembering that links the practitioner to the saint . . . the committed dhikr participant "knows" the movement up the spiritual ladder with his body in such a way as to circumvent self-conscious awareness . . . At the summit of dhikr, self-awareness is abandoned for the bodily merging into a higher presence of engagement than what the conscious self can arrange for it" (Waugh 2005, 33–34). Other aspects of dhikr important in its effectiveness include the spiritual tone of the chanter, the infused energy experienced by the devotees, the presence of God, the Prophet or the saint, the presence of experienced adepts, and whether the day itself was auspicious (Waugh 2005, 34). In the Sufi tradition, dhikr is not a performance for an audience but a practice of the brotherhood of a munshid and his devotees for their own spiritual transformation. It is important to constantly engage in dhikr even if God's presence is not felt. As Ibn Arabi puts it, do not abandon dhikr because you don't feel God's presence, for "perhaps He will take you from a dhikr of [your] forgetfulness to one with vigilance, and from one with the Presence of God to one wherein everything but the Invoked is absent" (Waugh 2005, 35). Performance and memory together are essential for this process of spiritual transformation. As

118 / WORD, CHANT, AND SONG

Waugh puts it, there are shifts in speed and theme as the dhikr moves through cycles to completion—shifting the devotee from an exterior to an inner focus. "There are moments of blending in which layer after layer of images are cadenzically arranged. . . . The munshid weaves replication and new articulation together to contribute to the rising emotional sophistication of the dhikr. There is, at the last, the climax, the deliberate mantric-like repetition, the merging of tune, image and motion in intensity until the whole transcends the part and a new experience of Presence is born. The birth of this moment signals the end of the dhikr process" (Waugh 2005, 40–41).

MUSIC IN DHIKR

As the preceding discussions make clear, Sufi chanting in dhikr is infused with rhythm and melody—in short it is a form of singing. Indeed, Waugh describes the chanting master (munshid) in dhikr as a "Master of Musical Performance" (Waugh 2005, 191). Says Waugh, the munshidun clearly understand that words are not neutral but powerful conveyers of truth that can move people to inspired heights. To accomplish this the munshidun require a sense of rhythm and sound so that the chant can be sung. And, claims Waugh, the music that is chanted is not just formulaic but calls up familiar sonic patterns in the mind of the singer and listeners. The music is a powerful part of the remembering or going-back process. "Whether it is the crying dhikr of the Aissawiyya, the Andalusian tunes among the Darqawiyya, or the drumbeat of the Ginawa, music is the power that drives the message into the heart . . . It is rooted in the religious reality. This is a tool from God to draw humans to Himself" (Waugh 2005, 191). At least, this is the way Moroccan Sufis see it.

Waugh shows how all this manifests in the life of Morocco's best-known munshid, Muhammad Bennis, who lives in Fez (Waugh 2005, 161–169). Born in 1955, Bennis learned Sufi chanting from his father and especially his grandfather, the leading munshid of Fez. In his family everyone knows dhikr, and one of his brothers, Abd al-Fattah, is a great munshid and performer in the Rabat Andalusian Orchestra. Bennis was interviewed by Waugh and described how he grew up going to Friday prayers with his father and listening to the chanting. After the noon prayer, the chanters were invited home by his father for dinner and more singing of Sufi texts. This led the young boy to commit most of these texts to memory. At the age of eight he became a student of the widely respected Sufi, Shaikh Muhammad al-Zaytuni and demonstrated a remarkable facility for memorizing texts and *qasaid* (song poems). By age twelve, he could memorize a seventy-verse poem in a single day. This ability along with his good singing voice he understood as gifts from Allah. Bennis not only wanted to know all of the songs or qasaid by heart but also their background and context. He also showed an interest in Andalusian music because it was the basis of both sama and popular love songs. To move to this broader musical spectrum, he eventually left Shaikh al-Zaytuni and became a student of Abde al-Wahhab Saqqat, "a formidable singer whose abilities were appreciated even beyond the borders of the Sufi circle to which he belonged, and he regularly chanted for funerals and sang for weddings and circumcisions" (Waugh 2005, 163). He did not charge for these outside performances so as to show that he had not sold out for money. Although illiterate, Shaikh Saqqat gave Bennis a deep grounding in the oral tradition of the songs and their contexts. This led Bennis to do deep research into the music, studying ancient sources to complement his master's instruction. At the same time Bennis became a more deeply committed Sufi in his personal life. Of his performance, Bennis told Waugh: "On any occasion in which I was singing, I would picture my shaikh standing right there in front of me and start singing like I was in his presence. . . . I almost became another person because I was carried away by my shaikh's presence, and then he (the shaikh) would bring a very deep and old qasida, one that was even forgotten by people, but they would recognize in me the stamp of Shaikh Saqqat that they once knew" (Waugh 2005, 163). When Saqqat died, Bennis was acclaimed as his heir and replaced him as the main munshid in the tariqa, the organization around a spiritual guide or congregation of believers.

Speaking about the role of the munshid, Bennis maintains that it is not the munshid that attracts people to the Sufi way, rather, it is the spiritual depth of the *inshad* (chanted texts) and sama poems. It is the content of the Sufi poems he sings that lead people to Allah and not to any particular Sufi group. The special quality of Moroccan munshidun is their faithfulness to what they sees as the true texts of the Sufi—namely, "We chant first and foremost Imam Busayri's texts.

Each Friday we go to the mosque of Mulay Idris to chant the *Hamziyya* and the *Bourda*" (Waugh 2005, 165). As to the special role of a munshid, Bennis says that he should not be distracted from the content of what he is chanting because he is chanting in God's presence. As munshid it is his responsibility to choose the theme of the inshad or sama session, and then the poems that will become the basis of the performance. It is then up to the munshid "to carry on through the various texts in a smooth and convincing manner. . . . [the session] starts with the Qur'an, then proceeds with the poems of madih and then the sama" (Waugh 2005, 166). A wise munshid will pay attention to the makeup of his audience and choose poems accordingly. The smooth transition from one kind of text to another depends upon the artistic ability of the munshid.

A particular concern of Shaikh Bennis is today's youth and the training of youth munshidun. Since the 1990s, Bennis, in association with the mosque of Tajmuti, has operated a school in Fez to teach youth the chanting/singing of songs to be used in dhikr or sama (inshad). His school has graduated many renowned munshidun, including his own brother Abd al-Fattah. Waugh notes that the teaching technique of Bennis differs from the way he learned from his own shaikh. Bennis places more emphasis on music as the context in which to understand the text. He teaches his students the basic elements of the Andalusian music tradition (the *qasida* or poem line form, theme scheme, and meter) along with an explanation of the song's content and the composer's biography. This more intellectual approach differs from the old shaikh tradition of teaching a text by mere memorization and repetition. His stated goal is "to get the munshidun to go beyond a rather shallow understanding of the texts" (Waugh 2005, 168). He complains that many lack spiritual depth—the young munshidun do not want the work of memorizing the deeper and more complex poems that are valued within the Sufi mystical tradition. Thus, when he sings for the wider Moroccan community he chooses the easier, more popular texts and reserves the deeply spiritual and more complex poems for Sufi insiders who know the complex songs (Waugh 2005, 168). However, he still feels a responsibility to educate the broader Moroccan community into an understanding of the deeper meaning of what they are hearing. Thus, he also supports the use of audio tapes and videos so as to bring some awareness of Sufism throughout the country. As Shaikh Bennis puts it: "The munshidun should strive to conserve Islamic patrimony and educate the audience instead of following the audience's [bad] taste that now appreciates only light and profane music. And I believe that when the munshidun shoulder this 'mission,' Allah will endow them with more gifts to aid in their role of calling people to Allah. They will have a tarbiyya [youth education role] to attract the youth to Allah, and Allah will grant them success (tawfiq)" (Waugh, 168–169). Waugh concludes that Muhammad Bennis, as a contemporary Sufi munshid, has made a most significant contribution to Islam in Morocco—"his commitment to developing a school of young singers will clearly impact on the growth of the genre of music and its place in Moroccan culture.... From his perspective the future of the munshidun in Morocco is bright" (Waugh 2005, 169).

Conclusion

Muhammad received the words of the Qur'an as revelations from God through direct dictations from the angel Gabriel in retainable portions, kept them in his memory, and passed them on to his followers through oral recitation. As in music where it is the voiced sound, not the written score, that is the music, so also in Islam it is the chanted and sung word, not the written text, that is the experienced Qur'an. To aid in its memorization and chanting, "the Qur'an abounds in a wealth of rhyme, assonance, rhythmic patterns, and recurring phrases, all of which enhance the meaning, and provide structure to the text as well as its sonic impact" (Qureshi 2006, 91). The chanting itself when well done is felt to evoke the moment and sound of the revelation in the devotee, just as Muhammad experienced it. Traditional chanting of the Qur'an is done in public liturgy, as in the five daily calls to prayer and in personal devotions. Reciting the Qur'an is done to keep Allah front and center in one's daily thought and actions, to expiate sin, and to ensure blessings in the afterlife. On the day of resurrection, says Islam, the pious person will be called upon to rise up and recite. Muhammad chanted the scripture and taught people to follow his example of melodiously reciting the Qur'an—and thus to live in the Qur'an. Wilfrid Cantwell Smith put it well when he said, "The meaning of the Qur'an ... lies not in the text, but in the minds and hearts of Muslims" (Smith 1980, 505). For the Muslim, the Qur'an is what Jesus Christ, not the Bible, is to believing Christians.

In this chapter, we have examined the unique ways in which the word of the Qur'an is anchored and sustained in Muslim life by practices such as salat or recitation in the five-times-daily prayers following the call to prayer by a trained chanter or muezzin from the minaret of the mosque. We saw how this tradition of salat reinforces and is anchored in memorization and recitation of key passages learned in childhood (e.g., the basmala and sura 1, the Fatiha). With regard to the role of meditational chant/singing in all of this, we followed a detailed analysis of tajwid, the rules for the use of aesthetic practice in chant and song, by summarizing Kristina Nelson's fine study of the art of reciting the Qur'an. She outlines how learning to recite according to the rules of tajwid, as commanded in the Qur'an, is the duty of every Muslim (Nelson 1985, 15). We came to understand how the student of tajwid learns the correct melodic sound of the recited Qur'an from a teacher orally—by repeating the teacher's chanted passages and learning the rules for letter sounds, duration of syllables, and phrasing by the use of pause and beginning. The rules of tajwid highlight the key aspect of Qur'anic chanting for the devotee, namely, that the Qur'an is meant to be spoken/heard rather than read; the recited Qur'an is of divine and inimitable beauty; and finally, the Qur'an is held to be the last of God's revelations and tajwid recitation ensures its correct oral/aural transmission. But most important is its emotional effect upon the listener—the ability of a skilled reciter to make people weep because of the truth they recognize, just as the prophet and his companions are reported to have wept on hearing the Qur'an recited (Qureshi 2006, 93).

A case study of tajwid practice in the Mappila Muslim community of South India was offered to demonstrate the continuity and variation in chanting introduced as Islam spread from Arabia to quite different cultures and contexts. Here we depended on Roland Miller's fine study of the Sunni Mappila Muslims' chanting and singing of songs as passed from mother to daughter from the seventh century to the present (Miller 2015, 306). These songs are mostly noninstrumental and include songs of praise and prayer, heroic song stories of the saints, and songs such as wedding airs. Recent song stories tell of social problems such as family separation due to Gulf employment of Mappila men (e.g., "Tears of Kuwait"). Mappila women learn these songs at home and pass them on to their daughters. At public performances, these songs are usually sung in groups in a rhythmic meditational chant. Today, says Miller, Mappila women have begun to sing their religious songs on the internet.

Among the Shi'a, Qureshi briefly introduced us to the powerful spiritual role that chant and meditational singing plays in the majlis assembly to commemorate the martyrdom of Imam Hussain and the tragedy of his massacre at Karbala (Qureshi 2006, 98). The key music motif here is one of call-and-response lamentations in the recalling of the martyr sufferings of Hussain's death, which involves the devotees rising and beating their own chests. Such hymns, engaging the devotees' physical expression of grief, turn attention away from their own life experiences and into an experience of suffering that is both universal and deeply personal. These experiences of chanted and sung grief are central to Shi'a piety and are understood to be spiritually transformative.

Finally, we focused on the Sufi sama practice of using music as a meditational means for spiritual advancement. Since the thirteenth century, Sufi mystics across North Africa, the Middle East, and South Asia have developed the tradition of sama or qawwali—an assembly for listening that uses words of the Qur'an, names of God, or mystical poetry set to music as means for realizing ecstatic union with God. From the many varieties of Sufi manifestations we selected Earle Waugh's excellent book on the Moroccan Berber chanting/singing of the munshidun for a case study. Waugh's detailed analysis of the religious memory and acts of remembrance underlying the Sufi performance of dhikr provided an in-depth understanding of this Sufi approach. The ability of music to carry religious memory into articulation yet not to limit its meaning is crucial for the munshidun. Dhikr refers to the Sufi meditational chanting/singing focused on the remembrance of God and leading ultimately to a personal encounter with God (Waugh 2005, 18). Sufi chanting in dhikr is infused with rhythm and melody—it is a form of singing. Waugh demonstrates how the munshid or chanting master in dhikr understands that words are powerful conveyers of truth and, when paired with rhythm and melody, can move people to inspired heights. Waugh reveals how this chanted music is not just formulaic but calls up remembered sonic patterns in the minds of the singers and listeners—it is rooted in a religious reality in which God uses the word/music as a means to draw humans into union with himself. Waugh notes that the meditational movement of the dhikr requires a careful leadership "in order to 'ride the waves' of emotional and spiritual mood to *hal* (state of mystical experience)" (Waugh 2005, 25). As in prayer or Hindu/Buddhist mantra practice, the dhikr devotees must be guided through the various postures, breathing exercises, and chants at an appropriate spiritual pace, for the shaikh knows that the framework is constructed on the basis of the spiritual progression practiced in the religious culture of his tariqa (meditational group of devotees) (Waugh 2005, 25). At the advanced level, says Waugh, "having learned to discipline their disruptive minds and spirits through the dhikr, the adepts are all at peace in their relationship to the transcendent presence . . . they experience no conflictual/separational situation between their human selves and the 'presence' they encounter" (Waugh 2005, 27).

Clearly, this is the understanding of the Moroccan Sufis. Waugh's case study of Morocco's best-known munshid, Muhammad Bennis, manifests this in contemporary experience. We saw how as a boy of eight he became a student of the Moroccan Sufi master Shaikh al-Zaytuni, from whom he learned in a traditional chanting and memorizing style until he could memorize a seventy-verse poem in a day. To gain a wider and deeper understanding of the songs, Bennis became a student of Shaikh Saqqat, who gave him a deep grounding in the oral tradition of the songs and their contexts. All of this led Bennis to become more deeply Sufi in his personal life so that he became Saqqat's heir and replaced him as a leading munshid among Moroccan Sufis. We learned how he safeguards against his fame obstructing his spiritual mission both to his own Sufi society and the wider Moroccan community. Bennis has also established a school to train youth in dhikr chanting, so that the Moroccan Sufi tradition will continue into the future.

As a closing note, Regula Qureshi adds a few comments about current trends and the future of chanting and singing in Islam (Qureshi 2006, 109). Recordings of Qur'an recitation, especially by renowned Egyptian masters, have a preserving and standardizing influence across the Islamic world. Regarding hymn recitation, here too recordings of talented na't and nauha singers have suggested standards of melodic and tonal excellence. Qureshi does note that in Sufi qawwali or meditational dhikr assemblies, outside musical influence has resulted in changes in preferred instrumental accompaniment—from the traditional barrel drum (dholak) to the tabla, and from the simple plucked sitar to the intrusive presence of one or more harmoniums. In Pakistan, qawwali has developed into a concert genre, like concepts of religious compositions in the West. However, remarkably, on stage or on records, leading qawwali performers (e.g., the Sabri brothers or Nusrat Fateh Ali Khan) have retained their spiritual repertoire and performance style—suggesting that "these international stars never stopped performing qawwali in ritual assemblies for the spiritual goals of Sufism" (Qureshi 2006, 109). Qureshi observes that in Indonesia, the role of women in leading Qur'an chanting is gaining attention.

As a final pointer to the range of contemporary developments in Islam, we will mention Samy Alim's exploration of the "Transglobal Hip Hop *Umma*" as a new research area (Alim 2005). Alim, a linguistics professor at the University of California, Berkeley, specializing in the language of hip hop, maintains that Islam is hip hop's official religion. Alim's research for this contention is offered in the 2005 book *Muslim Networks from Hajj to Hip Hop*, edited by Miriam Cooke and Bruce Lawrence. Their contention is that Muslim networks are global and key to the shaping of Muslim civilization. Alim examines this insight in terms of hip hop music, which he argues forms a transglobal *umma*, or community, within a borderless Islamic nation (Alim 2005, 265). This global hip hop youth culture movement developed some three decades ago, spreading from African Americans to Europe, Algeria, and other African countries by hip hop artists' performance from the stadiums to the streets. Alim identifies three dominant forms of Islam in the hip hop nation of the United States—"the Nation of Islam, the Nation of Gods and Earths (or the Five Percent Nation of Islam) and the Sunni Muslim community" (Alim 2005, 266). Hip hop artists maintain that the way in which the Qur'an was revealed to the Prophet, namely, orally through rhymed prose, parallels the mode of delivery found in hip hop lyrical production. Hip hop rapper Mos Def is quoted chanting Qur'an verses and saying:

> . . . there's a rhyme scheme in all of it . . . and it holds fast to your memory. And then you start to have a deeper

relationship with it on recitation. Like, you know, you learn *Surat Al-Ikhlas*, right. You learn *Al-Fatiha*. And you learn it and you recite it. . . . Then one day you're reciting it, and you start to understand! You really have a deeper relationship with what you are reciting. '*A'undhu billahi min al-shaitan al-rajim* . . .' You be like, 'Wow!' You understand what I'm saying? Hip Hop has the ability to do that—on a poetic level. (Alim 2005, 267)

Alim's analysis shows how hip hop music not only functions as a means of spiritual transformation for individuals, but it also has produced activist social protest movements in America, Britain, France, Canada, Japan, Italy, South Africa, and Palestine. For example, England's Da-Mental and France's IAM are involved in antiracist mobilization against white supremacy (Alim 2005, 269). In concluding, Alim leaves us with the question: Will hip hop music and its *umma* transform the way we teach youth as scholars or imams? (Alim 2005, 272).

CHAPTER 4

Sikh Spiritual Practice

Word, Chant, and Song

This chapter examines some ways in which the Sikh tradition engages the hearing, reciting, and singing of sacred word for spiritual transformation in individual and congregational practice. After a brief introduction to the Adi Granth as Sikh scripture, the function of Sikh sacred word/chant/singing (*kirtan*) will be examined in spiritual practices such as chanting the divine name, singing scripture, oral recitation of the *bani* (divine utterance) as musical performance, *Hukam* or taking Vak, and "rites of passage such as naming, initiation, marriage, and death." Wherever possible, attention will be given to changes resulting from living in diaspora settings.

Nanak and Sikh Scripture or Adi Granth

Nanak, the founding figure of the Sikh tradition, was born in a Punjabi village not far from the modern city of Lahore in 1469 CE—fourteen years before the birth of Martin Luther (1483–1546), a time of great change. In the Punjab of Nanak's day, the two dominant religions of the region were Hinduism and Islam. His youth was marked by spending long hours in meditation and devotional singing along with his work. One morning while bathing in the river he disappeared without leaving a trace and was feared drowned. Three days later he was found and his first words were: "There is no Hindu, there is no

Muslim." Nanak's radically new vision, which Sikhs understand to have resulted from his three-day audience with Vahiguru (the Divine) and the enlightenment he realized, formed the basis for a new religion. In 1499 Nanak launched a new community, the Sikh *panth*. After about twenty years of travel and itinerant preaching, reaching as far east as Assam and as far west as Mecca, he returned to his native Punjab in 1519 and spent the next twenty years teaching disciples meditation, right conduct, and two key spiritual practices: *nam-simaran* (remembrance/chanting of the divine name), and kirtan (singing hymns of praise). As Oberoi (2000, 118) puts it, Nanak conceived of the Divine as the creator who is eternal and all-pervasive. This Akal Purakh (Nanak's name for the Divine) is beyond time and is both with qualities/forms (*saguna*) and without or beyond qualities/forms (*nirguna*). The Adi Granth repeatedly proclaims that the Divine is One (Akal Purakh) and that there is only one Divine in all religions. Says Pashaura Singh:

> It conveys a consistent message that liberation can be achieved only through meditation on the divine name (*nam*) and the music of the divine word (*shabad*, Sanskrit *sabda*). . . . Nanak employs the word *nam* to reflect the manifestation of divine presence everywhere, yet people fail to perceive it due to their *haurnai* or self-centeredness. The Punjabi term *haurmai* (I, me) signifies the powerful impulse to succumb to personal gratification, with the result that the person is separated from the Akal Purakh and thus continues to suffer within the cycle of rebirth (*samsar*). However, Akal Purakh reveals himself through the Guru by uttering the *shabad* (divine word) which communicates to those able to "hear" it. The Guru is thus the "voice" of Akal Purakh, mystically uttered within the human heart, mind and soul (*man*). The *shabad* is the actual "utterance" and in "hearing" it one awakens to the reality of the divine name, immanent in all that lies around and within one. (Singh 2006, 144)

Before his death, Guru Nanak chose a successor, thus launching a spiritual lineage of nine successor Gurus between 1539 and 1708.

Each one contributed to the consolidation of the institutional Sikh tradition. Oberoi notes four key contributions in the evolution of the Sikh tradition. The fourth Guru, Ram Das (1534–1581), acquired land and founded the city of Amritsar. In Amritsar, the fifth Guru, Arjan (1563–1606), constructed the Golden Temple and in 1603 and 1604 gathered his own writings and those of the four Gurus before him into the first collected scripture, called the *Adi Granth* or the *Sri Guru Granth Sahib* by devotees. The Adi Granth (First Book) was installed in the newly constructed Golden Temple. The tenth and last living Guru, Gobind Singh (1666–1708), completed the compilation of the Adi Granth and created a new religious order called the Khalsa. Oberoi describes the context of the Khalsa as follows. From the time of the third Guru there had emerged a group of priests or ritual specialists (called *masands*) who stood between the Guru and the lay public. So, in 1699 Guru Gobind Singh called for an end to the office of the masands by launching the Khalsa order with the idea that all Sikhs could now directly relate to the Guru without having to go through the masands. In addition, all Sikhs were expected to make a new start by being baptized or initiated into a new religious discipline involving the dress marks referred to as the *panj kakke* or five Ks (because they all begin with the Punjabi letter *k*) including: *kes* (uncut hair held in place by a turban), *kangha* (a comb worn in the hair), *kirpan* (a sword for protection only), *kara* (a steel bracelet), and *kachh* (underwear shorts). (For an interpretative essay on the five *k*s, see J. P. S. Uberoi 1992, 320–334.) In addition, Gobind Singh decided to end the line of personal Gurus by naming the Sikh scripture, the Granth Sahib as the future Guru. Oberoi explains the theological and historical significance of this action as follows:

> Behind this formal recognition of the scripture as *Guru* was a doctrine that had been emerging from the time of Guru Nanak. All of the Gurus in their respective compositions repeatedly made the point that the mode of transmission between the Akal Purakh and humanity was *bani*, or divine utterance. And since the *Granth Sahib* was the most concrete representation of this *bani*, Gobind Singh declared it to be the future Guru. (Oberoi 2000, 120)

Or, as the Sikh prayer *ardas* puts it, "From the Timeless One there came the command . . . Acknowledge the Granth as Guru, For it is the manifest body of the Masters" (Oberoi 2000, 121).

The Place of Scripture in the Sikh Tradition

While most religions have scriptures, the place and function of Sikh scripture seems unique. In no other religion can one find a human Guru founder, followed by a series of human Gurus living parallel with a collection of scripture, ending in a breaking of the human succession and the scripture attaining full authority as Guru (Cole and Sambhi 1978, 43). Both the Gurus and the scripture are respected within the tradition because of Vahiguru's word, which they express. This has opened the way for the error of idolatry of the Gurus and the scripture. Guru Nanak guarded against idolatry of the Guru by making a distinction between himself as Waheguru's mouthpiece and the message he uttered: "I spoke only when you, O Waheguru, inspired me to speak" (Adi Granth 566, as quoted by Cole 1982, 55). Unlike Hinduism, pictures of the Gurus are not seen as suitable objects for devotion. Instead, the true picture of the Gurus is said to be the *gurbani* (Vahiguru's word spoken by the Guru). Although first spoken as oral revelations, the words were memorized and written down. The Adi Granth is housed in its own building or room, the gurdwara. It is placed on a cushion, covered by a canopy and wrapped in special cloths. It is physically located so that it will be in the most elevated position, and when being moved it is carried on the head—all of this to indicate its exalted status as Guru. Just as one would bow before the Lord, so one bows before the Adi Granth and is careful not to turn one's back to it. The book is ritually put to bed and awakened. Before entering a gurdwara, one must have bathed and removed one's shoes. Offerings are placed before the enthroned book, and after worship a *prasad* (a communion-like blessing of food from Vahiguru) is received. For many Sikhs, the very sight of the scripture is a means of receiving grace (Cole 1982, 62).

Wilfred Cantwell Smith has pointed out that for a text/words to have transforming power, it needs to be in a living relationship with a community (Smith 1993, 18). As Pashaura Singh says, for the

Sikhs this "living relationship" is demonstrated in the daily installation of the Guru Granth Sahib early in the morning at the Golden Temple in Amritsar:

> The sacred volume is carried in a golden palanquin in a procession from the Akal Takhat ("Throne of the Timeless One") to the Golden Temple, beginning with the beat of a large drum, *nagara*, and occasionally blowing of a *narsinga* (a large horn-like brass instrument) to invoke the sacred symbols of power. Thousands of chanting Sikhs participate in this early morning service. . . . the high point of this devotional activity comes when the scripture is majestically installed on a lectern under a canopy inside the sanctum sanctorum of the Golden Temple to the accompaniment of "Panegyrics of the Bards" (*bhattan de savayye*) by a group of Sikhs, and then it is opened at random by the *granthi* ("reader") to proclaim the Guru's Word (*Vak*) that is received by the audience as the divine command for the day. (Singh 2008, 661)

Through this living relationship between the Book and its people, the Guru speaks to his followers in the same manner that he spoke to them while present in the flesh. As W. H. McLeod notes, the extraordinary reverence shown to the physical copy of the Guru Granth Sahib is not bibliolatry or idol worship. "Rather, it shows a living relationship between the scripture and the community" (McLeod 1975, 64).

Verne Dusenbery has given a careful analysis of the way in which the "word as Guru" functions as the basis for the living relationship between the divine and the community. This is based in the unique philosophy of language developed by the Sikh tradition. Unlike the modern West with its emphasis on the semantic meanings of words in their abstract or impersonal written or printed form (termed dualistic language), the Sikh tradition experiences scriptural language as having the dynamic qualities of a living personal relationship—the Adi Granth being the spoken words of the mouth of the Guru (*gurmukhi*) and then recited or sung in Sikh spiritual practice, which Dusenbery calls nondualistic language (Dusenbery 1992, 389). It is this approach to language that gives the chanted and sung words of the Gurus and the Adi Granth their transforming power. As Dusenbery puts it, "The relationship between the Sikh Guru and devotee is not an impersonal and didactic relationship based on formal instruction in religious dogma or doctrine. Rather, Sikh Gurus are thought able to transmit to devotees certain divine benefits that are simultaneously both cognitive and physiological" (Dusenbery 1992, 390). Thus, Gurus (as it were) channel the Divine through their spoken words to the devotees, transforming the person in body and spirit: "Receipt of the Guru's substances in the course of Sikh worship, therefore, serves to establish the substantive and moral connectedness of Guru and devotee (despite their differences in purity and rank); it serves to make those who receive and exchange the worship substances partly alike in their personal natures (through the 'biomoral' transformation it effects in their persons); and it serves to make of these regenerated persons a recognisably distinct worship genus, the Sikh Panth [community]" (Dusenbery 1992, 391).

Transformation or personal regeneration is effected through uttered sounds (*Nam, shabad, bani*), the visual or oral emanations (*darsan*), the edible "benefits" (*karah prasad*), and the "nectar" (*amrit*) of the Guru. Dusenbery observes that from the Sikh Punjabi perspective, not only prasad and amrit but also uttered sounds and visual emanations have powers for transformation. Uttered sounds in the form of recited, chanted, or sung gurbani are especially effective for personal transformation, since the words of the Guru are the most powerful of all words that a Sikh might engage in during his or her life (Dusenbery 1992, 391–392). This is because the community holds Sikh scripture to be the actual embodiment of the eternal Guru—thus the name, the Guru Granth Sahib. For gurbani to transform one's consciousness, it must be vocalized. As Pashaura Singh puts it: "The vocalization of Sikh scriptures is thought to have transformative power only when enunciated exactly in the way of the Sikh Gurus, which is achieved through devotional singing and oral exegesis. In fact, singing is regarded as the earthly resonance of the divine Word. . . . Each individual Sikh tries to understand the meaning of life in the light of his or her daily experience of immersing himself or herself in *gurbani*. Indeed, Sikhs firmly believe that the eternal Guru is disclosed in the performance of memorized text" (Singh 2008, 671). Emphasis on vocalization of the memorized divine word fits well with Bhartrhari's

Grammarian philosophy (ca. 500 CE) in traditional Hindu thought. In Bhartrhari's view it is the vibratory power of the carefully enunciated divine word, chosen by one's guru and meditatively recited (*Vak Yoga*) that has the power to remove one's obscuring ego-selfish karma and realize liberation (Coward 1976). While Bhartrhari's Grammarian philosophy of language is basic to Hindu chanting, and influenced Buddhist mantra practice, it seems as if the Sikh approach also has much in common with Bhartrhari's understanding of the transformative and purifying power of guru-selected divine words—a "new every morning" encounter with the timeless truth of the Adi Granth. Just as for Bhartrhari, Vak (Word/Language) is equated with Brahman (the one reality) of which the Veda is the spoken manifestation (Coward and Raja 1990, 35), so also for Sikhs, says Dusenbery (1992, 390), the word (gurbani) is the manifestation of the Divine through Nanak, the historical Gurus and ultimately the Guru Granth Sahib. Perhaps Aurobindo's gloss on language, Vak, as having Divine origin (daivi vak) works for the Sikhs as well (if Adi Granth is substituted for Veda): "The Language of the [Adi Granth] itself is *sruti*, a rhythm not composed by the intellect but heard, a divine Word that came vibrating out of the Infinite to the inner audience of the man who had previously made himself fit for the impersonal knowledge. These words are [gurbani] expressions; hymns, revelatory knowledge and the contents of inspiration" (Aurobindo 1971, 8). For the Sikhs, in practice, the uttered sounds of the Divine Word channeled through the Guru in worship establish a connection between Vahiguru and the devotee and help overcome their "duality" or *dubidha*, which Nanak declares to be the essence of the human problem (Dusenbery 1992, 390n17). In their chanting of the Divine name, singing of hymns, hearing the scripture, and taking Vahiguru's word (Vak), Sikh devotees receive via the gurbani substances that transform them in body as well as spirit. As Marriott and Inden put it, in the Punjabi understanding, not only prasad and amrit but also uttered sounds in chant and song have substantial transformative properties. Sounds of chanted or sung gurbani can have material/physical/physiological as well as spiritual/mental/cognitive effects upon devotees (in Dusenbery 1992, 391n19). Each word (shabad) of the Guru's bani or speech has its own *rasa* or flavor, "which is at one and the same time a product of its aesthetic, physiological, and semantic qualities . . . the entire text is taken to be an embodiment of the Guru" (Dusenbery 1992, 390). In fact, says Dusenbery, "being a Sikh means incorporating into one's person the divine 'coded substances' of their Guru" (Dusenbery 1992, 390). It may be thought of as a "physiological engagement" between the devotee and the Supreme Being in the person of the Guru (Dusenbery 1992, 393). Let us see how this understanding of language (Vak) functions in the chants and hymns (kirtan) of Sikhs in the rites of passage and daily devotions.

Chanting the Divine Name (*Nam-simaran*)

Nanak conceived of a Supreme Being "who is eternal, infinite, and all-pervasive; self-existent; and a perennial source of well-being, compassion, grace, and love" (Oberoi 2000, 118). This Akal Purakh, the name Nanak often used for the Divine, responds to the devotion of all without distinctions of caste or gender. Says Oberoi, "Nanak instructed his followers that the central objective in human life was *mukti*, or release. Human life entailed sorrow and *samsara*—the constant cycle of birth, death and rebirth. Release from bondage, self-delusion, and the cycle of transmigration could be had by concentrating on God's Name" (Oberoi 2000, 118). Nanak taught that for Sikhs, the seed mantra for Vahiguru is Nam. By the meditative chanting of Vahiguru's name, union with the Divine is realized; the cycle of birth, death, and rebirth is broken; and mukti is attained. Guru Nanak suggested that Nam is the manifestation of the Divine, and that meditation on Nam through chanting (*nam japan*) is the path and the unity of divine presence.

Nam-simaran ("remembering the Name") is a daily discipline ranging from the simple repetition of an appropriate word through the devout singing of hymns (kirtan) to sophisticated meditation (O'Connell, Milton, and Willard 1988, 453). Pashaura Singh describes the ideal daily devotion of a devout Sikh as beginning with meditation on the divine Name. This occurs between three and six in the morning (the "ambrosial hours") immediately after rising and bathing. Says Singh, this "meditation is followed by the recitation of five liturgical prayers, which include Guru Nanak's *Japji* ('Recitation'). Similarly, a collection of hymns, *Sodar Rahiras* ('Supplication at the Door'), is prescribed for the evening prayers, and the *Kirtan Sohila* ('Song of Praise') is recited before retiring for the night" (Singh 2008, 664). These prayers are learned by heart in childhood and recited from memory throughout life as part of daily devotions. The chanting of these prayers (all passages from the Guru Granth Sahib) form a daily living relationship with scripture not just to read it or to appropriate its meaning but to interiorize it into one's consciousness so that it becomes a spiritual resource that automatically guides one's thought and behavior throughout the day, especially at times of personal or communal crisis. Dusenbery comments that the memorization and daily recitation of the gurbani, the natural sacred sounds of the Adi Granth, effectively incorporate "the Guru's divinely coded substances and play a central role in recomposing Sikh persons as a divine human genus" (Dusenbery 1992, 393). Says Dusenbery, the logic here is that, as Guru, the words of the Adi Granth in daily devotions and life-cycle rituals are transformative agents.

In ideal practice, one's daily devotion each morning at home is followed by congregational worship at the gurdwara. There, says Pashaura Singh, the Guru Granth Sahib is installed ceremoniously every morning, and worship consists in mainly singing of scriptural passages set to music led by professional and amateur musicians. The congregational singing of hymns (kirtan) is described as the heart of Sikh devotional practice. Through such kirtan, the devotees attune themselves to vibrate in harmony with the divine word (Singh 2008, 664).

Kristina Myrvold compares this ideal practice of daily devotion with the actual practice of Sikhs in Varanasi. In her careful ethnographic study that spanned two years, Myrvold found a strong engagement in devotional chanting:

> . . . no less than eighty-seven percent of male and female respondents of all ages—*Amritdhari* and others—in the semi-structured interviews claimed they knew specific *gurbani* hymns by heart, while the remaining part said they had not committed complete texts to memory but tried to follow recitations with the help of prayer books (*gutkas*). . . . Seventy-seven percent stated they had memorized parts or the complete texts of *Japji Sahib* and a

> slightly fewer number . . . knew the *Rahiras Sahib* by heart, whereas about half of the respondents were able to recite the remaining texts of the *nitnem* entirely or in parts from memory. (Myrvold 2008, 246)

Myrvold's field data suggests that the majority of devotees (either Khalsa or non-Khalsa) memorize gurbani and will recite Japji Sahib in the morning and Rahiras Sahib at dusk or listen to recitals in the gurdwara as part of their daily routine (Myrvold 2008, 246–247). A seventy-year-old Amritdari man who had memorized all seven compositions said, "For correct path I use a *gutka*. I keep a *gutka* of *Rahiras Sahib* with me. When I am not coming to the house at night I can still do the *path* of *Rahiras Sahib* wherever I am" (Myrvold 2008, 246n438).

Myrvold notes the special importance of the opening hymn of the scriptural corpus, Japji Sahib. At an early age, children learn and pronounce this *mulmantra* ("root mantra"), which in Sikh practice is frequently used for continuous repetitions (*jap*) and remembrance of divine qualities. "The illocutionary force of reciting the *mantra* is equal to a declaration of acceptance and adherence to the Sikh religion" (Myrvold 2008, 247). It also marks the transition from an ordinary speech context to a sacred performance context. The Japji Sahib mantra is conceived as Guru Nanak's instruction on the path toward mukti, and its recitation is said by some to grant the same result. In Myrvold's study, adult Sikhs of all categories often adopt morning routines of reciting the whole Japji Sahib or at least a few verses before going to work or starting housework. If for any reason (e.g., illness or disability) one cannot recite the entire Japji Sahib, then the minimum practice is to repeat the name of God (Vahiguru) 108 times daily (Myrvold 2008, 248).

In his autobiography, Tara Singh Bains, a Sikh immigrant to Canada, gives the following description of his daily chanting practice:

> As soon as I get out of bed or even while I am in bed . . . morning prayer begins with simaran. That is just repeating a couple of words, "Sat Nam Wahiguru" or "Wahiguru, Wahiguru" or "Ram." This simaran continues while I do bathing, and it takes two to two and a half hours. Then I recite gurbani (scriptures) from memory for an hour and

a half. During the day, whenever possible—during eating time and so on—simaran continues at heart without enunciation. In the evening, rahiras sahib (the evening prayer) takes about thirty minutes. Then my daily schedule ends at bed with another ten minutes of kirtan-sohila (singing the bedtime prayer) mixed with some simaran. (Bains and Johnston 1995, 217)

This Sikh discipline of reciting has the effect of keeping the whole of one's life focused on and immersed in the sacred word. It is a powerful form of Vak Yoga or Yoga of the Word (Coward 1990, 49–50). As Tara Singh Bains puts it, "Prayer is the vehicle for travel on the path of spirituality to the destination that is the Almighty. . . . The only time I understand the scatteredness of my inner individuality is when I get into prayer or recital. . . . Then I forget about my individuality and become totally absorbed in prayer" (Bains and Johnston 1995, 220).

Kirtan (Singing of Hymns)

In the Sikh tradition, hymns are scriptural passages from the Adi Granth set to music. Morning worship in the gurdwara consists mainly of the singing of hymns, often those of Nanak, with the accompaniment of instruments. Pashaura Singh has done field research at the Golden Temple in 2006 on the history and practice of kirtan and its impact in spiritual practice (Singh 2011). Says Singh, "Guru Nanak's So Dar hymn presents his personal experience of heavenly joys in the company of all liberated ones, who sing in eternity the praises of Akal Purakh. . . . There is divine music everywhere and in everything" (Singh 2011, 111). In Sikhism, a central focus is on the mystical meaning of the Guru Granth Sahib in its intellectual and aesthetic experience evoked by meditating on, singing, and listening to sacred hymns. In Indian philosophy, the physical vibrations of musical sound (*nada*) are inextricably connected with the spiritual world. "Sikh doctrine maintains that the inspired 'utterance of the Guru' (*gurbani*) embodies the divine word (*shabad* or *nada*). In his Ramakali hymn, for instance, Guru Nanak proclaims 'Gurbani embodies all the scriptural knowledge (*Veda*) and the eternally sounding melodious vibration (*nada*) that permeates all space'" (Singh 2011, 113–114). Pashaura Singh concludes, "A careful analysis of Guru Nanak's works reveals that he stressed the mode of devotional singing as the only efficacious means of liberation: 'It is through singing of divine praises that we find a place in the Lord's court.' . . . So also Guru Arjan proclaims: 'The true aim of my life lies in absorption in religious discourse, kirtan, and vibrations of the divine Word through singing and music'" (Singh 2011, 114–115). For Sikhs, the sequence and patterns of musical performance serve to structure ritual time and set it apart from ordinary time. This is seen in the role played by the written text in Sikh practice. The presence of the written text in the gurdwara and in the home provides what a living Guru would provide—the physical manifestation of Vahiguru. But the written words of the Adi Granth function quite differently from the written words of ordinary books or even of other scriptures. As Pashaura Singh has shown, in Sikh devotion, the written words fill the same function as that of a musical score in relation to the performed music. Just as written music has no value until it is performed, so the written text of the Adi Granth has spiritual power only as it is chanted or sung. This is evident in the very structure of the written text. It is poetry, and at the top of each hymn the name of the raga and rhythm to be used in its singing are clearly stated. And just as with the learning of music, if it is learned by heart in childhood it will never be forgotten. One may not bother with it for a while, but it will always be there in the unconscious and later in life one will likely come back to it. But if music is not learned in childhood, it is very difficult to learn it (especially by heart) later in life. As kirtan, or sung words, the Sikh experience of scripture is very similar. Its music and poetry, when learned in youth, has a formative influence throughout life. Once learned, the constant singing and chanting of the scripture is described by one devotee as "vibrating into you . . . clearing and opening your mind to God's grace" (Coward 2000, 209n14). Ultimately it enables one to "dwell within the house of the Guru's Word." In village India, where many adult Canadian Sikhs grew up, this kind of devotional immersing of oneself in scripture happened quite naturally and without great self-effort. As Ranjit Dhaliwal recalls, "I knew people in the village where I grew up as a child. . . . Those people had a very simple life. You get up in the morning and do prayers [together, as a family or community] and then go and do your work. In the evening you sit and there would be prayers and a wise man or priest who would interpret the *gurbani* [scripture], and people would sit there for two or three hours with no temptations to get away from it" (Coward 2000, 209n15). In this rural traditional environment, with no television, radio, computers, or other modern distractions, the divine music of the Adi Granth in Sikh devotions surrounded one and was naturally absorbed into one's consciousness. In modern urban life, notes Pashaura Singh, Sikhs attempt to surround themselves with Sikh devotions by playing musical recordings of kirtan in their homes, or while driving to work "they attune themselves to the sacred sound by listening to a CD of *kirtan*" (Singh 2006, 148). In Canada, kirtan singing plays a major role in identity maintenance, community building and solidarity. At the gurdwara, congregational worship consists mainly in devotional singing of scriptural hymns. Through such kirtan, devout Sikhs attune themselves to vibrate in harmony with the divine word and thereby immerse themselves in the deeper levels of spiritual experience. This is based upon the assumption that the singing of hymns evokes the divine word and is an earthly resonance of it. A direct correspondence is seen as existing between the physical vibration of the phenomenal chant and the noumenal vibration of the transcendent. The more the physical vibrations of the sung words or chant are repeated, the more transcendent power is evoked in experience until one's consciousness is purified and put into a harmonious relationship with the Divine. Then, as Singh puts it, "they experience the 'eternal Guru' as 'an intimate companion of [their] soul'" (Singh 2006, 148).

In her field research with religious Sikhs in Varanasi, Myrvold describes how kirtan in their devotional practice is presented in personal interviews. An elderly Sikh woman said kirtan is a way "to praise the qualities of God and whatever God has given to us." She adds, "if *kirtan* comes in you, the Guru will become happy. *Kirtan* is food for my soul" (Myrvold 2008, 289). Clearly, for these devotees, the power of kirtan lives within the aesthetic and spiritual experiences evoked. One devotee defined kirtan in terms of internal feelings that arise through the language of music. The combination of music and vocal components kindle the flame for spiritual longing in the human heart and soul and generate a "taste" (rasa) of the Guru's words. In this devotee's understanding, "*kirtan* is a spiritual experience of intensity and immediacy that transcends ordinary conscious strivings" (Myrvold 2008, 289). Ordinary Sikhs say they are drawn closer to Vahiguru by listening to gurbani set to music. For them, kirtan is seen as spiritual nourishment or "food for the soul"—a religious experience that is simultaneously emotional, sensual, and intuitive. Or, in the words of a young female student, "*kirtan* performances should not only touch the ears but go into people and touch their hearts" (Myrvold 2008, 287). Myrvold concludes, as a public and shared worship form, kirtan gives to all people—literate and illiterate—an equal chance of gaining the spiritual benefits invoked by singing and listening to gurbani. "Because of its aesthetical power *kirtan* entices people to go to the gurdwara and dedicate time to devotional practices in the busy hours of everyday life . . . when there is *kirtan* people go into deep concentration (*samadhi lagana*)" (Myrvold 2008, 289). Myrvold's interviews illustrate a key principle for Sikhs, namely, that the recitation of daily prayers or mantras by heart and singing of hymns (kirtan) have transformative and purifying effects. For the Sikh, as for the Hindu, participation in the divine word has the power to transform and unify one's consciousness. The purifying power of sacred scripture, especially when experienced in song (kirtan), is understood as a "combing" of negative thoughts from one's heart and mind that occurs as a regular part of one's daily discipline. As Pashaura Singh puts it,

> The simple repetition of the sacred word sanctifies the whole life of the individual in much the same way as a seed sprouts with continual watering and grows into a beautiful tree in a garden. It involves the cultivation of virtues like patience, contentment, charity, humility, fear of God, purity and truthful living. This process makes a person virtuous in thought, word, and deed. It results in experiences that develop progressively as meditation draws the individual nearer and nearer to God. At the highest stage, the process becomes internalized and *nam-simaran* continues automatically (*ajapa jap*). This is where one listens to the music (*dhumi*) of divine word within one's self. . . . There, the drum of the divine word resounds, with the accompaniment of the melody of the five musical instruments. . . . In his celebrated hymn "Anand" (Bliss),

Guru Amar Das refers to the five types of "mystic sounds" (*panch shabad*) that resound in the heart of the individual who feels the divine presence within and all around . . . the musical sounds heard in meditation correspond to the musical instruments used to accompany devotional singing. As Guy Beck aptly puts it, "The divine sounds of the drum, cymbal, *vina*, and flute . . . exhibit marked correspondences with the instruments employed in devotional music" . . . therefore music plays a threefold role. First, it satisfies one's aesthetic sensibilities. Second, its dominant sentiment (rasa) delights one's inner consciousness and offers spiritual nourishment. Third, it transports one's soul into a realm of ecstasy. (Singh 2006, 148)

In the Sikh tradition, music, in either individual chanting (simaran) or group singing, the evocation of the divine word, has the power to transform consciousness so as to vibrate in harmony with the Divine.

Taking the Guru's Word (*Vak laina*)

A guru is the channel through which the divine is revealed in a way especially suited to the time, place, and condition of the devotee. Within Hinduism, for example, God takes the human form of rsi, or guru, especially for this purpose—to speak the divine truth in a way that is suited to the needs (karma) of the devotee. Without the guru to individualize it, the divine word is in danger of remaining an abstract universal truth passing far above the life experience of the devotee. The guru engages the divine word in worldly life. When Nanak and the Gurus were alive, Sikh tradition was not unlike Hindu experience—the word was experienced as personalized through the Guru. The uniqueness of the Sikh approach appears when, after Gobind Singh, the written book, in addition to being the divine word, takes on the function of personal Guru, to Sikhs both in congregational worship and in personal devotion. The relation of the ten historical Gurus to the written book is nicely summarized by Pashaura Singh: "There were not ten different Gurus. Guru is the one and the same spirit, and that's the spirit of Nanak. It is manifested in ten different historical persons. Finally, it resides in the word of God, in Guru Granth Sahib" (Singh 1985).

Acceptance of the Adi Granth as living Guru is seen in the practice of "taking the Guru's Word" (Vak laina) or "seeking a divine command" (Hukam laina). Pashaura Singh describes the process: "The procedure functions in a liturgical fashion of opening the scripture at random. The first hymn at the top of the left-hand page (or when a hymn begins on the preceding page, one turns back to the actual beginning) is read aloud as the proclamation of the Guru's *Vak* [Word] for that particular moment or situation in life" (Singh 2008, 665). The Word is then appropriated by the congregation (if in the gurdwara) through "hearing." If at home, the individual or family gathers for morning prayers in the presence of the Guru Granth Sahib to receive God's command for the day ahead. Says Singh, "This *Vak* becomes the inspiration for personal meditation throughout the day. Again during evening prayers, one takes the *Vak* to conclude the day with its particular joys and sorrows. Similarly, in the corporate setting, the whole *sangat* ('Congregation') receives the *Vak* as a divine command at the conclusion of the different ceremonies" (Singh 2008, 665). It is through these personalized experiences of Vak laina in the context of individual daily devotion and congregational experiences that God's grace is understood in such a way as to break the bonds of karma and purify one's body and mind.

Rites of Passage and the Guru Granth Sahib

In the Sikh tradition, the performance of life-cycle rituals, from birth to death, is inseparably connected to the Guru Granth Sahib and its recitation.

Naming. Soon after the birth, the family takes the baby to the gurdwara and offers *karah prasad* or sweet porridge (sanctified food made of flour, sugar, butter, and water). After offering thanks and prayers of petition, the Guru Granth Sahib is opened at random and a name is chosen beginning with the same letter as the first composition on the left-hand page. Says Singh, "The underlying principle is that the child derives his or her identity from the Guru's word and begins life as a Sikh" (Singh 2008, 665). After the name chosen is announced to the congregation, six stanzas of the hymn "Anand Sahib" are sung and the *granthi* or priest performs an *Ardas* prayer in which blessings for the child are invoked (Myrvold 2008, 360).

Initiation (amrit sanskar). Oberoi (2000, 130) describes the initiation ceremony as follows: As the child grows up, he or she may choose to be initiated into the Khalsa order of Sikhism (there is no fixed age for this initiation). This key initiation ceremony—known as *amrit sanskar*—can only be performed in the presence of the Guru Granth Sahib. A collectivity of five Sikhs who are already initiated lead the ceremony. Each recites from memory one of the five liturgical prayers while stirring the sweetened water (*amrit*) with a double-edged sword. The novice then drinks the amrit five times to purify the body, and five times the amrit is sprinkled on the eyes to transform one's outlook on life. Finally, the amrit is poured on the head five times to sanctify one's hair so that one will preserve one's natural form and listen to the voice of conscience. Singh notes that "throughout the ceremony the Sikh being initiated formally takes the oath each time by repeating . . . : *Vahiguru Ji Ka Khalsa! Vahiguru Ji Ki Fateh!* ('Khalsa belongs to the Wonderful Lord! Victory belongs to the Wonderful Lord!). Thus, a person becomes a Khalsa Sikh through the transforming power of the sacred word" (Singh 2008, 666). At the conclusion of the ceremony a Vak laina or word is taken from the Guru Granth Sahib and is understood to be a command or hukam from God. As Oberoi (2000, 131) notes, without the transforming power of the sacred word, the initiation ceremony could not function.

Marriage. Like "initiation" and "naming," marriage can only be performed in the presence of the Guru Granth Sahib. Pashaura Singh describes the *Anand* or "Bliss" ceremony as follows:

> . . . in the presence of the Guru Granth Sahib the performance of the actual marriage requires the couple to circumambulate the sacred scripture four times and take four vows. Before each round they listen to a verse of the 'wedding hymn' (AG, 773–4) . . . being read by a scriptural reader. Then, they bow before the Guru Granth Sahib and get up to make the round while professional musicians and the congregation sing the same verse. During their clockwise movement around the scripture four times, they take the

following vows: (1) to live an action-oriented life based on righteousness and to never shun obligation to family and society; (2) to maintain a bond of reverence and dignity between them; (3) to keep enthusiasm for life alive in the face of adversity; and (4) to cultivate a "balanced approach" in life, avoiding all extremes. (Singh 2008, 665–666)

While the couple is performing the Anand ceremony, often a trio of *ragis* sing prescribed hymns from the sacred text. Once again, it is the sacred sound of the recited and sung scripture passages that provides the legitimacy for the marriage ritual. Myrvold comments, "The organization of linguistic and bodily acts within the structure of the wedding ceremony makes a marriage binding only if it has been recognized and blessed by the Guru" (Myrvold 2008, 372).

Death. "For Sikhs, a good death occurs when one has completed a lifetime and fulfilled all social responsibilities." Myrvold notes, "The most significant means to secure a good death is to die to the sounds of *gurbani*. Persons who envisage their own death will commit themselves to a recitation of *Sukmani Sahib* . . . if the dying person is too weak to recite, family members will read and sometimes whisper sacred words in his or her ear. Many also say that listening to recitals and singing of any gurbani hymn will assist the dying in the life after death" (Myrvold 2008, 377). Both in the period preceding the cremation and in the post-cremation rites, hymns from the Guru Granth Sahib are sung. In the pre-cremation period, professional readers or members of the family continuously read from scripture. In addition, a recited reading of the entire Guru Granth Sahib takes place at home or in a gurdwara. "At the conclusion of the reading within ten days, a *bhog* ('completion') ceremony takes place when final prayers are offered in memory of the deceased" (Myrvold 2008, 666).

In the aforementioned life-cycle rituals and daily devotional practices it is clear that reciting/chanting/singing of the Adi Granth (understood as the living Guru) is the basis for spiritual transformation in the Sikh tradition. Oberoi concludes that Sikh scripture has turned into a meta-resource for Sikh identity, cultural practices, personal piety, and collective liturgical practices. But what is even more unique is that the Sikh experience of having a "textual Guru" is certainly uncommon. Says Oberoi, "in the Indic religious environment a Guru is generally a living person who communicates divine knowledge and aids his disciples by providing them with a cognitive map for salvation. In the Sikh religion, after the tenure of the ten living Gurus, this role has been performed by the holy book. Simply put, the Guru speaks through the book" (Oberoi 2000, 131). And, we might add, the Guru's word when recited, meditated upon, and especially when sung as kirtan has demonstrated power to transform lives and communities.

Changes from Living in Diaspora Settings

Living in North America, or perhaps more correctly, living in modern Western society, is introducing changes in both the devotional and the intellectual experience of the Adi Granth by Sikhs. Modern society has many distractions and pressures that militate against the natural and simple experience of village India. The individualistic and rationalistic nature of modern society tends to emphasize the study of, as opposed to the devotional approach to, the Adi Granth. The crucial importance of one's being immersed in learning the singing of the scripture as a child poses a major challenge to Sikh parents in modernity, especially in diaspora communities.

A Canadian Sikh describes the pressures to drink and to eat meat, and the lack of time for the daily discipline of saying morning and evening prayers (which usually takes two hours): "I think we need to go back to more devotion. Living in the Western context, you are torn apart by these things. So many Sikhs, even those who have taken *Amrit*, have betrayed the religion . . . I can easily opt out of so many things, accept only twenty percent of Sikhism, and live the other life for eighty percent of the time" (Gahuma 1985). He feels himself pulled apart by the pressures toward egoism, selfishness, and competition. All of these tendencies go directly against the Guru Granth Sahib. In this situation, many are moving to see the full commitment to scripture required by Amrit as the only solution. This seems very hard at first, but once the discipline has begun and Amrit taken, the practice seems quite possible and the obvious solution to the problem. Thus, there may turn out to be greater stress on the need for Amrit, for Sikhs living in modern society, if they are to have the full experience of scripture chanting and singing. In modern life, television, computers, and smart phones, not the Adi Granth, is what one naturally absorbs. Special discipline is therefore essential if the lived scripture experience is to be had. Saying prayers morning and evening is not something that happens "naturally" in modern urban life; it requires considerable self-discipline. Kirtan revival movements in diaspora communities, especially after 1984, have played an important role in globalizing Sikh devotional consciousness (Purewal and Lallie 2013, 399).

The rational emphasis of the modern West is another influence that produces differences from the Sikh experience of village India. Congregational services in the gurdwara (following the Protestant example) give more emphasis to sermon and rational interpretation than is the case in traditional India. Pashaura Singh (2000, 270) says that *katha* or the tradition of scriptural interpretation began in the court of the historical Sikh Gurus. In her excellent essay, Myrvold notes that while in the various diaspora settings the recitations from the Guru Granth Sahib are held constant, the tradition of katha allows for the contextualizing of the words and deeds of the Gurus to the everyday concerns of the present-day communities. Recently the use of global TV and internet technologies have added tremendous "reach and consolidation to the *katha* teachings of leading orators of Sikh scripture" (Myrvold 2013, 327). While katha teaching may help the devotee understand the meaning of the recited Guru Granth Sahib and motivate moral actions, the devotional chanting and singing remains foundational in daily devotional routines (Myrvold 2013). In their Canadian homes, Sikhs are more tempted to spend their valuable time in study and interpretation of the text rather than in oral devotional practice (Gahuma 1985). In addition, there is the problem that children in Western schools and society are being trained to be critical and rational. Unless the family and gurdwara make a strong effort against the flow, the devotional approach to scripture will not be given value or development in the child's experience. In this connection, a fundamental prerequisite is the teaching of the Punjabi language to the children—something that is being done with vigor both in the gurdwara and in the families studied (Coward and Goa 1986).

Kirtan in the Diaspora after 1984

In their excellent essay "Sikh *Kirtan* in the Diaspora," Purewal and Lallie (2013) trace developments in kirtan singing in diaspora communities throughout the history of Sikh migrations. They identify modernizing influences in the contemporary globalized Sikh diaspora resulting in a rich diversity of kirtan practice from religious folk and revivalist projects to a return to traditional forms of kirtan performance. In the diaspora, one of the key ways Sikh identity and religious practice has been carried out and maintained is through kirtan (Purewal and Lallie 2013, 384). This was especially so, say Purewal and Lallie, in the years after the 1984 storming of the Golden Temple in Amritsar, "when links between diasporic locations and the Punjab became stronger than had previously been the case" (Purewal and Lallie 2013, 399). In 1984 and after, the consciousness roused in the diaspora focused on Sikh identity through new forms of cultural and religious activism. Kirtan singing was a key way in which this globalizing consciousness spread. The authors identify several important religious musical practices within Sikh kirtan during this period, including: Akhand Kirtani Jatha (AKJ), *dharmik geet* (religious folk), *satsang* styles, and revivalist projects to return to traditional forms of kirtan in terms of the prescribed *raags* and *taal* (Purewal and Lallie 2013, 383). Let's look briefly at each of these.

AKJ *kirtan* "has a distinctive form which emphasizes *gurumantra*, nam-simaran (meditation on the Divine name), the *Dasam Granth* of Guru Gobind Singh in addition to the *Guru Granth Sahib*, and of the *amrit* (baptism) ceremony" (Purewal and Lallie 2013, 399). Instead of traditional recitation of kirtan within denoted raag and taal with traditional instruments, the AKJ style is simple and repetitive so that devotees can sing along to easy, accessible tunes accompanied by harmonium and tabla. The collective singing of the *gurumantra* through repetition with increasing speed and intensity builds to an ecstatic and rapturous kirtan experience. According to Purewal and Lallie, the potent simplicity and power of kirtan through the repetition of Vahiguru led to an awakening of Sikh consciousness for the diaspora youth from the mid-1980s to the mid-1990s. Since then, say the authors, AKJ kirtan practice remains popular and, although not classical in form, "has made a significant mark on *kirtan* in the diaspora" (Purewal and Lallie 2013, 400)

Influences from folk and world music have also stretched the boundaries of *kirtan*. Purewal and Lallie give the example of Dya Singh's World Music Group from Australia. They comment, "Not only does Dya Singh's group use the harmonium and tabla in its renditions of *shabad kirtan*, but also the aboriginal didgeridoo, the European gypsy violin, the electric guitar and other instruments in their recordings and performance, stretching the imagination and boundaries of *kirtan*" (Purewal and Lallie 2013, 381). The authors recount how Dya Singh's group came to a California town to run a Sikh youth camp, teaching the children Gurmukhi gurbani kirtan using their world music style. While the youth responded positively to the music and learned a great deal, gurdwara committee members became quite upset over Dya Singh's style of teaching and kirtan, refusing the group payment. However, others in the community were appreciative of the impact the week had had on their youth in evoking interest in Sikhism and kirtan. Either way, say the authors, Dya Singh's "style, melodies and method . . . remain a source of listening enjoyment. His CDs have circulated globally making his world music style a hallmark of diaspora *kirtan*" (Purewal and Lallie 2013, 382). Also during the past decade Snatam Kaur Khalsa, a Colorado-born, California-raised member of the 3HO American Sikh community introduced a style combining Celtic, Native American chants, Indian raags, Western folk, and jazz in veering away from the classical kirtan in raag and taal (Purewal and Lallie 2013). A 2017 Scripps Senior Thesis by Paolina Marielle Sigueira-Koo titled "How Can We Explore the Connection of Sound with the Experience of Religion?" focuses on an analysis of the 3HO Sikh musical Kundalini Yoga as taught by Yogi Bhajan in California (Sigueira-Koo 2017).

In response to such modernist evolutionary kirtan styles, say the authors, the Sikh diaspora has witnessed a revivalist movement that aims to bring the singing of kirtan back to its classical roots. Among the *raagis* or professional performers of kirtan across the Sikh diaspora, there has been a recent move toward revival of the traditional classical form of kirtan, and a shift away from the modern movements. For example, classical instruments have been reinstated in the Golden Temple (Purewal and Lallie 2013, 401). Also, in the

United Kingdom, the Raj Academy and the Gurmat Sangeet Academy "have adopted a strong method of teaching and commitment to the practice and preservation of *kirtan* as a classical art form . . . drawing on the expertise and heritage of the Namdharies" (Purewal and Lallie 2013, 383). They promote kirtan as the sacred art of "singing and playing hymns from the Siri Guru Granth Sahib in the prescribed ragas using the original string instruments (Purewal and Lallie 2013, 392). The revival push has come from many directions and "has seen many *raagi jathas* making steps towards performing within the classical or traditional mode and strategically moving away from the modern" (Purewal and Lallie 2013, 401).

The conclusion offered by Purewal and Lallie in their analysis of the development of kirtan in the Sikh diaspora after 1984 is as follows: "The diaspora dimension of *kirtan*'s evolution . . . shows both a desire to connect with a global Sikh identity while also asserting a historical tradition which predates the colonial encounter and exhibits a musicality symbiotically connected with the scriptures for which they were composed" (Purewal and Lallie 2013, 401–402).

I have said little about the important role of kirtan recordings by records, cassettes, CDs, DVDs, and more recently the plethora of internet sites from which kirtan can be downloaded and listened to. This task I leave for someone more skilled in music and contemporary technology. But, in my understanding, it is not enough just to listen to kirtan via TV or on a CD, DVD, or internet download. It is my view that in order to have the power to transform one's consciousness, music should be personally performed. For kirtan, this suggests that one needs to engage in the recitation or singing oneself in one's own morning or evening devotions and by singing kirtans with the congregation in a gurdwara, or youth camp, or some other group setting. As Pashaura Singh puts it: "The singing of hymns (kirtan) in a congregational setting is the heart of the Sikh devotional experience. Through such kirtan, the devotees attune themselves to vibrate in harmony with the divine word, which has the power to transform and unify their consciousness" (Singh 2008, 664).

Conclusion

Walter Ong in his *The Presence of the Word* points out that early humans had a true, if at the same time confused, sense of the mystery, power, and holiness of the word. Today, says Ong, "the oral word is still with us. . . . But to know it for what it is, we must deliberately reflect on it. The spoken word, the center of human life, is overgrown with its own excrescences—script, print, electronic verbalism—valuable in themselves but, as is the case with human accomplishments, not unmixed blessings" (Ong 1967, 314). Ong's suggestion that the original spoken, chanted, or sung word has become "overgrown with its own excrescences" is an apt observation of what happens in religious traditions when the holy and powerful word develops into a closed institutional system or ideology that obstructs the original revelation. Modern structuralist and post-structuralist thinkers have shown how language can become an alien system weighing upon human consciousness. Feminists turn away from traditional hierarchical approaches typical of the masculine use of language. Nagarjuna, a second-century CE Buddhist monk in India, was fully aware of this imprisoning quality of language. Nagarjuna taught that words ensnare us when we make them into a philosophical, theological, or ideological system and then become ego-attached to that system (Nagarjuna 1970). Rather than experiencing reality, we construct our own "excrescences," as Ong puts it—our own philosophy, theology, or way of describing reality as absolute—and these word systems can then become obstacles to our direct experiences of nature or the divine. Indeed, this seems a good description of my own life experience, which began in childhood with a strong spiritual experience of the spoken parables of Jesus at my mother's knee, and a powerful congregational hymn-singing experience standing at my father's side. This clear Christian childhood experience of the spoken and sung word moved me deeply, but then became obscured in my Sunday School and university seminar training as to how to do Bible study. Only as my curiosity to learn about other religious traditions led me to study the Hindu tradition with my teacher T. R. V. Murti and a guru-student reading of Patanjali's *Yoga Sutras* did I come to understand the spiritual power of mantra chanting and kirtan singing so as to recover and deepen my own Christian experience of the word. In this book, we have made an introductory study of how devotees of the Hindu, Buddhist, Islamic, and Sikh traditions each have their own experiences of spiritual transformation through word, chant, and song. By way of conclusion, let us recall some of the differences and similarities encountered.

Scriptural Chant and Meditation

As the earliest religious tradition of India, Hinduism set the pattern for word understanding and practice that strongly influenced the later Buddhist, Islamic, and Sikh spiritual practices. The foundational notions of karma (memory traces/impulses from freely chosen good or bad thoughts and acts) and samsara or rebirth (caused by karma carried forward from past lives to this life and on to the next) are Hindu presuppositions adopted by both Buddhism and Sikhism. Sunni Muslims came to South India in the seventh century (to form the Mappila Muslims of our chapter 3 case study) and together with Sufi missionaries arriving in Northwest India from the tenth century on influenced Hindu and Sikh practice in the Punjab region. With this in mind, let us examine conclusions from each chapter regarding "word as revelation," "word chanting," "hymn singing," and "modern developments" as forces for spiritual transformation.

WORD AS REVELATION

In the Hindu view, the seer (rsi) who had purged off all karma and thus had a crystal-clear perception of Sabdabrahman (Divine Word Consciousness), spoke the words of the Veda (all Hindu scripture) as a direct revelation of the Divine. It is this view of the words (mantras) of the Veda as Daivi Vak (Divine Word) that establishes the basis for mantra chanting as a powerful practice for spiritual transformation in the devotees. And it is this understanding that led Hindu teachers such as Patanjali and Bhartrhari to speak of Vak Yoga or mantra chanting as the Yoga of the Word offering moksa or release from rebirth for all.

Gautama the Buddha was born into the Hindu culture and religion. In setting forth his own path to release, he accepted the basic ideas of karma and samsara as conditions we all possess at birth, but he rejected the Hindu teaching of the Veda as divine revelation or Daivi Vak. For him, all language was conventional and not divine, including even his own teachings, which his followers passed on as Buddhist sutras. Thus, unlike Hinduism, Islam, Sikhism, Judaism, or Christianity, Buddhism claims no "revealed" words or scripture. As we saw in chapter 2 with the Theravada Buddhists of Sri Lanka, the words of the Buddha's sutras are remembered and chanted as an aid-to-memory to help the devotee follow the example and teachings of the historical Buddha in his or her own life, but they have no divine power beyond that. It was fascinating to follow Buddhist development into the Mahayana and Mantrayana traditions, as practiced by Tibet, China, and Japan, where chants such as Om Mani Padme Hum and Namu Amida Butsu seem to have become "revealed mantras," which when chanted have power to remove obstructing karma and attain nirvana. This development has the appearance of a full circle return to the Vak Yoga mantra practice of Hindu devotees.

When we examined Islam, there was no doubt that the words spoken by the prophet Muhammad as the Qur'an are experienced as the revealed words of Allah (God) dictated to Muhammad by the angel Gabriel. Just as Muhammad had to memorize these words of Allah, revealed to him through the angel, so also his followers have to remember the revealed words of the Qur'an recited in their five-times-daily prayer or salat and in all their individual and congregational chanting and singing. It is because they are God's words to his people that the Quranic words have the power to keep one on the spiritual path of submission to Allah.

Growing up in a fourteenth-century Punjab village not far from the modern city of Lahore, Nanak, the founding figure of the Sikh tradition, was born in a culture composed of both Hindu and Muslim influences, and he spent much time in the devotional singing of songs from both traditions. In chapter 4 we saw how, while still young, Nanak had a three-day disappearance in the river, which he described as an audience with Vahiguru (the Divine) resulting in his enlightenment and radical new vision: "There is no Hindu, there is no Muslim." Nanak's teachings and those of his nine successor Gurus were collected into a scripture, the Adi Granth, understood, by Sikhs, as Vahiguru's words spoken by Nanak and the other Gurus when inspired. Thus, these words are revelations that were at first memorized and then written down. The last human Guru, Gobind Singh (1666–1708), completed the compilation of the Adi Granth and, declared that henceforth there would be no more living Gurus. Instead, the Adi Granth, also called the Guru Granth Sahib, would be the future Guru whom all Sikh's would follow. This living relationship between the devotees and their revealed word, the Guru Granth Sahib, is symbolized in the sacred volume being treated as a living Guru by being enthroned in the temple each morning, giving the teaching for the day, providing the words for hymns (*kirtan*), life rituals, and individual meditation. At night, the Guru Granth Sahib is carried from the temple with all the respect one would give to a living person and then reinstalled ritually in the temple early the next morning. For Sikh devotees, all of this symbolizes a living relationship with the scripture, which is what gives its word such transforming power in chanted rituals such as nam-simaran (chanting God's name).

CHANT

As we saw in the introduction, it was the Hindu sensitivity to the power of chanted word to transform consciousness that first drew me to the study of Indian religious life and helped me understand how the Roman Catholic chanting of the rosary was much more than just an empty superstition. The Sanskrit term mantra refers to the ability to hear the divine sound in the chanting of the Veda as Hindu devotees perform their morning prayers with the rising and setting of the sun. For them, the mantra is not just a Vedic text but rather a manifestation of Brahman, the source of sacred sound that evokes all of life to include not only the speaking of humans but also of animals and is heard in the voices of fire, thunder, and rain. Hearing and saying a mantra such as Om is an act of worship that "tunes" one to the basic sound or vibration of the universe. By a continual hearing and chanting, one purifies and transforms one's consciousness until all of one's life vibrates in harmony with the divine—the yoga of the word (Vak Yoga) as explained by Patanjali and Bhartrhari. They offered a technical description of how mantra chanting works. Speaking or singing a mantra lays down a karmic memory trace in the unconscious. Chanting a mantra over and over reinforces that karmic trace (samskara) until a deep root or habit pattern (vasana) is established. Correctly chanting a mantra such as Om for the Hindu or Om Manipadme Hum for a Tibetan Buddhist reinforces good karma and removes negative karmas or seed impulses so that they do not "blossom" or mature but wither away, leaving no trace behind. The more powerful the mantra, the more good karma will be reinforced and negative karma will be removed from one's storehouse consciousness (one's unconscious in modern psychology). In this way mantra chanting or singing can be seen to be a powerful tool for purifying and transforming consciousness. Key chants such as Om and Om Manipadme Hum are seen by devotees as "shorthand" or symbolic chants that include and evoke all other manifestations of the divine and thus have great power—especially in Hindu and Buddhist tantric understanding and practice (where there is considerable similarity). In Japanese Jodo Shinshu Pure Land Buddhist practice, we saw how Shinran identified the dimension of complete "sincerity" in the devotee's chanting of the mantra Namu Amida Butsu. To compete with each other to see how many thousand chants of the Nembutsu one could do in a day (as the Buddhist monks on Mt. Hiei were doing) was leading in the wrong direction because it was fostering ego-pride in one's own self-power (*jiriki*), the opposite of what the Buddha had taught. Shinran's life experience taught him that only when one chants Namu Amida Butsu without calculation or self-interest (no jiriki) could enlightenment be realized. Only one completely sincere chant of the Nembutsu could do that—and that could only happen when one gave up trying to do it to achieve spiritual merit for oneself (jiriki or self-power) and surrendered to Amida Buddha so that it was not oneself but Amida who originates and does the chant through one (Nembutsu as an "other power" or tariki practice). In Chapter 2 we saw how Shinran's Jodo Shinshu diaspora Buddhist practitioners in North America are engaged in this Buddhist mantra practice. Shinran's teaching regarding mantra chanting illustrates the Buddhist fine tuning of the Hindu notion of karma by placing the emphasis on its motivation or intent aspect.

When it comes to Islam (chapter 3), spiritual practice is centered on the devotee committing the words of Allah in the Qur'an to heart through recitation or chanting. Learning how to "read" the Qur'an means learning how to chant and remember the Arabic words and their meaning. To aid in its memorization and chanting, the Qur'an abounds in assonance, rhyme, rhythmic patterns, and recurring phrases that enhance its meaning and sonic impact. Notations have been developed that, when superimposed on the text according to the rules for chanting (tajwid), are held to enable the devotee to hear and experience the sound of God's words, the revelation, just as Muhammad heard them dictated from Allah to him by the angel Gabriel in the cave on Mt. Hira. Thus, the written pages of the text are not the real Qur'an. Only when the words are remembered and chanted (as they are each day in the salat or five-times-daily prayer) does God's word come alive to the devotee as revelation. To the extent that the devotee memorizes and chants the Qur'an, he or she is said to "live in the Qur'an." As was the case with the Buddhist chanting of the Nembutsu where ego attachment to the number of mantra chants per day became an obstruction to its purifying power, so also in the Qur'an chanting, the musical style of singing and the beauty of the chanter's voice must not take center stage, for then it draws attention to the person chanting rather than highlighting God's words. Thus, the Muslim injunction for chanting, "Do not seek to adorn the Qur'an with your voice, rather, adorn your voice with the Qur'an." Again, it is a matter of ego: the emphasis must be upon the aesthetic beauty of the sacred word in itself (i'jaz) rather than upon the chanter's voice, thus guarding against the sin of pride. Chanting the Qur'an not only purifies the life of the devotee but is also seen to be necessary for the well-being of the rest of humanity and the maintenance of order in nature and the cosmos. This idea of the power of the recited Qur'an parallels the Hindu experience of chanted Vedic mantra as necessary for maintaining both personal and cosmic order (rta). Reciting the Qur'an is done to keep Allah front and center in one's daily thought and actions, to expiate sin, and to ensure blessings in the afterlife. On the day of resurrection, says Islam, Allah will call upon the pious person to rise up, recite, and be judged—a quite different end goal than the Hindu view of Vedic chanting as removing karma until one's consciousness is clear of obstruction, so that one is no longer reborn but realizes eternal union or communion with the Divine. But in both cases the focus is on the power of the chanted word to transform one's life.

Turning finally to the Sikh tradition, we find a similar understanding of the central position of the chanted and sung word, but also something quite unique. As Cole and Sambhi observed (1978, 43), in no other religious tradition can one find a human Guru founder, followed by a series of human Gurus living parallel with the collection of scripture, ending in a breaking of the human succession and the scripture attaining full authority as itself Guru (Guru Granth Sahib). Thus, for the Sikh devotee, the holy word is a living Guru with whom one engages in a daily relationship via recited and sung gurbani or divine word. What results is a living relationship between scripture, the word as Guru, and the community embodying qualities of moral compassion in all relationships. Living in a context of the Hindu and Muslim religions, Nanak, the founding Guru, and the revealed scripture, Guru Granth Sahib, proclaim that the Divine is One (Akal Purakh), that there is only one Divine in all religions, and that liberation can only be achieved through the chanting of the divine name (nam) and the singing of divine word (kirtan). As Pashaura Singh puts it, the Guru is the "voice" of the Akal Purakh and the shabad is the divine "utterance." By hearing and chanting it, "one awakens to the reality of the divine name, imminent in all that lies around and within one" (Singh 2006, 144). And, as Dusenbery adds, the Sikh Gurus are thought, as it were, to channel the Divine through their spoken words, the Guru Granth Sahib, which have the power to transform devotees in body and spirit and make of these regenerated persons a distinct Sikh Panth or Community (Dusenbery 1992, 391). For the gurbani or Sikh scripture to have transforming power, it is to be enunciated exactly in the way of the Sikh Gurus through chanting the divine name and singing. This is regarded by the Sikh tradition as the earthly resonance of the divine word. As Singh puts it, each individual Sikh tries to understand the meaning of life through immersing him- or herself in gurbani. "Sikhs firmly believe that the eternal Guru is disclosed in the performance of memorized text" (Singh 2008, 671). Sikh emphasis on vocalization of the memorized divine word fits well with Muslim, Buddhist Mantrayana, and Hindu spiritual practices. As the Grammarian Bhartrhari theorized, it is the vibratory power of the carefully enunciated divine word, chosen by one's guru and meditatively recited in Vak Yoga, that has power to remove one's obscuring ego-selfish karma and realize release. While Patanjali's Yoga psychology and Bhartrhari's philosophy of language are basic to Hindu chanting and influenced by Buddhist tantric mantra practice, the Sikh approach also seems to have much in common with this Hindu understanding of the transforming and purifying power of guru-chosen divine words. Just as Om for Hindus and Om Manipadme Hum or Namu Amida Butsu for Buddhists function as powerful "seed mantras" for the chant of lay devotees, so also for Sikhs, there is nam-simaran (remembering the Name), the seed mantra for Vahiguru, through which union with the Divine is realized and mukti or release from rebirth attained. The salat, or five-times-daily chanted prayers from the Qur'an, fulfills a parallel function for pious Muslims. Only for the Sri Lankan Theravada Buddhists do we find a significant difference. For them, the chanting of the Triple Refuge by laypeople is understood quite differently from the Hindu Vak Yoga or the Mahayana power mantras. While the teachings and life experience of the historical Buddha were passed on as memorized and written sutras, for lay Theravada devotees, the daily chanting of the Triple Refuge ("I go for refuge to the Buddha, Dhamma, and Sangha") has as its goal the establishment and maintenance of trust (saddha) in the historical Buddha. This Triple Refuge chanting (along with the family upbringing) helps the person remember, know, and emulate the example of the historical Buddha in his or her life. Chanting the Triple Refuge in daily morning and evening worship at home in a space or room with an altar and statue keeps the Buddha, his teachings for virtuous living, and his community (the Sangha) front and center in one's life. Constant repetition of the chant helps to keep one on track in the attempt to follow the Buddha in one's daily life. As Williams notes, in Theravada chanting there is little engagement of music except for a few basic notes indicating the beginning and ending of the chant (S. Williams 2006, 173). Chanting the Triple

Refuge is also seen as a "merit-making" practice for both Theravada householders and monks—a notion completely rejected by Shinran's Japanese Buddhism.

SONG

It seems that almost from the beginning of religious chanting, the addition of music has been often understood to give more spiritual power and aesthetic appeal to the devotee's practice. This is seen in the addition of simple musical modes to the biblical chants of Jews and Christians prior to 500 CE and is strongly present in the melodious reciting of the Qur'an by Muslim devotees following the example of Muhammad. Islam also developed the practice of tajwid or musical recitation of the Qur'an by professional singers/chanters with groups of lay devotees gathered to listen in homes, mosques, or in the street (as in the Cairo example in chapter 3). The excellence of such professional singer/reciters in Islam is evidenced when listeners are moved by the beauty of the chanted words, and when devotees are moved to tears in response to the truth of the recited Qur'an. In addition to the traditional chanting of prayers and Qur'an, our study of the Mappila Muslim community demonstrated a great love for songs often sung by women and passed on to their daughters—songs extoling the lives of prophets such as Abraham or Joseph, the virtues of early companions of the Prophet Muhammad, war songs of military martyrs, instructional songs, wedding songs, and songs expressing the social problems of contemporary life on the internet (e.g., the songs of family separation due to Gulf employment of Mappila men such as "Tears of Kuwait"). In addition to the Mappila songs of Kerala, vernacular devotional hymns are common in Sunni, Shi'a, and Sufi practices in Pakistan and India. Such hymns are usually sung in Urdu using raga scales and tala rhythms along with harmonium and barrel drum, or dholak, and are usually sung at devotional song gatherings held in homes rather than mosques (Qureshi 2006, 96). Special festival assemblies or milad celebrate the birth of the Prophet Muhammad or special family events with recited Qur'an passages, followed by a series of na't poems and hymns that musically evoke feelings of devotion, exultation, veneration, and submission (Qureshi 2006, 97). These milad devotional assemblies, says Qureshi, may well achieve states of spiritual transformation comparable to Hindu and Sikh group singing.

In the Shi'a traditions of South India, the majlis is a recitational and hymn assembly held to mark the martyrdom of Imam Hussain that features simple dirges of intense grief building to a climax in which devotees rise and beat their chests in mourning (matam). Says Qureshi, majlis hymn singing creates for the devotees an involvement in suffering that is both deeply personal and spiritually transformative. Majlis hymns constitute a repository of Shi'a heritage and sentiment that their recitation brings to life for the whole community (Qureshi 2006, 98). Such sung lamentations turn the focus of worshipers away from their own lives and onto Husayn and other imams (the *ahl-al-bayt*) "so that these experiences become tools of reflection upon their own lives" (Schubel 1993, 100).

Within Islam, it is perhaps some Sufis that give music the most significant role, namely, as a means to spiritual union with the divine (Nelson 1985, 32). Since the thirteenth century, Sufi mystics across North Africa, the Middle East, Iran, and South Asia have developed the practice of reciting and meditational listening to mystical poetry and words as a spiritual way to achieve nearness to Allah. In this tradition, a sama or qawwali is an assembly for listening that uses mystical poetry set to music as a means of realizing ecstatic union with God (Qureshi 2006, 18). In our case study of the Moroccan Berber chanting/singing of the munshidun, Waugh offered a detailed analysis of how the munshid or Sufi chanting master uses chanted music to call up remembered sonic patterns in the minds of the singers and listeners, which God uses to draw humans into union (Waugh 2005, 25). In this process called dhikr, careful leadership is required to guide the dhikr devotees through various postures, breathing exercises, and chants/songs so that they successfully "ride the waves" of emotional and spiritual mood to hal, the state of mystical union—all of which is mindful of the guru's role in Hindu/Buddhist mantra practice. Success at the advanced level, says Waugh, comes when, having learned to discipline their disruptive minds and spirits through the dhikr, the devotees are at peace in their relationship to the transcendent presence—they experience no separation between their human selves and the "presence" they encounter (Waugh 2005, 27). We saw all of this manifested in the case study of Morocco's best-known munshid, Muhammad Bennis.

Our look at Hinduism (chapter 1) demonstrated that down through the centuries and still today, devotional singing has been the favored means for moksa realization for most Hindus. Especially from the seventh century on, most Hindu devotional songs were in vernacular dialects, rather than Sanskrit, and thus could be sung by all regardless of caste groups or gender. In such bhakti song, the rhythm or tala gives benefits to the singers of removing karma, enabling communion with the Lord, and ultimately the realization of moksa. This devotional singing for the Hindu masses rapidly spread throughout India. Every linguistic region of India had its own composer of bhakti songs (high and low caste, male and female), all understood as manifestations of Nada-Brahman (Divine Sound) with Vishnu and his incarnations as Krishna and Rama as favorites. As Beck noted, today there are many skilled singers of kirtan who freely improvise—a little like spontaneous improvisation in modern jazz. And in Hindu religious gatherings today, bhajan or informal devotional singing has largely replaced earlier more formal types of song because of its open audience participation for all, regardless of class, caste, gender, or social background. Such bhajan sessions may go on for hours or even days and are popular across India and throughout the Hindu diaspora (Beck 2006, 132–133). The Hindu development of devotional song occurred alongside and influenced Sikh kirtan.

Kirtan, or the singing of hymns, occupies a central place in Sikh spiritual practice. As we saw in chapter 4, Sikh hymns are scriptural passages from the Adi Granth set to music, and they occupy a major part of congregational worship in the gurdwara. Kirtan was initiated by Guru Nanak in saying that God's word (gurbani) embodies all scriptural knowledge (Veda) and the eternally sounding melodious vibration (nada) that permeates all space (Singh 2011, 113–114)—a statement with which most Hindus would agree. Singh also goes on to suggest that for Nanak devotional singing was the most efficacious means of liberation, and that Guru Arjan agrees (Singh 2011). It is when the Adi Granth is sung that it has spiritual power, just as a piece of written music has no value until it is performed. As one devotee put it to me, once learned, the constant singing of the scripture vibrates into you, clearing and opening your mind to God's grace (Coward 2000, 209n14). Kirtan ultimately is what enables most Sikhs to dwell in the house of the Guru's Word. Through kirtan Sikhs attune themselves to vibrate in harmony with the divine word and thereby immerse themselves in the deeper levels of spiritual experience. Singing of the hymns is experienced as evoking the divine word and is an earthly resonance of it—a direct correspondence is seen as existing between the physical vibration of the phenomenal singing and the noumenal word sound of the transcendent. The more the devotee sings, the more divine power is evoked until one's being is purified and put into a harmonious relationship with the Divine and an experience of the "eternal Guru" as an intimate companion of their soul (Singh 2006, 148). In her field research on lay Sikhs in Varanasi, Myrvold reports their devotional experience of kirtan as "internal feelings that arise through the language of music," "the flame of spiritual longing in the heart," "food for my soul," and "a spiritual experience of intensity and immediacy that transcends ordinary conscious striving" (Myrvold 2008, 289). Myrvold concludes that as a public and shared worship form, kirtan gives to all people, literate and illiterate, an equal chance of gaining the spiritual benefits involved in singing and listening to gurbani (God's word). Myrvold's interviews demonstrate that for lay Sikhs, as for lay Hindus, the chanting of daily prayers or mantras by heart and the singing of hymns (kirtan) have powerful transformative and purifying effects.

Turning finally to our analysis of Buddhism, we found that in our Jodo Shinshu case study the Nembutsu mantra chanting and congregational singing expanded the monastic focus of much Buddhist spiritual practice so as to give room for the equal engagement of both male and female laypeople. Only after leaving the monastery, marrying, and living as a layperson did Shinran discover the decadence of his own karmic nature. The more he tried to reach nirvana through jiriki or self-power practice (such as counting the number of Namu Amida Butsu chants he did in a day), the more karmically trapped he became. Only by throwing himself in total surrender on the compassion of Amida Buddha was he rescued into Amida's Pure Land—not due to his own surrender, but as a free gift of grace from Amida (tariki or other power). Our field study of Jodo Shinshu congregations in Alberta demonstrated that for laypeople, their chanting and singing hymns in congregational Sunday worship and funeral services (which exhibit Protestant Christian influence) has a spiritually sustaining and transforming effect. As one participant put it, "Although I am chanting and singing, Amida speaks it, Amida hears it, and I am the union" (Coward and Goa 1983, 275). Or as another layperson put it, "You are one with Amida Buddha in the nembutsu," adding that in the congregational worship she feels closest to her husband and her parents—all are one in Amida (Coward and Goa 1983, 275). However, it is clear that in Buddhist practice, music and hymn singing plays a lesser role in lay spirituality than it does in the other religions studied. As Williams observes, in Japanese Buddhist chanting, music plays a limited role (Williams 2006, 182). In our own Alberta field study of Jodo Shinshu congregations, the piano accompanying the opening nembutsu chant as a collective invocation, and a couple of hymns (gatha) accompanied by piano were the key uses of music—and that owing to considerable Protestant Christian influence. For all laypeople and ministers it is the straight Nembutsu chanting without musical accompaniment that is the focus of their experience of Amida's presence and grace. Bells and chimes are used but only to indicate the start and stop of each section of chant. Thus, in the Buddhist practice studied here, music plays a limited role when compared with the powerful hymn singing or kirtan of the Sikhs, Hindus, or for example in Muslim musical engagement in the emotional milad and majlis songs of South Asia or the Sufi dhikr musical singing of the Moroccan munshidun.

References

Alim, H. S. 2005. "A New Research Agenda: Exploring the Transglobal Hip Hop *Umma*." In *Muslim Networks from Hajj to Hip Hop*, edited by Miriam Cooke and Bruce Lawrence, 264–274. Chapel Hill: University of North Carolina Press.
Alper, Harvey P., ed. 1989. *Understanding Mantras*. Albany: State University of New York Press.
Alper, Harvey P. 1989a. "The Cosmos as Siva's Language Game." In *Understanding Mantras*, edited by H. Alper, 249–294. Albany: State University of New York Press.
Arberry, A. J. 1955. *The Koran Interpreted*. London: Allen & Unwin.
Aurobindo, G. 1971. *The Secret of the Veda*. Pondicherry: Sri Aurobindo Ashram.
Ayoub, Mahmoud. 1984. *The Qur'an and Its Interpreters*. Albany: State University of New York Press.
Bains, Tara Singh, and H. Johnston. 1995. *The Four Quarters of the Night: The Life Journey of an Emigrant Sikh*. Montreal: McGill-Queen's University Press.
Bando, S. 2014. "Significance of the Nembutsu." *Muryoko: Journal of Shin Buddhism*. http://www.nembutsu.info/bandonem.htm.
Barua, Mitra. 2014. Personal communication. August 3 email.
Beck, Guy L. 1993. *Sonic Theology: Hinduism and Sacred Sound*. Columbia: University of South Carolina Press.
Beck, Guy L. 2006. "Hinduism and Music." In *Sacred Sound: Experiencing Music in the World Religions*, edited Guy L. Beck, 113–139. Waterloo: Wilfrid Laurier University Press.
Bharati, A. 1970. *The Ochre Robe*. Garden City: Doubleday.
Bharati, A. 1970a. *The Tantric Tradition*. London: Rider.
Bloom, A. 1965. *Shinran's Gospel of Pure Grace*. Tucson: University of Arizona Press.

Choy, F. K. 2012. "Saccakiriya: The Belief in the Power of True Speech in Theravada Buddhist Tradition." PhD thesis, Singapore University.
Coburn, Thomas B. 1984. "Scripture in India." *Journal of the American Academy of Religion* 52: 435–459.
Cole, W. O. 1982. *The Guru in Sikhism*. London: Darton, Longman.
Cole, W. O., and P. S. Sambhi. 1978. *The Sikhs: Their Religious Beliefs and Practices*. Delhi: Vikas.
Cooke, Miriam, and Bruce Lawrence. 2005. *Muslim Networks from Hajj to Hip Hop*. Chapel Hill: University of North Carolina Press.
Coward, Harold. 1976. *Bhartrhari*. Boston: G. K. Hall & Co.
Coward, Harold G. 1983. "Psychology and Karma." *Philosophy East and West* 33: 49–60.
Coward, Harold. 1985. "The Yoga of the Word (*Sabdapurvayoga*)." *Adyar Library Bulletin* 49: 1–13.
Coward, Harold. 2000. "Scripture in Sikhism." *Scripture in the World Religions*, 130–137. Oxford: Oneworld.
Coward, Harold. 2010. "Religions of Canada in the Twenty-First Century." In *The Penguin Handbook of the World's Living Religions*, edited by John R. Hinnells, 870–895. London: Penguin.
Coward, Harold, and David Goa. 1983. "Sacred Ritual, Sacred Language: Jodo Shinshu Religious Forms in Transition." *Studies in Religion* 12.4: 363–80.
Coward, Harold, and David Goa. 1986. "Ritual Word and Meaning in Sikh Religious Life: A Canadian Field Study." *Journal of Sikh Studies* 8.2: 13–32.
Coward, Harold, and David Goa. 2004. *Mantra: Hearing the Divine in India and America*. New York: Columbia University Press.
Coward, Harold, J. Lipner, and Katherine Young. 1989. *Hindu Ethics, Purity, Abortion, and Euthanasia*. Albany: State University of New York Press.
Coward, Harold, and K. Raja. 1990. *The Philosophy of the Grammarians*. Princeton: Princeton University Press.
Cragg, K. 1969. *The House of Islam*. Belmont: Dickenson.
Dasgupta, S. B. 1977. *Aspects of Indian Religious Thought*. Calcutta: Firma KLM Pvt.
Davids, T. W. Rhys, trans. 1969. *Buddhist Sutras*. New York: Dover.
Davidson, R. M. 2004. *Indian Esoteric Buddhism: A Social History of the Tantric Movement*. Delhi: Motilal Banarsidass.
Dusenbery, Verne A. 1992. "The Word as Guru: Sikh Scripture and the Translation Controversy." *History of Religions* 31: 385–402.
Earhart, B. 1997. *Religion in the Japanese Experience*. Belmont: Wadsworth.
Eck, Diana L. 1998. *Darshan: Seeing the Divine Image in India*, third ed. New York: Columbia University Press.
Eck, Diana. 2001. *A New Religious America*. San Francisco: Harper.

Eliade, Mircea. 1969. *Yoga: Immortality and Freedom*, second ed. Trans. Willard Trask. Princeton: Princeton University Press.
Findly, Ellison Banks. 1989. "*Mantra kavisasta*: Speech as Performative in the Rgveda." In *Understanding Mantras*, edited by Harvey P. Alper, 15–47. Albany: State University of New York Press.
Gahuma, H. 1985. Personal communication. February 16.
Garfield, J., trans. 1995. *Nagarjuna's Mulamadhyamakakarika*. New York: Oxford University Press.
Garfield, J. L. 2002. *Empty Words: Buddhist Philosophy and Cross-Cultural Transformation*. Oxford: Oxford University Press.
Gonda, J. 1963. "The Indian Mantra." *Oriens* 16: 261–268.
Gonda, J. 1963a. *The Vision of the Vedic Poets*. The Hague: Mouton.
Graham, W. 1985. "Qur'an as Spoken Word" In *Approaches to Islam in Religious Studies*, edited by Richard C. Martin, 25–40. Tucson: University of Arizona Press.
Graham, W. 1987. *Beyond the Written Word*. Cambridge: Cambridge University Press.
Hawley, M., ed. 2013. *Sikh Diaspora: Theory, Agency, and Experience*. Leiden: Brill.
Hori, Victor. 2014. Personal communication. January 20 and April 15 emails.
Ikuta, Susumu. 1981. Taped interview. September.
"Islamic Arts." 1989. *Encyclopedia of Britannica*. Vol. 22: 44–102.
Iyer, K. A. Subramania, trans. 1965. *The Vakyapadiya of Bhartrhari*. Poona: Deccan College Research Institute.
Jayatilleke, K. N. 1980. *Early Buddhist Theory of Knowledge*. Delhi: Motilal Banarsidass.
Kassis, Hanna. 2000. "The Qur'an." In *Experiencing Scripture in World Religions*, edited by Harold Coward, 63–84. Maryknoll: Orbis.
Kaufmann, W. 1975. *Tibetan Buddhist Chant*. London: Indiana University Press.
Kawamura, Leslie. 1977. "Changes in the Japanese True Pure Land Buddhism in Alberta." In *Religion and Ethnicity*, edited by Harold Coward and Leslie Kawamura, 37–56. Waterloo: Wilfrid Laurier University Press.
Kawamura, Leslie. 1986. "Shinran's View of Karma." In *Karma and Rebirth*, edited by Ronald Neufeldt, 191–202. Albany: State University of New York Press.
Kawamura, Y. 1981. Taped interview. September.
Laack, I. 2015. "Sound, Music and Religion: A Preliminary Cartography of a Transdisciplinary Research Field." *Method and Theory in the Study of Religion* 27: 220–246.
Lancaster, Lewis. 1979. "Buddhist Literature: Its Canons, Scribes and Editors." In *The Critical Study of Sacred Texts*, edited by Wendy Doniger, 215–226. Berkeley: Berkeley Religious Studies Series.

Long, T. O., ed. 1970. "Mantrayana." In *A Dictionary of Buddhism*. New York: Scribner's.
MacQueen, Graeme. 1981. "Inspired Speech in Early Mahayana Buddhism." *Religion* 11: 303–345.
Main, John. 1977. *Christian Meditation: Prayer in the Tradition*. Montreal: Benedictine Priory of Montreal.
Martin, Luther. 1961. *Works* as quoted by Willem Jan Koorman. *Luther and the Bible*. Philadelphia: Muhlenberg Press.
Matics, M. 1970. *Entering the Path of Enlightenment by Santideva*. London: Macmillan.
McLeod, W. H. 1975. *The Evolution of the Sikh Community*. Oxford: Clarendon Press.
Miller, Roland E. 1995. *Muslim Friends: Their Faith and Feeling*. Saint Louis: Concordia.
Miller, Roland E. 2015. *Mappila Muslim Culture: How a Historic Muslim Community in India Has Blended Tradition and Modernity*. Albany: State University of New York Press.
Miller, Roland E. 2016. Personal communication. April 18.
Murti, T. R. V. 1974. "Some Comments on the Philosophy of Language in the Indian Context." *Journal of Indian Philosophy* 2: 321–331.
Murti, T. R. V. 1980. Foreword. Harold Coward, *The Sphota Theory of Language*, vii–xv. Delhi: Motilal Banarsidass.
Murti, T. R. V. 1983. "The Philosophy of Language in the Indian Context." In *Studies in Indian Thought*, edited by Harold Coward, 357–376. Delhi: Motilal Banarsidass.
Myrvold, Kristina. 2008. "Inside the Guru's Gate." PhD thesis, Lund University. www.anpere.net.
Myrvold, Kristina. 2013. "Translating the Guru's Words to Local and Global Contexts: *Katha* for Contemporary Sikh Communities." In *Sikh Diaspora*, edited by Michael Hawley, 321–350. Boston: Brill.
Nagarjuna. 1970. *Mulamadhyamakakarika*. Trans. K. K. Imada. Tokyo: Hokuseido Press.
Narayanan, Vasudha. 2000. "Dialogic Hinduism: Liberation and Lentils." *Journal of the American Academy of Religion* 68.4: 761–779.
Nelson, K. 1985. *The Art of Reciting the Qur'an*. Austin: University of Texas Press.
Neusner, J. 1985. *The Memorized Torah*. Chicago: Scholars Press.
Nishiyama, Reyko. 1981. Taped interview. September.
Oberhammer, G. 1989. "The Use of Mantra in Yogic Meditation: The Testimony of Pasupata." In *Understanding Mantras*, edited by Harvey P. Alper, 201–223. Albany: State University of New York Press.

Oberoi, Harjot. 2000. "Sikhism." In *Experiencing Scripture in the World Religions*, edited by Harold Coward, 113–137. Maryknoll: Orbis.
O'Connell, J. T., I. Milton, and O. Willard, eds. 1988. *Sikh History and Religion in the Twentieth Century*. Toronto: University of Toronto, Centre for South Asian Studies.
Ong, Walter. 1967. *The Presence of the Word*. New Haven: Yale University Press.
Otto, Rudolf. 1958. *The Idea of the Holy*, second ed. Trans. J. W. Harvey. New York: Oxford University Press.
Patanjali's Yoga Sutras. 1978. Second ed. Trans. Rama Prasada. New Delhi: Oriental Books.
Perera, A. 2000. *Buddhist Paritta Chanting Ritual*. Sri Lanka: Buddhist Cultural Centre, Nedimala.
Purewal, N. K., and H. S. Lallie. 2013. "Sikh *Kirtan* in the Diaspora: Identity, Innovation, and Revivalism." In *Sikh Diaspora*, edited by Michael Hawley, 381–404. Boston: Brill.
Qureshi, Regula. 2006. "Islam and Music." In *Sacred Sound: Experiencing Music in World Religions*, edited by Guy L. Beck, 89–111. Waterloo: Wilfrid Laurier University Press.
Raju, P. T. 1985. *Structural Depths of Indian Thought*. Albany: State University of New York Press.
Ricoeur, Paul. 1979. "The 'Sacred' Text and Community." In *The Critical Study of Sacred Texts*, edited Wendy Doniger O'Flaherty, 274–275. Berkeley: Graduate Theological Union.
Robinson, R. 1970. *The Buddhist Religion*. Belmont: Dickenson.
as-Said, Labib. 1975. *The Recited Koran*. Princeton: Darwin Press.
Schubel, V. J. 1993. *Religious Performance in Contemporary Islam: Shi'a Devotional Rituals in South Asia*. Columbia: University of South Carolina Press.
Shinran. 2001. *The Collected Works of Shinran* (CW). Trans. Dennis Hirota et al. http://www.shinranworks.com.
Shinran. 2012. *Shinran's Kyogyoshinsho*. Trans. D. T. Suzuki. Oxford: Oxford University Press.
Shinran. 2014. *Shinran's Concept of Practice*. ww.nembutsu.info/indshin/readings/Chapter4/Concept.pdf.
Sigueira-Koo, Paolina Marielle. 2017. "How Can We Explore the Connection of Sound with the Experience of Religion?" Scripps Senior Thesis, 1009. Claremont.
Singh, Pashaura. 1985. Personal communication, January 18.
Singh, Pashaura. 2006. "Sikhism and Music." In *Sacred Sound: Experiencing Music in the World Religions*, edited by Guy L. Beck, 141–167. Waterloo: Wilfrid Laurier University Press.

Singh, Pashaura. 2008. "Scripture as Guru in the Sikh Tradition." *Religion Compass* 2.4: 659–673.
Singh, Pashaura. 2011. "Musical *Chaunkis* at the Darbar Sahib." In *Sikhism in Global Context*, edited by Pashaura Singh, 103–129. New Delhi: Oxford University Press.
Smith, B. L., ed. 1976. *Hinduism: New Essays in the History of Religions*. Leiden: Brill. See essays by Joseph O'Connell, 33–52, and Norvin Hein, 15–32.
Smith, Wilfred Cantwell. 1971. "The Study of Religion and the Study of the Bible." *Journal of the American Academy of Religion* 39: 133–143.
Smith, Wilfred Cantwell. 1980. "An Empirical Historian's Nonreductionist Interpretation of the Qur'an." *International Journal of Middle East Studies* 11: 490–505.
Smith, Wilfred Cantwell. 1993. *What Is Scripture? A Comparative Approach*. Minneapolis: Fortress Press.
Staal, Frits. 1977. "Rigveda 10.71 on the Origin of Language." In *Revelation in Indian Thought*, edited by Harold Coward and K. Sivaraman, 3–14. Emeryville: Dharma.
Staal, Frits. 1979. "Oriental Ideas on the Origin of Language." *Journal of the American Oriental Society* 99: 1–14.
Stace, W. T. 1961. *Mysticism and Philosophy*. London: Macmillan.
Studholme, Alexander. 2002. *The Origins of Om Manipadme Hum: A Study of the Karandavyuha Sutra*. Albany: State University of New York Press.
Tabari. 2000. *Ta'rikh al-rusul wal-muluk* (History of Messengers and Kings). Ed. M. J. De Goeje et al. (Leiden: Brill, 1879–1901), 1: 1150. In Hanna Kassis, "The Qur'an," in *Experiencing Scripture in World Religions*, edited by Harold Coward, 65. Maryknoll: Orbis, 2000.
Tilakaratne, A. 2012. *Theravada Buddhism: The View of the Elders*. Honolulu: University of Hawaii Press.
Uberoi, J. P. S. 1992. "The Five Symbols of Sikhism." In *Religion in India*, edited by T. N. Madan, 320–334. Delhi: Oxford University Press.
Unno, T. 2002. *Shin Buddhism: Bits of Rubble Turn into Gold*. New York: Random House.
Veda, Yoshifumi, ed. 1991. *Hymns of the Pure Land*. Kyoto: Hongwanji International Center.
von Denffer, A. 1983. *'Ulum Al-Qur'an*. London: The Islamic Foundation.
Waugh, Earle H. 2005. *Memory, Music, and Religion: Morocco's Mystical Chanters*. Columbia: University of South Carolina Press.
Welch, A. 1979. "Introduction" to "Studies in Qur'an and Tafsir." *Journal of the American Academy of Religion* 47: 620.
Welch, A. 1981. "Al Kur'an." In *The Encyclopedia of Islam*, 403. Leiden: E. J. Brill.

Wheelock, W. 1980. "A Taxonomy of the Mantras in the New and Full Moon Sacrifice." *History of Religion* 19: 349–369.
Wheelock, W. 1989. "Mantra in Vedic and Tantric Ritual." In *Understanding Mantras*, edited by Harvey P. Alper, 96–122. Albany: State University of New York Press.
Williams, Paul. 2000. *Buddhist Thought: A Complete Introduction to the Indian Tradition*. London: Routledge.
Williams, Sean. 2006. "Buddhism and Music." In *Sacred Sound: Experiencing Music in World Religions*, edited by Guy L. Beck, 169–189. Waterloo: Wilfrid Laurier University Press.
Woods, J. H. trans. 1966. *The Yoga-System of Patanjali*. Harvard Oriental Series, vol. 17, third ed. Delhi: Motilal Banarsidass.
Yun-Hua, J. 1976. "Dimensions of Indian Buddhism." In *The Malalasekera Commemorative Volume*, edited by O. H. de A. Wyesekera, 162. Colombo: Sri Lanka.

Index

Adi Granth (Sikhism; "The First Book"; sacred text; living Guru), 8, 127–35, 137–39, 142, 144–46, 154, 161
Akal Purakh (Sikhism: the divine), 128, 129, 134, 137, 157
Akhand Kirtani Jatha (Sikhism: kirtan practice popularized in the late twentieth century), 147, 148
akhar (Hinduism: kirtan phrases improvised in vernacular language), 43
altar, 12, 44, 56, 85
Amida Buddha, 74–86, 89, 153, 155, 158, 162, 163. See also Shinjin
Amrit sanskar (Sikhism: initiation into Khalsa Sikhism), 143, 145, 147
Arabic, 92, 93, 96, 98, 99, 100, 102, 103, 108–13, 156
Astasahasrika Prajnaparamita, 30, 61
ascetic, 11, 12, 53, 65, 75
Avalokitesvara (Buddhism: bodhisattva of compassion), 68–72, 74, 88

bani (Sikhism: divine utterance), 127, 129, 132, 133. See also gurbani

bells, 13, 84, 163
Berbers, 105, 115, 123, 160
Bhagavad Gita, 39, 41, 44, 70
bhajan (Hinduism: informal sessions of devotional song), 9, 43–45, 161
bhakti (Hinduism: devotional singing), 37, 40–45, 70, 161
Bhaktivedanta, A. C. (1977 CE), 37, 38, 44
Bhartrhari (5th c. CE), 6, 21–26, 41, 45, 132, 133, 153, 155, 158. See also Vakyapadia
bhavana (Buddhism: meditation), 57
bija (Hinduism: mantra seed syllables), 25, 30
bodhisattva (Buddhism: those who help others on path to Buddhahood), 53, 61, 63–65, 68–72, 74, 79, 87, 88. See also Avalokitesvara
Brahman (Hinduism: the divine), 15, 21, 23, 41, 42, 49, 60, 63, 73, 133, 154. See also Nada-Brahman; Sabdabrahman
Brahmanic, 18
breath, 36, 45
breathing exercises, 29, 124, 160
Buddha nature, 72, 80, 86

buddhavacana (Buddhism: words of the Buddha), 59 64, 66, 87
"by heart" recitation of
  prayers, 135, 136, 138, 140, 162
  Qur'an, 94, 98, 102, 104, 109
  qusaid poetry, 119
  textual chant, 2, 55

call and response format, 40, 56, 57, 123
chant
  divine name and, 127, 128, 133–37, 154, 157 (*see also* nam-simaran)
  experience of, 1, 3, 4, 30, 83–85, 99, 100, 103–105, 110, 111, 125, 132, 144, 146, 148, 156, 163
  japa and, 26, 35
  kirtan and, 9, 134, 138–41 (*see also* kirtan)
  mantra and (*see under* mantra)
  meditation and, 4, 7, 29, 115–18, 123, 160
  memory and, 92, 98, 124
  refuge and, 54–59
  teaching and, 2, 5, 73
  word and, 6, 8, 10, 44–46, 65, 68, 121, 122, 131, 151 (*see also* tajwid)
  worship and, 11, 12, 38, 43, 93–96, 102, 106–109, 119, 120
caste, 36, 38, 41–45, 68, 76, 108, 134, 161
chimes, 84, 163
congregational
  lamentation, 112, 113
  prayer, 103, 142, 146, 153
  song and chant, 2, 40, 82, 85, 135, 143, 149, 151–53, 161–63
  worship, 5, 84, 135, 139, 163 (*see also* majlis; sangat)
consciousness, 37, 45, 83, 86, 98, 117, 147, 154, 162
  devotion as sole occupant of, 3
  divine word and, 4, 5, 7, 10, 14, 21, 22, 34, 84, 132, 135, 139–41, 146, 149, 152, 155 (*see also* Samadhi; Sabdabrahman)
  enlightenment and, 72, 74
  language and, 151
  purification of negative karma and, 15–17, 25, 26, 61, 63, 155, 157
cymbals, 13, 40, 42, 44, 73, 141

Daivi Vak (Hinduism: Divine Word), 17, 18, 133, 153
darshan (Hinduism: exchange of vision between image and worshipper), 13, 14
devotional singing, 7, 40–43, 45, 111, 127, 132, 138, 139, 141, 154, 161. See also bhajan; bhakti; milad; song
dhamma. *See* dharma
dharma (Buddhism: teachings of the Buddha), 49, 50, 52, 54, 55, 58, 61–64, 66, 67, 69, 72, 73, 77, 158
dhikr (Islam: remembrance of God via group litanies), 103, 104, 115–18, 120, 123–25, 160, 163
dholak (barrel drum), 111, 114, 125, 159
diaspora and immigration
  Buddhist, 59, 81–85, 89, 155, 162
  Hindu, 13, 39, 43–46, 161
  Muslim, 126
  Sikh, 127, 136, 139, 145–49
diksa (Hinduism: initiation of devotee by guru), 35, 36

drum(s), 13, 40, 42, 44, 56, 114, 131. *See also* dholak
  beat of the, 114, 118
  of the Dharma, 73
  of the divine word, 140, 141
Durga, 11, 12, 30

emotional
  affliction, 76, 82
  impact of song and chant, 41, 42, 95, 107, 112, 113, 118, 122, 124, 140, 160, 163 (*see also* hal; ragas)

fasting, 35, 94, 95
flute, 13, 73, 141

Ganesha, 11, 12, 30
Ganges River, 10–12
gatha (Buddhism: hymn), 85, 163
Gautama Buddha (ca. 560–ca. 480 BCE), 48–50, 63, 87, 154. *See also* Sakyamuni
God(s), 29, 50, 56, 58, 65, 102, 103, 109, 111, 113, 117–20, 125, 141
  encounters and relationships with, 16, 27, 28, 35, 42, 116, 138
  existence of, 20
  images of, 11, 44
  messenger of, 91, 92 (*see also* Muhammad)
  name(s) of, 30, 38–40, 115, 123, 134, 136, 154
  remembrance of (*see* dhikr; Nam-simaran)
  singing to, 39, 41, 139, 140 (*see also* kirtan)
  spiritual unity with, 2, 15, 110, 114, 160
  word and, 6, 17, 18, 21, 93–96, 98–102, 106, 107, 121, 122, 124, 142, 143, 153, 156, 161, 162 (*see also* gurbani; Qur'an; Vak)
goddess, in Hinduism, 11, 17, 19, 39, 42, 44
Golden Temple, Amritsar, 129, 131, 137, 147, 148
Grammarian philosophy (Hinduism: philosophical school), 18–21, 25, 28, 41, 64, 133, 158. *See also* Bhartrhari
Great Goddess, 28, 29
gurbani (Sikhism: divine word uttered by the Guru), 130, 132, 133, 135–40, 144, 148, 157, 161, 162
gurdwara, 130, 135–40, 142, 144, 146–49, 161
gurumantra, 147
gurmukhi (Sikhism: words of the Guru), 131, 148
guru(s)
  eternal, 139, 158, 162
  God in Hinduism as, 141
  and mantra in Hinduism, 33, 34, 35, 36, 37, 160
  relationship with student in Hinduism, 2, 29, 30, 31, 32, 44
  relationship with student in Sikhism, 132, 133, 152, 158
  scripture in Sikhism as, 128–31, 135, 139, 142, 145, 154, 157 (*see also* Adi Granth; Vak)
  as Ten historical figures in Sikhism, 128, 133, 141, 142, 145, 146, 154
Guru Gobind Singh (1666–1708), 154
Guru Nanak, (1469–1539) 127–30, 133–38, 141, 153, 154, 157, 160, 161

Guru Granth Sahib, 132, 133, 135, 137, 142–47, 149, 154, 157. See also *Adi Granth*

hal (Islam: state of mystical experience), 124, 160
Hare Krishna. See International Society for Krishna Consciousness
hafiz (Islam: one who can recite the *Qur'an* from memory), 93, 102
harmonium, 40, 44, 111, 114, 125, 147, 148, 159
hearing, 1, 2, 4, 7
 and the divine, 11, 157
 and kirtan; shabad, 127, 128, 133, 142
 and mantra, 13, 14, 16, 22, 26, 28, 154, 155
 the name of Buddha, 81, 86
 the *Qur'an*, 108, 122
 and salvation, 5
 Sufi verse, 120, 121
hip hop, 125, 126
hukam (Sikhism: divine word command), 127, 142, 143
Hukam laina (Sikhism: seeking a divine word command), 142
Hussain. See Imam Hussain
hymn(s), 1, 4, 5–7, 10, 39, 41, 43, 85, 152, 154, 163. See also gatha; kirtan; milad
 Shi'ia, 106, 111–13, 115, 123, 124, 159, 160
 Sikh, 128, 133, 134–44, 149, 161, 162
 Vedic, 17, 18

i'jaz (Islam: incomparability of *Qur'an*), 98, 99, 156
Imam Hussain (626–680 CE), 106, 112, 113, 123, 160

improvisation, musical, 43, 114, 161
instruments, musical, 149. See also cymbal; drum(s); flute; harmonium; piano
Internet, 110, 123, 146, 149, 159
International Society for Krishna Consciousness (ISKCON), 37–40
Isvara (Hinduism; Buddhism: master yogi), 7, 20, 25–27, 40, 42, 70

Jainism, 19, 28, 35
japa (Hinduism: chanting of a sacred syllable), 26, 34, 35, 44, 45
Japji Sahib, 134–36
Jesus, 1, 4, 5, 7, 48, 101, 122, 151
Jodo Shinsu (True Pure Land School) Buddhism, 47, 74, 75, 81–85, 89, 155, 162, 163

Kali, 11, 12, 19, 44
karma, 5, 152, 157
 bakhti music and, 42, 161
 Buddhist doctrine of, 76, 77, 79, 80, 85, 87, 156
 merit-making (punya-karma) and, 55
 Nada-Yoga and, 41
 obstruction removed by mantra and, 14, 15, 17, 23, 36, 37, 48, 71, 74, 75, 133, 153, 155
 freedom from, 60, 61, 63, 64, 152 (*see also* pratibha)
 Vak and, 141, 142, 158
Khalsa (Sikhism: Sikh religious order requiring initiation), 129, 136, 143
kirtan (Hinduism: worship through mantras and devotional singing; Sikhism: hymns of

praise), 2, 9, 38–45, 127, 128, 134, 135, 137–41, 145–49, 152, 154, 157, 161–63
Koran. See Qur'an
Krishna, 11, 12, 14, 37–40, 42, 43, 161

madhyama (Hinduism: inner thought sound), 6, 24, 66
Mahayana Buddhism, 48, 50, 52–54, 56, 58–66, 68–73, 87–89, 153, 158
majlis (Islam: assembly; session to commemorate martyrdom of Hussain), 112, 113, 123, 160, 163
Malayalam, 108–10
mantra (Buddhism: syllabic vehicles of salvation; Hinduism: speech as divine word and sound in chant and worship; Sikhism: chanted meditation on the divine). See Mantrayana; mantrin; Nam; Nam-simaran; Namu Amida Butsu; Om; Om Manipadme Hum; prajnaparamita; Vak Yoga
   as form of fixed concentration (see Samadhi)
   chant and, 9, 12–16, 18, 19, 23, 25–28, 31, 32, 34, 37, 39–42, 47, 48, 51, 63, 64, 69–72, 74–82, 87–89, 133, 152, 153, 155, 156, 158, 162
   diksa and, 35, 36
   guru and (see under guru(s))
   karmic obstacles and (see under karma)
   repetition of, 6, 10, 12, 16, 22–26, 34, 35
   seed, 11, 20, 23, 25, 30, 31, 50, 52, 134, 158

Vedas and, 9, 10, 13, 16–25, 27, 28, 31, 32, 36, 41, 44, 59, 70, 72, 102, 133, 152–54, 156
Mantrayana (Buddhism: movement for mantra sounds as vehicles of salvation), 20, 29, 48, 65, 67–69, 72–74, 88, 153, 158
mantrin (Buddhism: secret, powerful mantra), 69
Mappila Muslim community, South India, 105–11, 115, 122, 123, 152, 159
meditation, 11, 12, 21, 27, 29, 36, 37, 54, 57, 74, 85, 110, 127, 128, 134, 140–42, 147, 152–54, 160. See also bhavana; Nam-simaran
meditational song, 112, 114–17, 122–25. See also dhikr
melodies, 40, 41, 73, 98, 105, 113, 114, 118, 121–24, 137, 140, 148, 159, 161. See also raga
memorization, 84, 93, 96, 98, 102, 104, 120–22, 135
milad (Islam: assembly to celebrate the birth of the Prophet Muhammad), 111, 112, 159, 160, 163
Mimamsa (Hinduism: philosophical school), 17–20
moksa (Hinduism: release from cycle of birth and death; complete communion with the divine), 5, 12, 15, 19, 21, 25, 34, 39, 40–43, 45, 64, 153, 161
morality of music, 113, 114
muezzin (Islam: one who makes the call to prayer), 103, 107, 122
Muhammad, Prophet (632 CE), 91–98, 101, 103, 105, 106, 108–11, 115, 121, 153, 156, 159

mukti (Sikhism: release from samsara cycle of rebirth), 134, 136, 158
munshid (Islam: Sufi chant master), 106, 115–21, 123, 124, 160, 161, 163
murti (Hinduism: divine image), 43
Murti, T. R. V. (1902–1986), 2, 3, 21, 152

nada (Sanskrit: physical vibrations of music), 137, 138, 161
Nada-Brahman (Hinduism: sacred sound), 40–42, 45, 161
Nam (Sikhism: seed mantra for Vahiguru), 132, 134, 157
nam-kirtan (Hinduism: singing the names of God), 39, 40, 44
Nam-simaran (Sikhism: remembrance of God's name), 134–37, 140, 147, 154, 158
Namu Amida Butsu (Buddhism: Nembutsu mantra chant), 74, 80–82, 85, 86, 153, 155, 158, 162
Nam-yoga (Hinduism: chanting of God's names), 41
Nanak. *See* Guru Nanak
na't (Islam: poem chanted to commemorate the birth of Prophet Muhammad during the milad), 111, 112, 124, 159
nature, 10, 41, 151, 156
  divine in, 11
  order in, 96
Nembutsu (Buddhism: Pure Land meditation/recitation), 48, 69, 74–86, 88, 89, 155, 156, 162, 163
  in English, 82

Nirvana (Buddhism: enlightenment; release from suffering), 47–50, 55, 57, 71, 72, 76, 87, 88, 153, 162
offering, 11, 38, 44, 57, 84, 130, 142, 153
Om, 7, 10, 11, 12, 14, 21, 25–27, 31, 40, 41, 44, 45, 48, 155, 158. *See also* japa
Om Manipadme Hum (Buddhism: mantra chant), 69, 70–74, 88, 89, 155, 158
oral
  devotional practice, 146
  recitation, 57, 93–100, 121, 127
  rhetoric, 5
  scripture, 8, 132
  teachings, 4, 106, 122
  tradition, 11, 119, 124
  transmission, 5, 20, 51, 107, 125, 130
  word, 6, 91, 104, 151
Other Power (Buddhism: tariki practice generated by Amida Buddha; living in Amida), 77–79, 85, 89, 155, 162

Pali, 55–57, 59
Panth (Sikhism: community), 128, 132, 157
Paritta (Buddhism: protective Theravada chanting ritual), 57–59
parivartina (Buddhism: revelation of the hidden), 15, 50
pasyanti (Hinduism: supersensuous seeing of the meaning-whole), 6, 24
Patanjali. *See Yoga Sutras*

piano, 85, 163
piety, 38, 100–102, 105, 110, 123, 144
prajnaparamita (Buddhism: perfection of wisdom), 62–63, 87
prajna-paramita (Hinduism: condensed meaning of *Vedas* in a seed mantra), 30, 31
pratibha (Buddhism; Hinduism: perception clear of any obstructing karma), 60, 61, 63, 64
pratibhana (Buddhism: state of having pratibha), 61–64, 87
prayer
  in Buddhism, 69, 73, 124
  in Christianity, 6, 7
  in Hinduism, 9–12, 15, 17, 44, 124, 154, 162
prayer in Islam, 116, 118, 122, 158, 159. See also salat
  call to, 106, 107, 109, 121
  five daily, 102, 103, 109, 122, 153, 156
  Qur'an in, 94, 104
  saints and, 110, 111
prayer in Sikhism, 130, 142–46
  kirtan and, 137–40
  Nam-simaran and, 134–37
puja (Hinduism: worship), 32, 43, 44
Punjabi, 132, 133, 146
punya-karma (Buddhism: merit-making through chant), 55

qasaid (Islam: song poem), 119
qawwali (Islam: public recitation assembly), 113–15, 123, 125, 160
qira'at. See Ten Readings

Qur'an, 8, 91–109, 111, 113–17, 120–25, 153, 156, 158, 159. See also revelation; tartil. See also under "by heart"; hearing; prayer; recitation; revelation; women

ragas (Hinduism: musical scales and melody patterns), 41–43, 72, 111, 138, 149, 159
Rama, 37, 39, 40, 42, 161
rational thought, 3, 4, 7, 15
  in opposition to devotional, intuitive thought, 82, 145, 146
reality
  divine order of, 16, 41, 128, 157
  evocation of, 24
  experience of, 49, 66, 81, 87, 151
  religious, 115, 116, 118, 124
  seen, 7, 60
  ultimate, 20, 47, 133
recitation
  in dialect, 52
  oral (*see under* oral)
  public discourse and teachings and, 51, 54, 64, 68
  Qur'anic revelation and, 91–115, 121, 122, 124, 126, 153, 156, 157, 159, 160. See also hafiz; Qur'an
  worship practice and, 16, 19, 57, 59, 70, 72–74, 77, 79, 80, 83, 87, 89, 127, 131–37, 140–47, 149, 158
repetition, 109, 112, 118, 120
  of chant, 56, 69, 70, 88, 158
  of divine names, 114, 134, 136, 140, 147
  of mantra (*see under* mantra)
  of scripture, 41, 44, 98, 104

revelation
   Buddhist ideas regarding, 49, 50, 53, 54, 60–63, 68. *See also* parivartina
   gospels and, 6
   oral, 130
   Qur'anic, 91–94, 96–99, 101, 106, 107, 109, 121, 122
   Vedic, 17, 19, 22, 35, 48, 49, 72, 87, 153
   word as, 8, 151–54, 156
Rgveda (Hinduism: canonical Vedic text), 15–18
rhyme, 93, 121, 125, 156
rhythm, 12, 16, 29, 73, 93, 100, 105, 110–13, 118, 121, 123, 133, 138, 156, 159, 161. *See also* sruti; tala
ritual, 6, 7, 9, 10, 18, 19, 23, 28, 31, 32, 36, 38, 44, 52, 58, 59, 65, 67, 69, 72, 82–85, 88, 103, 109, 112, 115, 116, 125, 129, 130, 135, 138, 142, 144, 154
rsi (Hinduism: "seer;" one purged of ignorance allowing her/him to speak the *Vedas*), 17–19, 22, 24, 25, 48–50, 60, 63, 64, 87, 141, 152
rta (Buddhism: melodic change chant), 73
rta (Hinduism: cosmic order), 16, 18, 20, 28, 29, 96

sabda (Hinduism: word as divine, eternal, authorless), 19–21, 128
Sabdabrahman (Hinduism: divine word-consciousness), 20–25, 41, 152
Sabdapurvayoga (Hinduism: yoga of the word), 25, 64

sacred sound, 12, 13, 15, 45, 72, 73, 105, 106, 135, 139, 144. *See also* Nada-Brahman; Sabdabrahman; shabad; sphota; tajwid; Vak
Sakti. *See* Great Goddess
Sakyamuni Buddha, 50, 62, 63, 71, 78, 80. *See also* Gautama
salat (Islam: daily prayer), 101–104, 122, 153, 156, 158
sama (Islam: assembly for listening; spiritual music), 105, 113–16, 119, 120, 123, 160. *See also* qawwali
samadhi (Hinduism; Sikhism: state of consciousness with no subject-object distinction) 7, 25, 26, 140
samsara (Buddhism; Hinduism: cycle of death and rebirth) 14, 15, 50, 55, 57, 71, 78, 134, 152, 153
samvriti (Buddhism: conventional language to access conventional truth), 66
sangha (Buddhism: community of lay and/or monastic followers), 48, 51, 52, 54, 55, 75, 87, 158
Sangita-Ratnakara by Sarngadeva (ca. 1250 CE), 41
Sanskrit, 2, 3, 10, 41, 43, 44, 60, 128, 154, 161
scripture. *See also under* guru; oral; repetition
   Buddhist, 47–54, 65, 66, 68, 69, 83, 87, 153 (*see also* sutras)
   Christian, 3, 5
   Hindu, 2, 9, 10, 11, 15, 16, 31, 41, 44, 152 (see also *Vedas*)

Islamic, 98, 100, 101, 121. See also *Qur'an*
Sikh, 127–33, 135, 136, 138–40, 142–46, 149, 154, 157, 161 (see also *Adi Granth*; Guru Granth Sahib)
spoken, 5, 6, 17
vision and, 4, 17, 64
writing and, 8
shabad (Sikhism: music of the divine word), 128, 132, 133, 137, 141, 148, 157
Shi'a (Islam: followers of the family lineage of the Prophet Muhammad), 106, 111–13, 123, 159, 160
Shinjin (Buddhism: moment of loss of self and confirmation by Amida), 79, 80, 81, 83, 86
Shinran (1173–1262 CE), 74–81, 83–86, 88, 89, 155
Shiva (Hinduism: Brahman as divine creator), 11, 12, 23, 27–31, 34, 35
siddha (Buddhism: "perfected" laypeople), 65, 67, 68, 88
song. *See also* kirtan; qasaid; sama
pilgrimage and, 105
poetry and, 119
spiritual practice and, 1, 41–45, 73, 106, 109–11, 115, 120, 122–24, 133, 135, 154, 159–63
transformative power of, 51, 152
wedding (*see* wedding songs)
word and, 8, 54, 140
sonic, 32, 93, 111, 118, 121, 123, 124, 156, 160
experience, 13, 28
theology, 13, 30, 41, 91

sound, 7, 38, 40, 99, 132. *See also* sacred sound
chant and, 6, 30, 83, 84, 93, 107, 109, 118, 121, 122, 133, 154–56
cosmic order and, 19
divine origin of, 10, 11, 13, 14, 33, 91, 94, 137, 141, 154, 162
perception and, 22–24, 26, 28
salvation and, 20
in Tantrism, 29, 30, 40, 41
text and, 3
sphota (Hinduism: meaning-whole; unitary idea), 6, 22–25. *See also* Grammarian philosophy
sruti (Hinduism: heard text), 11, 16, 133. See also *Veda(s)*; rsi
Sufi (Islam: one seeking a direct connection to God through mystical practice), 103, 105, 106, 111, 113–25, 152, 159, 160, 163
Sukhavati (Buddhism: Pure Land of the Buddha), 70–72, 88
sura (Islam: chapter of the *Qur'an*), 94, 99–104, 108, 122, 126
sutras (Buddhism: sayings and teachings of the Buddha), 8, 47, 48, 51–53, 59, 60–64, 68, 70–72, 85, 87, 88, 153, 158
sutra-pitaka (Buddhism: revelation as possessed by the community), 51, 60, 61
svadhyaya (Hinduism: communion with the divine via scriptural study), 3, 4, 25
svara-sadhana (Hinduism: spiritual practice involving musical notes), 44

syllable
  Nembutsu, 81, 82
  sacred, 21, 35, 64 (*see also* Om)
  seed (bija), 25, 29, 30, 31
  six-syllable formula (Om
    Manipadme Hum) and, 71, 72,
    73
  tajwid, 107, 122

tajwid (Islam: aesthetic rules of
    Qur'anic recitation), 94, 95,
    98, 104–108, 122, 156, 159
tala (Hinduism: musical rhythm),
    42, 111, 159, 161
tariki. *See* Other Power
tariqa (Islam: spiritual path;
    community), 115, 116, 119,
    124
tartil (Islam: slow deliberate
    Qur'anic recitation), 93, 95, 96
tashif (Islam: misreading of words
    during Qur'anic recitation),
    96, 98
Tantric (Hinduism: philosophical
    school), 20, 24, 27–33, 36, 40,
    72, 88, 155
tantrism (Buddhism: practice of the
    tantric texts), 70, 72, 88, 155,
    158
temple
  Hindu, 11–13, 40, 43–45
  Japanese Buddhist, 84
  Krishna, 37–39
  Sikh, 154 (*see also* Golden
    Temple; gurdwara)
  Theravada, 56, 59
  Tibetan Buddhist, 70
Ten Readings (Islam: acceptable
    oral variations in the recitation
    of the *Qur'an*), 97
Theistic Buddhism, 49, 62–64

Theistic Hinduism, 27, 28
Theravada Buddhism, 48, 50,
    52–59, 69, 73, 87, 89, 153,
    158, 159. *See also* Triple Refuge
Tibetan Buddhism, 47, 48, 69, 70,
    72–74, 88, 155
Transcendental Meditation (TM),
    37, 38
Triple Gem (Buddhism: Theravada
    chant of refuge in virtues
    of Buddha, Dhamma, and
    Sangha), 54, 55, 57–59
Triple Refuge (Buddhism: Theravada
    chant implying Triple Gem), 48,
    54–57, 87–89, 158
truth, spiritual, 7, 12, 16–18, 20,
    22–25, 27, 49, 50, 59, 61, 63,
    64, 66, 73, 81, 87, 100, 108,
    111, 118, 122, 123, 133, 140,
    141, 159

Urdu, 111, 115, 159

Vahiguru (Sikhism: the divine),
    128, 133, 134, 136, 138, 140,
    147, 154, 158
vajrin (Buddhism: secret, powerful
    mantra), 69
vaikhari (Hinduism: level of
    uttered sound), 6, 24. *See also*
    Grammarian philosophy
Vak (Hinduism; Sikhism: language;
    divine word), 133, 134, 142.
    See also Daivi Vak
Vak laina (Sikhism: taking the
    Guru's word), 141–43
Vakyapadia, 21–25, 45. *See also*
    Grammarian philosophy
Vak Yoga (Hinduism: mantra
    chanting as Yoga of the Word),
    64, 133, 137, 153, 155, 158

Varanasi, 10–12, 135, 139, 162
Veda(s) (Hinduism: scripture; scriptural knowledge; collection of mantras), 8, 9, 10, 13, 14, 16–25, 27, 28, 31, 32, 36, 41, 42, 44, 48, 49, 56, 59, 60, 63, 64, 70, 72, 87, 102, 133, 137, 152–54, 156, 157, 161. See also *Rgveda*
vibration. *See also* nada
  chant and, 14
  cosmic order and, 19
  kirtan and, 137, 138, 139, 161, 162
  universe and, 13, 16, 133, 155
  words and, 18, 82
Vinaya (Buddhism: rules of conduct for the monastic community), 47, 51–53, 61, 66
Vishnu (Hinduism: Brahman manifested as divine father), 11, 12, 27, 41, 42, 44, 161
vision. *See also* darshan
  as false, 49
  spoken as scripture, 4, 17, 64
  as Tantric experience, 24
  via chant, 4, 27, 70–72

water, 10, 12, 38, 44, 140, 142, 143
wedding songs, 57, 110, 119, 122, 143, 144, 159
women
  abstinence from, 66
  bhajan and, 43
  bhakti and, 40
  conversion and, 108
  incarnation of Great Goddess as, 29
  kirtan and, 139
  reciting *Qur'an*, 125
  in religious orders, 12, 116
  song transmission and, 110, 111, 123, 159
word
  chant and, 6, 8, 10, 44–46, 65, 68, 121, 122, 131, 151 (*see also* tajwid)
  knowledge and, 5, 16, 21, 95, 133, 145, 161
  spiritual limitations of, 47, 81, 87
  transcendence of the, 27, 32, 118, 124, 139, 140, 160. *See also* Daivi Vak; sabda; Sabdapurvayoga; shabad; Vak; Veda(s). *See also under* God(s); mantra; oral; revelation; song; vibration
yoga, 2, 17, 19, 25–29, 41, 64, 148, 158. *See also* Nada-Yoga; Sabdapurvayoga; Vak Yoga
Yoga Sutras by Patanjali, 2, 3, 4, 7, 20, 25, 26, 27, 152